# Speak for Yourself, John

John Mason Brown (1952)

# Speak for Yourself, John

## The Life of John Mason Brown, with Some of His Letters and Many of His Opinions

George Stevens

The Viking Press | New York

Copyright © 1974 by George Stevens
All rights reserved
First published in 1974 by The Viking Press, Inc.
625 Madison Avenue, New York, N.Y. 10022
Published simultaneously in Canada by
The Macmillan Company of Canada Limited
SBN 670-66203-8
Library of Congress catalog card number: 73-17786
Printed in U.S.A. by Vail-Ballou Press, Inc.

*Page 292 constitutes an extension of this copyright page.*

Acknowledgment is made to the following for permission to quote material:

The Associated Press: From Charles Mercer's report of one of John Mason Brown's lectures which appeared in the Louisville *Courier-Journal* on July 14, 1957.

Columbia Broadcasting System, Inc.: Excerpts from broadcasts of *The Last Word, Of Men and Books,* and *Invitation to Learning,* © 1973 Columbia Broadcasting System, Inc. All rights reserved.

Dodd, Mead & Company: From *Our Hearts Were Young and Gay* by Cornelia Otis Skinner and Emily Kimbrough. Copyright 1942 by Dodd, Mead & Company, Inc. Copyright © renewed 1970 by Cornelia Otis Skinner and Emily Kimbrough. Reprinted by permission of Dodd, Mead & Company, Inc.

Esquire, Inc.: From *One Man Chautauqua* by Serrell Hillman. © 1960 by Esquire, Inc. Reprinted by permission of *Esquire* magazine.

To
Catherine M. Brown
and
Laura B. Stevens

# Foreword

Customarily, in a biography the subject is called by his surname; in a memoir, if the author wishes, by his first name. This book purports to be a biography rather than a memoir, but I cannot call John Mason Brown anything but John. I knew John too long and too well to start calling him Brown now, especially since I begin this biography with his boyhood. We were college class-mates, and for ten years close neighbors in New York. Where my memories of him are included, I usually refer to myself as "a friend." I am not the only friend so designated; it should not be assumed that this phrase always refers to me.

John expressed himself so well and so fully that it would be a disservice to the reader to paraphrase when I could quote—from his books and his letters, especially the latter: he never wrote a perfunctory letter, and after he got married in 1933 and subse-quently acquired a secretary, he made carbon copies and never threw anything away. Fortunately for the years before 1933 there are many other sources: a long diary, letters that his friends have kept, and the recollections those friends retain of him.

I have not hesitated to insert footnotes where I thought they might be informative or amusing; no ibid.'s or loc. cit.'s. Against my will and better judgment I have felt obliged to use the British spelling of "theater": i.e., "theatre." In a book about a drama critic the word must be used often. John invariably spelled it "theatre," and so does Harvard, his alma mater. This seems to me inconsistent, since both John and Harvard use the American spelling of "center"; it would have been odd indeed if Harvard had called the Loeb Drama Center the Loeb Theatre Center. Unfortunately I found no way, in Chapter Eleven, to avoid writing "theatre center." Moreover, one of my best sources has been the Harvard Theatre Collection.

Belatedly—in fact, when the writing of this book was almost finished—I came across the interviews with John recorded by Serrell Hillman. These consist of ten double-sided LP records; each of the ten interviews lasts about fifty minutes. I had known of these records—WNYC had been broadcasting one or another from time to time on its program "Spoken Words." Finally I found a friend who had a set and who lent the records to me.

This set of recorded interviews is one of several series produced —with different interviewers and different celebrities—at the instigation and expense of a Texas architect who apparently wanted to do something to spread culture throughout the United States. Accordingly the records (or tapes) were made available to recording studios the country over. Mr. Hillman reports that many small stations must have had them, "judging by the number of friends who have unexpectedly heard us in the most unlikely places." Mr. Hillman, at the time of the interviews, which he recalls as having taken place in 1957, was a member of the editorial staff of *Time* magazine.

John's series with Hillman is called "The Humanities." The individual interviews are titled as follows: 1. "The World of the Theatre," 2. "What Is Greatness?" 3. "The Artist and His Times," 4. "The Art of Laughter," 5. "The Development of Style," 6. "The Revelation of Character," 7. "Biography and Autobiography," 8. "What Constitutes a Classic?" 9. "What Determines Taste?" 10. "Men and Ideas." References to them, or quotations from them, are to be found here and there throughout the book.

As far as John was concerned, the interviews were spontaneous and unrehearsed; Hillman and John did map out a broad outline, but only Hillman came to the sessions provided with notes, and those in casual form. He brought a book or two if he foresaw an appropriate place to read a short quotation. And the records are indeed spontaneous; the pity is that they are not available for John's friends, they so effectively bring John into the living room. I had noticed, for instance—and so had another friend, who mentioned it to me—that in the first record John sounds impatient. In all the rest he is relaxed, witty, charming.

It remains to quote a brief paragraph from one of Mr. Hillman's letters. He had first met John when he was about fourteen and John in his early thirties.

> I think John was better with young people than anyone I ever knew. He was enormously interested in youngsters without being inquisitive; he remarkably lacked pomposity in himself. . . . It could never be said of him, as he once said to me about John Gunther (when I was working on a *Time* cover on Gunther) that "Gunther isn't a name-dropper; he's just a name-inhaler." Perfect!

In the interview "Biography and Autobiography" John says that "letters and diaries are the very core of biography," thus justifying me after the event in the decision I made to let John speak for himself as far as possible. Hence the title.

# Acknowledgments

This book has depended for its existence on the help of many people who contributed information, advice, and suggestions, and who gave generously of their time in doing so. More than a few of them appear in the text, notably those whose assistance was most indispensable: Mrs. John Mason Brown (Cassie) and her sons, Preston and Meredith; and John's closest friend, Donald M. Oenslager.

Although geographical identification cannot generally be given, it is convenient to begin with a special category of John's friends and relatives in Louisville, and others there who have been helpful in ways that I hope the book itself will show. Mrs. Thomas J. Wood (Ellen Barret) and Mrs. Roland Whitney (Mary Churchill) John grew up with and knew all his life; likewise Mr. Arthur Peter, Jr., and Mr. Richard Peter. John's half brother, Mr. James C. Stone, Jr., and Mrs. Stone have given generous assistance. So have Miss Thelma Dolan and Mr. James R. Bentley of the Filson Club, specially acknowledged herein; Mrs. Josephine Johnson, Librarian of the *Louisville Courier-Journal;* and members of the staff of the Louisville Public Library. I am grateful to Melville O. Briney (Mrs. Russell Briney) for permitting me to quote from her book, *Fond Recollection,* and to its publisher, *The Louisville Times.*

From here on, until we reach the final category, we may as well list our acknowledgments in roughly alphabetical order.

Most, but not all, were John's friends; many, but by no means all, live in New York. To save space I shall not place "Mr." before each masculine name; as to the women, any one who wants to be called "Ms." must look elsewhere. More or less alphabetically, then, here are the names of those who have helped me. Stephen A. Aaron, Richard Aldrich, Mrs. Reginald Allen (Helen Howe), former Senator Clinton P. Anderson, Mrs. Vincent Astor, Brooks Atkinson, Louis Auchincloss, David W. Bailey, George Pierce Baker, Jr., Mrs. August Belmont, Barry Bingham, Sr., Chairman of the Board, *The Courier-Journal* and *The Louisville Times,* for permission to quote from those papers, and for some choice anecdotes. Mrs. Charles S. Bolster, McGeorge Bundy, Mr. and Mrs. William A. M. Burden; Cass Canfield of Harper & Row, John's last publisher, and his helpful associate, Mrs. Beulah Hagen; Mrs. Henry Cave, and Mr. Robert H. Chapman, Director of the Loeb Drama Center at Harvard.

Edward C. Cole of the Yale School of Drama and my old friend John J. Pullen helped with research at Yale. Miss Katharine Cornell received me most graciously. Norman Cousins of *Saturday Review/World* has been kindness itself, and—as will appear—encyclopedic in knowledge and elephantine in memory. Here is the place to express my thanks to his assistant, Mrs. Emily Suesskind. Mrs. Norris Darrell (née Mary Hand), Mrs. Russell W. Davenport, Alfred de Liagre, Jr., Dr. Kenneth T. Donaldson. Miss May Dowell of the Columbia Broadcasting System (Director of Special Projects, CBS News) took a lot of time and trouble digging out records of some of John's broadcasts. The late Dudley T. Easby, Jr., Wolcott Gibbs, Jr., Miss Rosamond Gilder; Thornton D. Grant, Headmaster of what is now The Morristown-Beard School; Hamish Hamilton, John's London publisher and close friend; Serrell Hillman, John K. Hutchens, Norris Houghton, Lewis M. Isaacs, Jr., Miss Emily Kimbrough, the Rev. Arthur Lee Kinsolving, Mrs. Alan G. Kirk; Louis Kronenberger, Mrs. Adrian Lambert, Professor Harry Levin of Harvard, Walter Lippmann, Bertram K. Little, the Honorable Henry Cabot

Lodge, Walter Lord, Archibald MacLeish. By no means all of David McCord's contributions are identified in the text.

H. G. Merriam, Theodore Morrison, George Oppenheimer, the late Mrs. J. Robert Oppenheimer, Peter Oppenheimer, Laurence O. Pratt, Mrs. Ralph Pulitzer (Margaret Leech), the late Doris Fielding Reid. Axel Rosin, Warren Lynch, Ralph Thompson, and Miss Elizabeth Easton of the Book-of-the-Month Club were hospitable and informative. Colgate Salsbury; Miss Dorothy Sands, whose importance to the book will be apparent; Miss Elizabeth Schenk of the Keedick Lecture Bureau; James M. Seward, Executor of the Estate of Edward R. Murrow; Miss Elisabeth Sill, who was for years John's secretary and who has been invaluable as my editorial associate; Miss Cornelia Otis Skinner (Mrs. Alden Blodget), Dr. and Mrs. Henry DeWolf Smyth, Mrs. Richard Stillwell (Celia Sachs), Richard Watts, Jr., Edward Weeks, William H. Wells. And at the end of the alphabetical progression, Herbert Warren Wind; his permission and that of *The New Yorker* to quote him so copiously are acknowledged with special gratitude. *The New Yorker* also added its kind permission to that of Mr. Wolcott Gibbs, Jr., to quote from an article by the late Wolcott Gibbs.

I am placing librarians in a special category; without them there would have been no book, and no thanks can be sufficient. John left his correspondence to the Houghton Library at Harvard, where I spent two weeks, greatly indebted to William H. Bond, Librarian; Rodney G. Dennis, Curator of Manuscripts; and the ladies of the Reading Room, who suffered my presence: Misses Carolyn E. Jakeman, Toni Boldrick, and Marte Shaw, and Mrs. Jill Karhan; likewise Mr. Joseph McCarthy, who trundled seventeen large cartons of Browniana, one by one and two by two, from the basement and back. The author is grateful to Mr. Bond for permission to publish letters and excerpts from letters from the Houghton Library collection, on pages 19(2), 22, 24(2), 26, 34, 37, 89, 106, 108, 128, 153(2), 154(2), 156, 157, 158, 159, 160, 164, 165, 169(2), 173, 179, 182, 185, 199, 201, 204, 205(2), 206, 209,

219, 220, 236, 237(2), 243, 258, 262, 265, 278. I am likewise indebted to Miss Helen D. Willard, who at the time of my researches in Cambridge was Curator of the Harvard Theatre Collection—she retired in the summer of 1972. Her successor, Miss Jeanne T. Newlin, has added further to my information.

The correspondence between John and George Pierce Baker on pages 113–116 is at the Sterling Library at Yale, and is reproduced by the kind permission of the Sterling Library, as conveyed by Miss Judith A. Schiff.

In Princeton I have had almost daily assistance, over a period of months, from my very good friend Mrs. Mina R. Bryan, Librarian of the Scheide Library; she has looked up or checked innumerable facts and dates. So has Miss Mary Ann Jensen, Curator of the Theatre Collection at the Princeton University Library.

I am indebted to the staff of the Theatre Collection of the New York Public Library; to Miss Margery B. Leonard of the Washington Athletic Club, Seattle, where one of John's lectures was recorded and transcribed, for permission to quote from it; to Lounsbury D. Bates, Librarian of the Harvard Club of New York, who helped in many ways, most conspicuously in digging up John's review of the Passion Play; and finally to Louis Rachow, Librarian of the Players Club, and Carl Willers, Associate Librarian, who allowed me to listen to the tape recording of the Pipe Night in John's honor and to take notes.

To any one whom I may have overlooked, profound apologies. Two whom I shall not overlook: my wife, Laura B. Stevens, who read the manuscript twice and made excellent suggestions; and my old friend Marshall A. Best, John's classmate and mine at Harvard, long an executive of The Viking Press, who edited this book with patience, consideration, and unerring judgment.

—GEORGE STEVENS

# Contents

# Speak for Yourself, John

# Prologue

John Mason Brown was called to the theatre as others have been called to the bar or the ministry. He heard the call before he was ten years old, and found it irresistible. His *métier* was to be drama criticism, and his published books, of which twelve are devoted either entirely or in substantial part to the drama, combine to form an unpremeditated but nevertheless comprehensive history of the American theatre for more than four decades—from the early 1920s to the mid-1960s. Some of the contents of the books are reprints of reviews—many of them considerably revised—from *Theatre Arts,* the *New York Evening Post,* the New York *World-Telegram,* and, after the Second World War, *The Saturday Review.* Others of this group of twelve were written as books and did not depend on the nagging inspiration of newspaper and magazine deadlines. The four and a half decades of John Mason Brown's theatre-going happened to be a memorable period, producing Eugene O'Neill, Sidney Howard, Elmer Rice, Thornton Wilder, and Robert E. Sherwood; the Theatre Guild and the Federal Theatre; Lynn Fontanne and Alfred Lunt and Katharine Cornell and Helen Hayes. All of this John saw, and part of it he was.

A climax in John's life, perhaps *the* climax, was the Second World War. He enlisted in the Navy as soon as possible, participated in the invasions of Sicily and Normandy, and wrote two of his most memorable books about those experiences. Undoubtedly

3

the war changed him: it would be inexact to say that it decreased his interest in the theatre, but it increased his interest in public affairs: the Nuremberg trials, the conventions and election of 1952, the case of J. Robert Oppenheimer; and he wrote of these in his later books. His last book, the biography of Robert E. Sherwood—the second volume of which he did not live to finish—was a perfect combination of the two fields of interests, for Sherwood began as a playwright and became director of the European branch of the Office of War Information, and later the author of *Roosevelt and Hopkins*.

All this is on the record, and John Mason Brown's books are there for those who wish to read them. What remains for the biographer is of course the chronological account of his life, and more particularly the attempt, both necessary and impossible, to bring his personality to the printed page. It is his personality that his friends most vividly remember, and he was especially fortunate in his friends, owing to his effortless talent for human relationships. He was alive with an unceasing nervous energy which, like alternating current, was receptive to the personalities of others while it conveyed his own to them. An indefatigable lecturer as well as a drama critic, later well known to radio and TV audiences, he was never at a loss for words. He had many serious things to say and to write. He has been quoted as saying, "A good conversationalist is not one who remembers what was said, but says what someone wants to remember." * This is not characteristic; John was quite capable of being outrageous, but not of being conceited; and a man whose friends included Dean Acheson, Hamilton Fish Armstrong, McGeorge Bundy, Walter Lippmann, and Henry Cabot Lodge was unlikely to dominate every conversation. The special quality of John's own conversation was wit, and his wit was invariably spontaneous. Any one who was lucky enough to be exposed to it could not doubt that his wit sprang from a geyser rather than from a fountain, for a fountain can be turned on and off. John's wit rose from the occa-

* *Town and Country*, March 1973.

sion and to the occasion. Like Falstaff (though not in other respects), he was not only witty in himself "but the cause that wit is in other men." If his friends could recall a tenth of his *bons mots,* a substantial anthology could be compiled.

To dwell upon his wit would be to slight his gift for friendship. Besides his professional associations and his meetings with friends at lunch, dinner parties, and other social gatherings—not to speak of the friends he made on his lecture tours from coast to coast—he spent a great deal of time on the telephone, passing the time of day, or night, never allowing his personal relationships to stagnate.

He was much written about and otherwise recognized for the charming and distinguished man he was. No doubt the most deeply satisfying recognition was that accorded him on the occasion of a "Pipe Night" at the Players Club in New York on November 12, 1967. An account of this tribute, or series of tributes, is given at the appropriate place in this book. These tributes were anything but solemn, conventional eulogies—none of the praise came out of a treacle well; on the contrary, John's own capacity for being outrageous when the spirit moved him, as it often did, was matched by the quality of the bouquets thrown at him on this occasion. It came when John's health was failing, but in time for him to enjoy every minute of it.

But let us begin at the beginning.

# Chapter One

# The First Nineteen Years

According to the census of 1900, the population of Louisville, Kentucky, was 204,731; and whether that final digit may be taken to represent John Mason Brown depends on whether the census was taken before or after the date of his birth, July 3 of that last year of the nineteenth century. Louisville is on the left bank of the Ohio River, which may be the widest river in the United States, since it separates the South from the North. But not altogether: Kentucky split off from Virginia and became the fifteenth state (though, like Virginia, she calls herself a Commonwealth) in 1792; and although a slave state from the beginning, she did not secede from the union seventy years later. Nevertheless, any one who listens to the speech of the Louisvillians, tinged, and often more than tinged, with the sound of the South, and then crosses the river into Indiana to hear the Hoosier voices in the twang which Elmer Davis was to make famous on the radio, will not underestimate the Ohio River.

Louisville itself was laid out when it was still part of Virginia, and was named by the Virginia legislature in honor of Louis XVI, who had supported the colonies during the American Revolution. Louis survived long enough to learn of this honor, and one hopes that he did. George Rogers Clark built a fort there in 1778, before his successful campaigns in Illinois during which he captured the notorious British General Henry Hamilton, the "hair-buyer," at Vincennes. The enduring importance of Louis-

ville comes from its location at the Falls of the Ohio, where—
until a canal was built—shipping was interrupted and Louisville, on the route of portage, became a commercial center. A visi-
tor to Louisville today is impressed by the accessibility of the
river to the residential section of the city, the commercial struc-
tures along the waterfront being carefully segregated.

Many if not most native Kentuckians have ancestors on both
sides of the Civil War. John Mason Brown did. Many if not most
Kentuckians consider themselves Southerners. The southern quality of the Commonwealth, kept vividly alive by—among other
things—horses and the production of bourbon whiskey, was given
an enduring romantic flavor by the Pennsylvanian Stephen Foster in "My Old Kentucky Home"—though the nearest he came
to having a Kentucky home was to spend two years as a book-
keeper in Cincinnati.

To make ourselves at home in the Louisville of 1900, we turn
with pleasure to Melville O. Briney's book *Fond Recollection,*
published by the *Louisville Times;* the chapters of Mrs. Briney's
book were first published separately as articles in that newspaper.
Indeed, some of her most interesting recollections go back well
before her own time. For instance: George Keats, brother of the
poet, lived in Louisville for twenty-two years. He died, as his
brother had, of tuberculosis, and almost twenty-one years later:
December 24, 1841. Along with George Rogers Clark, and many
of John Mason Brown's forebears, he was buried in Louisville's
Cave Hill Cemetery.

Mrs. Briney also tells of the actress Mary Anderson, famous in
her day; she was born in 1859 in California, but brought up in
Louisville. After retiring from the stage in 1889, Mary Anderson
wrote her autobiography, *A Few Memories* (1896), in which she
said that she had told Sarah Bernhardt that "she would look 'far
better with less paint on her cheeks and lips. She [Sarah] followed
the suggestion at once.' "

Coming to 1900, Mrs. Briney describes Central Park in Louis-

ville, which had been created largely owing to the efforts of John
Mason Brown's grandfather (1837–1890), also named John Mason
Brown, who had been instrumental in getting a bill passed making what had been du Pont Square, a private estate, into a pub-
lic park. "Children born at the turn of the century," writes Mrs.
Briney, "remember Central Park as the domain of the nursemaid.
That now almost extinct species sat in throngs upon its benches;
kept a wary eye on the wicker baby carriages; rose, when occasion demanded, to administer justice to the recalcitrants of the
tricycle set." John Mason Brown was brought up in a house on
Park Avenue, facing Central Park. His parents, (John) Mason
Brown and Carolyn Carroll Ferguson, had been married on April
28, 1897.

When John was two, his parents were divorced, and John was
raised by his mother and her mother, who was also separated
from her husband, John Moore Ferguson, an insurance man. After a year in Switzerland, they settled into the house on Park
Avenue; the household also included John's sister, Mary Miller
Brown, his elder by two years and a few months. Besides Mrs.
Briney's, there are many other reminiscences. Those of his neighbor Ellen Barret (literally the girl next door), with whom John
grew up, although she was four years younger, and Mary Churchill Jungbluth, daughter of John's godmother, are copious and
valuable. (Ellen Barret is now Mrs. Thomas J. Wood, and Mary
Churchill is Mrs. Roland Whitney, both of Louisville.) Similar
memories flow from Arthur Peter, Jr., and his brother Richard.
Judge Arthur Peter, Sr., was John's godfather. When John had
grown up, his godmother took an occasion to ask him if he were
satisfied with his religious upbringing. "Why, yes, Aunt Mimi
[Amelia]," replied John; "every time I pass a church I think of
you passing one, too." Apparently the same was true of the judge.

One of the earliest episodes in John's life to have been recorded has, interestingly enough, been recorded twice, and the
two versions are contradictory. In his *Saturday Review* article

"The Going-Home Train" * John speaks of the Gavin H. Cochran School, where, he alleges, he had a teacher in the first grade who maintained discipline with "a black butter paddle, which raised blisters because of the holes cut in its surface." The use of this instrument was preceded by the warning, "Do you want me to warm your jacket for you?" As John remarks, "She meant something else." Less than a month later John wrote to a friend: "[In the Gavin H. Cochran School] it was a woman named Miss Preston who, in the first grade, roughed my spank-spots with that butter paddle. Isn't it funny how in retrospect it is the strictest teachers you remember longest and admire most?"

A different version was given by Floyd Edwards in the *Louisville Times* for March 20, 1969—only a few days after John's death. (This article is evidently a follow-up to the obituary.) He speaks of Mrs. W. E. Render, née Flora Gray, who taught John in the first and third grades. To Mrs. Render, he was a "brilliant and loveable child."

Flora Gray could hardly have been Miss Preston. Edwards's version is backed up by the recollection of one of John's friends that his third-grade teacher had said he was the cutest little boy she had ever taught.

John also told a friend that his mother used to spank him with the French heel of her slipper. According to his account, he seems to have had an upbringing like that of the Elephant's Child, without the opportunity to travel to the great gray-green greasy Limpopo River and find out what the crocodile had for dinner. Whatever happened to him, he seemed to have harbored no resentment.

A few more of Mrs. Briney's background reminiscences are appropriate. She mentions that in 1903 George Ade, best known for his *Fables in Slang*, "had three productions running simul-

---

* November 16, 1946. A piece describing his feelings whenever he returned to Louisville, it has been widely reprinted and appears in his book *Seeing More Things*.

taneously on Broadway. . . . A Kentuckian, John Fox, Jr., was topping best-seller lists with his 'Little Shepherd of Kingdom Come.' " "Sweet Adeline" was composed that year. *Mrs. Wiggs of the Cabbage Patch* by Alice Hegan Rice of Shelbyville, Kentucky, opened October 5 in a dramatization by Anne Crawford (Mrs. Abraham) Flexner.* *Mrs. Wiggs* was widely played: "The Louisville legend is that more people have appeared in stage, stock, cinema, and radio versions of *Mrs. Wiggs* than in versions of any play except *Uncle Tom's Cabin*." Mae West once played in it.

Mrs. Briney writes delightfully of fans and front porches, of mosquito nets, of ladies' white dresses of muslin or dotted swiss; of calomel and quinine, and of wonderful superstitions and taboos pertaining to food. More specifically appropriate is her description of Miss Meme Wastell's dancing class, which John and Mary Miller attended; so did Mary Churchill and some of their other friends—Ellen Barret not until later, because of the difference in ages. When John became a teen-ager he transferred to Miss Wellington's dancing class because Miss Meme did not encourage teen-agers. Miss Meme's sounds like every other dancing class of that period, and many have been described. John seems to have distinguished himself by refusing to take his partner by chance out of a circle—thus setting himself apart from his fellow pupils, as well as from Marco and Giuseppe in *The Gondoliers*. (Mrs. Briney, in her description of Miss Meme's, calls attention to the chapter on dancing school in John's book *Morning Faces* —but John says nothing there about his own experiences.)

The children—except Ellen, who was too young—used to play in an alley off Ormsby Avenue—a wide alley with carriage houses and barns. And in John's back yard, according to Mary Churchill Whitney, frequent funeral services were conducted; an old sand pile served as a cemetery for "Cordelia, Ophelia, Polonius, poor Yorick, [buried] over and over again according to the number of

---

* Is it necessary to point out that the Flexners were one of Louisville's most distinguished families?—especially Dr. Abraham Flexner and his brother, Dr. Simon Flexner.

dead birds, squirrels, mice, even beetles" they found. At these services John would sometimes appropriate one of Mary Miller's nightgowns for use as a surplice; it made her furious.

However John may have felt about the proper manner of selecting dancing partners, it is obvious that he was never unwilling to play with girls, and never went through a period of boyhood misogyny. In fact a tendency which was to manifest itself in his young bachelor days in New York—a tendency to think of every girl as a potential fiancée—was exemplified, or anticipated, in two boyhood episodes. When he was about nine, John became enamored of a friend of his sister's—presumably his sister's age. Wishing to give a demonstration of his affectionate regard, he collected an armful of books and carried them to the young lady's house. When she put in an appearance, he offered them to her, proclaiming, "These are for you, my paramour."

The other episode concerns a diamond ring that John bought at the ten-cent store to give to Ellen Barret. She was about eight, so John must have been twelve or so. When John presented the ring to her, Ellen haughtily declined to accept it; and this diamond, as will appear, became a stone of contention. John continued to upbraid Ellen for her ingratitude—or whatever he thought it was—off and on for literally the rest of his life: when she last saw him, four months before his death, he brought the matter up again. To some extent, of course, he was pretending; but John was quite capable of pretending to mean something and meaning it too.

The names of the unfortunate corpses already mentioned suggest John's interest in the theatre—the interest that was to be central to his career. In the brief introduction which he wrote in December 1962 to *Dramatis Personae: A Retrospective Show* \*— he said: "I have been stagestruck ever since, when eight, I was taken to Macauley's Theatre in Louisville, Kentucky, to see

---

\* An anthology of John Mason Brown's writings over three decades. His classmate and old friend, Marshall A. Best, was his editor at The Viking Press, which published it in 1963.

Robert B. Mantell play King Lear, one of the few parts, I realize now, that he was still young enough to act." (This is perhaps unfair. That same year, 1908, Mantell played a Shakespearean season of eight weeks in New York. Moreover, he was only three years older than E. H. Sothern, another Shakespearean actor, whom John admired.)

John's next recorded visit to a theatre took place in 1911, when Maude Adams brought Rostand's *Chantecler* \* to Louisville. About this time, John acquired a puppet theatre. It had been in the Barret family—Ellen's aunt had played with it—and Ellen's father, Alexander Barret, gave it to John. It was kept on a table in an alcove, in a bedroom on the second floor of the Park Avenue house. Sometimes the audience for John's puppet show performances consisted of Ellen alone; sometimes John's mother and grandmother, Mary Miller, and Ellen's parents and her aunt came. The first puppet show Ellen recalls was *Hamlet*— presumably not in an uncut version; John's mother broke a date with an admirer in order to attend. It also seems reasonable to suppose—again from the names bestowed upon the buried animals—that other plays of Shakespeare were performed, in John's versions. Obviously he was precocious in his knowledge of Shakespeare. It was Mr. Barret who had taken Ellen and John to see *Chantecler,* and this was probably the first of several paper figures he made for them to play with—Ellen recalls their playing with it, and with other paper birds made for them by her father, on the stair landing before the puppet theatre was set up. *L'Aiglon* also figured in these performances.

Possibly even before he had the puppet theatre John was giving live performances in the attic. For these productions he pressed into service any of his friends and relatives who could be persuaded to join him. In an interview with Maurice Hecksher, published in the *Louisville Courier-Journal* in January 1940,

---

\* *Chantecler* is an allegorical satire in which the characters are dressed as birds; Chantecler himself believed that his crowing caused the sun to rise. Evidently the play is difficult to produce successfully, in spite of many felicities, largely owing to the costumes.

John told about the plays they used to give in the attic. In *Lear,*
"none of us could remember more than a dozen lines or so, but
we were very serious, and I remember toward the end carrying
the body of the dead Cordelia—my small cousin Mary Churchill
[cousin by courtesy—no relation]—in my arms, swathed in a
window curtain for a regal robe, crying 'Howl, howl, howl, howl!
O! you are men of stones.' " Mary Churchill also played Ophelia.

In the same interview John said that he had had an unnatural
childhood, spending every afternoon at the movies. When there
were plays, the local theatre manager was very friendly, and often
let the children go onstage as supers. John himself wrote a play
about Benedict Arnold "with a great love scene ending when he
suddenly jumped out of the window and fled into the snow."

Other memories—these from Ellen Barret Wood—are of being
taken with John to see Sothern and Marlowe, and a play called
*Joseph and His Brethren,* in which Pauline Frederick appeared
as Potiphar's wife. John went backstage to get her autograph,
and talked about it afterwards for weeks. From Mary Churchill
Whitney comes the information that the audience at the attic
productions usually included herself (when she was not a member of the cast), Richard Peter, and John's cousins Churchill
Newcomb and Franklin Starks. Sometimes Mary Miller conde-
scended to attend. But the players did not want their parents to
attend the live performances—from apprehension of being pa-
tronized? And much later, John told Herbert Warren Wind, who
was interviewing him for a "Profile" which appeared in *The New
Yorker* in 1952, that the servants were made part of a captive
audience. One hopes they were captivated.

In November 1946 Alfred Lunt asked John to write a short
essay on a collection of nineteenth-century toy theatres to be
shown at the Museum of the City of New York. The result appeared in *The Saturday Review* of January 4, 1947, under the
title "Children of Skelt." Skelt was a nineteenth-century entre-
preneur who, in partnership with one Webb, put out packages
of "papers bulging with actors, properties, and settings for the

possession of which children . . . were separated from their coppers." Apparently John got much of his information from a chapter by Robert Louis Stevenson in his *Memories and Portraits,* "A Penny Plain and Twopence Colored." "Stevenson," wrote John, "worshipped the very name of Skelt—so stagey and piratical.' " Skelt was particularly to be admired for his pre-realism: he left much to the child's imagination, unlike certain manufacturers of expensive and elaborate toy theatres today. Mr. Lunt's exhibition filled three rooms of the museum. John's article modestly made no direct mention of his own toy theatre in Louisville.

John attended an institution of learning uniquely designated as the Louisville Male High School, later called the Boys' High School, where he seems to have distinguished himself only in English. In May 1917 John won a gold medal for a speech called "Hyphenated Americans." The speech has not survived, but presumably, like Calvin Coolidge's preacher in respect to sin, he was against them. It was just a month after America had entered World War I, and patriotism was at a high temperature. Other records of his teen-age years are fragmentary. During this period, immediately after the movies, he often visited the emporium of Miss Jennie Benedict (a confectioner mentioned in *Fond Recollection*) and, according to Mrs. Wood, he would eat not one but two banana splits. He admired Robert W. Service, and Kipling's "If." He used to quote "I've Got a Little List," substituting his own *bêtes noires* for Koko's. And—this from the interview with Maurice Hecksher—Henry Watterson, the famous Marse Henry of Kentucky journalism, wrote a piece in the *Courier-Journal* denying the authenticity of Shakespeare's authorship of the plays. John wrote him a letter defending the Shakespearean authorship, and received a reply "ending with the phrase—I remember it because at the time it seemed to me so inept—the phrase, 'What boots it?' "

After absorbing what education the Louisville Male High School could give him—or some of it—John spent two years,

1917–19, at the Morristown School in Morristown, New Jersey. No doubt he chose this because his second cousin, (John) Churchill Newcomb, had already spent three years there and had two more to go. The boys were nearly contemporaries; Churchill Newcomb was seven months older. It was at the Newcomb family's farm in Virginia that John had spent parts of several summers. Newcomb's grandmother was a Ferguson—sister of John's grandfather.

John's records at Morristown are a little sketchy. The school itself is attractively situated, with a pleasant campus and buildings. Both the cousins were interested in the school Dramatic Club, and in April 1918 Churchill played the wife to John's Colonel Bowie in *The Dictator* by Richard Harding Davis. There are photographs of them, as well as of the entire cast, in an old scrapbook of John's; two pictures of John show him with his collar becoming detached from the neckband of his shirt, while he himself was nonchalantly twirling a handlebar moustache. Churchill, in a blond wig, a straw "sailor" hat, and an enormous sash, looks rather more convincing as a girl than most boys do in school and college dramatic productions. The following year, in March 1919, John played in *The Magistrate* by Arthur Wing Pinero; evidently Churchill was not in this one. The program is not preserved in the scrapbook.

There is also a photograph of the 1918 football squad, incredibly showing John in football uniform. It is not known what position he played, or how often.* A handwritten, unsigned note in the school file says that John was "not a natural athlete," a judgment with which no one would conceivably take issue. This paper, dated July 16, 1919, apparently a final report on John by one of the masters, states that John rose from "a New Boy to the Head of the School, as Chairman of the Committee of Seven." This corresponded to what would elsewhere be called the Stu-

---

* When the author visited the Morristown School, he was treated with every consideration and courtesy, but unfortunately the class yearbooks for the two years John was at Morristown were missing.

dent Council; both John and Churchill were on it. The same note discloses that John's scholastic average was 75 per cent, "but he has marked capacity for expression both in writing and speaking." He graduated with distinction in English and history. The note speaks of his "admirable qualities, devotion to duty and to right doing." His chief danger was considered to be "lack of judgment and a tendency to court popular favor." In his senior year John was chairman of the Chapel Committee.

In January 1918 he had measles, and wrote a letter of reassurance to his mother. She and her second husband, James C. Stone, had hesitated to have him come home for Christmas in 1918 because of the world-wide epidemic of what was called "Spanish influenza," which killed at least ten million people during that year; it was considered safer to stay away from big cities with concentrated populations. They changed their minds, and telegraphed the school on December 21 to send John home, but evidently this change of mind came too late, for there is a letter in the school files written by John and dated December 26.

Meanwhile he had applied for admission to Harvard and to Williams. In the Harvard entrance examinations he failed in Latin and algebra, but passed four other subjects. (He was duly admitted to the freshman class at Harvard in 1919.) During the summer of 1918 he had the war much on his mind. He became eligible for the draft on his birthday that year, July 3. There is some haziness in the records at Morristown; apparently John thought of entering Williams in the fall of 1918 in order to attend the SATC (Students' Army Training Corps), but changed his mind; he preferred another year at Morristown, then Harvard, but unquestionably his sense of duty in wartime was uppermost in his mind. In the end he went to Williams in the summer of 1918 and attended the ROTC there,* then returned to Morristown in September. The war by then had less than two more months to run.

* So he stated in a letter to Lieutenant (later Captain) Edmund S. DeLong, dated December 23, 1941, applying for a Naval Reserve Commission.

Undoubtedly the principal event in John's life at Morristown was the beginning of a feud between John and his cousin Churchill, which ultimately involved both families. (Although they came from the country of the Hatfields and the McCoys, the feud consisted of reciprocal silence and the breaking of relations.) Apparently one of the masters at Morristown either said or wrote that in his opinion the Russian Revolution had been necessary. This enraged Churchill, who was highly conservative in his views and evidently was inspired by the intolerance of youth. He got his family to attempt to have the master discharged or at least reprimanded. John promptly came to the defense of the master and of free speech. Presumably before they ceased to speak to each other, tempers flared and things were said that left deep wounds.

In any event, John and Churchill entered Harvard together, but quite separately. For one who knew them both, but at quite different times, the situation after all these years is not easy to interpret. John could certainly lose his temper, but he was not one to bear a grudge or to "stay mad"; apparently Churchill, under what seemed to outsiders an unruffled exterior, could keep his internal fires burning. But this is conjecture.

Churchill was twenty when he entered Harvard, which is perhaps a couple of years older than the average. He was an out-and-out Tory, opposed to Woodrow Wilson, the Treaty of Versailles, and the League of Nations. He used to tell of his exploits as a Morristown student—these exploits chiefly consisting of trips to New York for entertaining evenings spent in what were then called cabarets. He had a particular penchant for a cabaret called the Pré-Catalan, and liked to boast about the goings-on there.

After graduation from Harvard, Churchill lived for a few years in the Greenwich Village section of New York. In the sixth anniversary report of the Class of 1923, he gave his profession as journalism, and listed a number of published articles, most if not all of them having to do with horses. But this may have been the last report he made to his classmates; in the twenty-fifth report, published in 1948 in time for the class reunion in June, the class secretary had to say that Churchill had not returned his questionnaire. By this time he was living the life of a gentleman farmer in Virginia.

The end must come as a shock: on February 28, 1962, John Churchill Newcomb was murdered at his Virginia home. No one was ever apprehended; no one knows who did it; it remains a mystery. In John's files there are two letters, one to his friend Barry Bingham, editor and publisher of the *Louisville Courier-Journal*, thanking him for sending the newspaper clipping of the story: "I was in Phoenix on a lecture trip when your note reached me," he wrote on March 19. On the same date he also wrote to Arthur Peter, Jr., who had also sent him a clipping:

"I was horrified by the story about Churchill which you thoughtfully sent me. . . . For many, many years I have regretted the Morristown School feud, and, though its hurt has remained, its heat has long since left me. I think back only to the time when you, and Mary Churchill, and all of us were kids out at the Newcomb place, and then to my summers in Virginia with Churchill, and then . . . at Morristown until the foolishness of the feud erupted. It was a wounding and divisive affair all the way around, and one which I deeply regret because it cost me one of the closest friends I had had in my youth."

This brings us back to John's boyhood in Louisville.

# Chapter Two

## Browns and Fergusons

The statement that John and Mary Miller were brought up by their mother and grandmother must be corrected. John's mother was quite content to leave his grandmother in charge. From all accounts, Carrie Ferguson Brown—"petite, with black curly hair and great dark eyes"—was a perpetual southern belle. Just what her grounds for divorce were in 1902 is not recorded in the family documents, but in those days there were not many causes for which divorces were granted. In any event, Carrie was a strict high-church Episcopalian; if not too high-church for divorce, at least she refused to remarry until her first husband was dead. In 1913, a year after the death of John's father, she married James C. Stone, a distinguished agriculturalist. In the 1920s he was president of the Burley Tobacco Growers Cooperative Association. He was appointed by President Hoover, in March 1931, to the Federal Farm Board, of which he became vice-chairman.

Meanwhile he had formed a close attachment to his stepson, which John heartily reciprocated until the end of Stone's life. A similar attachment developed between John and his stepbrother, James C. Stone, Jr., born in 1914. Stone Senior was evidently the strongest masculine influence in John Mason Brown's life, together with Ellen's father, Alexander Barret, and Arthur Peter, Sr.—and John's colorful Uncle Preston Brown.

The Stones lived at first in Louisville, later moved to Lexington, Kentucky; after Carrie's second marriage John's grandmother gave up the Park Avenue house and moved, with John, to an apartment on Reesor Place, not far from Central Park. Mary Miller was at Miss Wright's School in Bryn Mawr, Pennsylvania. The parents of John's cousin Churchill Newcomb had a farm in Virginia, near Charlottesville, and John often visited them during the summers. Later, when he was fourteen or fifteen, he and Mary Miller and several others, including Ellen Barret, would go to northern Michigan with Mrs. Ferguson and the Stones. One summer they all went to Atlantic City; Ellen managed to get caught in a bowl-like contraption on the Steel Pier; John, embarrassed, had to get the machinery turned off in order to rescue her.

Carrie Ferguson Stone gave to young Jim Stone all the maternal feeling that had been lacking in her relations with John and Mary Miller, and John never resented it. After Jim's birth, John was heard—and being John, he must have been heard more than once—to refer to his mother as "the careless virgin." In 1923 Mary Miller suddenly decided to marry her first husband, Pelham Turner; there was no possibility of a church wedding because Turner had been divorced. Mary Miller asked her mother to have the wedding and reception in the Stones' house in Lexington, but Carrie refused on the ground that she had just put summer covers on the furniture, and also that she was preparing to take Jim to Colorado Springs because of his hay fever. The breach between Mary Miller and her mother was not healed for years. Mrs. Ferguson came to the wedding, but none of the Stones; nor did John, though he was very fond of Mary Miller, because he was teaching in Montana that summer.

The episode of the slip covers shows a characteristic of Carrie's that led to John's calling her "Craig's Wife"—after the title of the Pulitzer Prize play of 1926 by George Kelly, uncle of the present Princess of Monaco. The play concerned Mrs. Craig's preference for her furniture over her husband, and the consequent break-up of their marriage.

Nothing of that sort happened to the Stones' marriage, which was evidently happy and successful. John continued on affection-ate terms with his stepfather, whom he called Dad. And it was not in him to be otherwise than courteous, generous, and affec-tionate with his mother, except when a witty remark came into his head. These he could never resist, and he almost certainly never tried.

If Carrie did not undertake to bring up John and Mary Miller, she was unquestionably affectionate with them. There are those in Louisville who assure us that John and Carrie loved each other, in their own fashions. She played with her children, and with Ellen; sang to them, read to them, acted out plays. Perhaps Carrie's love for John was more that of an elder sister than of a mother, but it was genuine. They were together for summer vaca-tions in Michigan during John's teen-age years. Habitually he went to see her—often going out of his way from Louisville to Lexington—on his fairly frequent trips to Kentucky made in the course of his lecture tours, over several decades. But in February 1946—John had been on active service in the Navy and the state of the world was much on his mind—he wrote to Mrs. Arthur Peter, Sr., wife of his godfather—her name was Louise, and he called her Aunt Ouida: "Please persuade Mother not to go out too much at night. Also ask her if she doesn't think it's in rather questionable taste to give so many lavish parties when the world is in such a sorry shape."

James C. Stone, Sr., died in December 1949 at the age of seventy-one. Carrie was about the same age. She was to survive un-til 1964, but her last years were spent in a state of senility. John wrote Jim Stone in April 1960 that he was shocked by their mother's appearance, and even more when she did not recognize Jim.

Meanwhile, however, he had written affectionate letters to his mother; here is one that survives from January 1948:

"Mother darling,

"I am home, safely home, and really not at all tired. The Pittsburgh weekend, during which I dug in and wrote my SRL piece, proved immensely restful. . . . Chiefly I worked, getting to bed for two nights at diaperishly early hours.

"The high point of my trip was, of course, my Louisville visit. And the high point of that was seeing you, Dad, and the Jumbos.* Your party was one of the best I have ever been to in my life. . . .

"I did so enjoy my dinner with you and Dad out in the country. Your house is truly beautiful. I have thought back so many times to the warm comfort of your porch room, the graciousness of your dining room, the fine sweep of the front hall, and the distinction of your living room. I have thought back, too, to the blissful comfort of your bedrooms upstairs and the loveliness of that view of the Ohio. Yes, and of the charm of the exterior of the house, the flagged courtyards, and the gardens. It's a perfect spot—just what you two perfect people deserve."

But in a letter (to another correspondent) ten years later he wrote: "My mother . . . has for the last six years or so been an invalid in Louisville." And finally, after her death in 1964, when she was well into her eighties, John wrote to Mrs. Robert Vaughan of Louisville (Ellen Wood's aunt) in reply to her letter of condolence:

"Madeleine darling,

"That was a lovely letter you wrote me about Mother. I deeply appreciate not only your writing but writing as you did. It was a tragedy, wasn't it, that someone, such as Mother, who brought every gift to life, had no gift for living? I like to look back on the happiness of the early days. I will never forget that summer at Ramona Park [the place where they all vacationed in Michigan] with Bob 'whitecapped as a wave,' and all of us laughing through those gay days.

"I had a fine time with Ellen in Louisville, and we all talked

---

* The Stones had moved from Lexington to Louisville in 1946. The Jumbos were Jim Stone, his wife Faith, and their two boys.

much about you and Bob, Uncle Alec and Aunt Nell,* Mother and Grandmother and Park Avenue."

In the nature of things, John's relations with his own father were not close. (John) Mason Brown, the second to bear this name, was born in Lexington in 1874, and was graduated from Yale in the class of 1896. He was admitted to the bar, and became first assistant city attorney in Louisville. Later he was in the Law Department of the Office of the Comptroller of the United States Treasury in Washington. He and Carrie were married in 1897. After their divorce, he did not share her scruples about remarriage, and indeed was married, in November 1904, to a young lady aged nineteen, Miss Grace Dudderen of Maryland. He was to live only eight years longer.

The only story that seems to have survived about John and his father is that when John was about ten, his father offered to give him a pony—an offer which John spurned, with the melodramatic words, "You can't buy my affections!" The loyalties of childhood are arbitrary and uncompromising.

Long afterwards—in July 1953—his stepmother wrote John, evidently in reply to a letter of his that has not survived. She said that she regretted not having seen more of Mary Miller and John, and would have liked to talk to him about his father. "At the expiration of his office lease, when cleaning his desk I found photographs of you and your sister with bits of poetry, on your various birthdays, attached. I have always wanted you to know you were never replaced by anything or anyone in your father's interest or affections. . . ."

John replied on July 28:

"Dear Mrs. Brown,

"Both Cassie [John's wife, Catherine M. Brown] and I were deeply happy to have your letter and immensely touched by it. It was sensitive, kind, and generous. Indeed, it had all the qualities that I have always heard were yours.

"I sympathize with your feeling of 'bitter and anguished re-

* Uncle Alec and Aunt Nell were Ellen's parents. Bob was Robert Vaughan.

sentment against fate' because Father was not permitted to have the long life he merited. I, too, have always felt this resentment. But what has consoled me is the knowledge that long before he died he had found himself—and you. Life at the beginning of his career was cruel and unjust to him. Thank God, it treated him not only mercifully but splendidly during those happy, happy years he had with you. . . ."

John's paternal grandfather, John Mason Brown, besides being the public-spirited citizen responsible for the act creating Central Park in Louisville, had been a colonel in the Union Army during the Civil War. After his death in 1890, he was referred to as "a man of the noblest character, deeply concerned for the public good." He was married in 1869 to Mary Preston, daughter of the Confederate Minister to Mexico. Unfortunately the Minister never reached Mexico, and we are therefore deprived of what might have been some enlightening observations on Maximilian and Carlotta. Maximilian was in Europe when General Preston set out for Mexico; he got only as far as Cuba, and waited there for Maximilian's return. The author is indebted to Mr. James R. Bentley, Curator of Manuscripts of the Filson Club,* for this information.

General Preston's sister Henrietta was the first wife of the distinguished Confederate General Albert Sidney Johnston. It was Preston's Confederate daughter who, anticipating the plot of *The Birth of a Nation,* married Colonel John Mason Brown, USA.

John's own papers contain considerably more about the Browns than about the Fergusons, or any other of the tributary branches. The first recorded Brown was the Reverend John Brown, who seems to have come to the United States from Londonderry. His

* The letterhead of the Filson Club, the excellent local historical society, informs us that it was "organized May 15, 1884, for collecting, preserving, and publishing historical material, especially that pertaining to Kentucky." It is named in honor of John Filson, called "the first historian of Kentucky." The Filson Club contains a large quantity of information about General Preston— as about many of John Mason Brown's other ancestors—including family papers and letters. It is beyond the scope of this book to pursue this very interesting material.

dates were 1728–1803. His son John (1757–1837) was the last surviving member of the Continental Congress and one of the first
two United States senators from Kentucky upon the admission of
that Commonwealth to the Union. Apparently there was a canard
about Senator Brown—an accusation, or at least a rumor—that
he had associated himself with the notorious General James Wilkinson in a plot to detach Kentucky from the other states of the
Union and turn it over to Spain. This was disproved in an article
by Elizabeth Warren in the *Filson Club History Quarterly* for
April 1962. The magazine containing the article was sent to the
Senator's great-great-grandson by T. Kennedy Helm, Jr., of Louisville, now one of the directors of the Filson Club, and John wrote
to thank him on May 9, 1962.

"Dear Helm,

"Profound thanks for your thoughtfulness in sending me the
Filson Club Quarterly. . . . I have long been a subscriber but
am delighted to get an extra copy so that I can give it to my
elder son, Preston [twenty-five years old at that time], who shares
my interest in such things.

"For many years I have been interested in that fascinating tan-
gle which was the conspiracy and in Wilkinson's shameful part
in it. The old Senator's loyalty I have never doubted, in spite of
the rumors and innuendoes. I still remember Theodore Roosevelt's clearing Brown and the other Kentuckians in *The Winning
of the West* and pointing out how these men were really trying
to get better trading terms from Virginia and the Continental
Congress. I am grateful, however, to have Miss Warren's ably
written and more fully documented explanation of the Senator's
role. My grandfather, John Mason Brown, in *The Political Beginnings of Kentucky,* made the same point that T.R. and Miss
Warren do, but Grandpappy, being a grandson of the old John
Brown, naturally seemed to some (not me) to be writing out of
family loyalty. . . ."

The old Senator begat Mason Brown (1799–1867), who—not

necessarily in this order—became a judge and begat John's grandfather, whose distinguished career has been discussed.

We must remember that when we get back as far as the Senator, John's great-great-grandfather, there were seven other great-great-grandfathers as well as eight great-great-grandmothers; nobody knows who they all were; * you can't see the family tree for the woods.

But before we come to the main Ferguson line, there is one other great-grandfather, Captain Silas F. Miller, paternal grandfather of John's grandmother, Carrie's mother. Captain Miller— a river-boat captain on the Ohio who later went into the wool business (with Ellen Barret's grandfather) and prospered—turns up in the Brown archives altogether by serendipity. In an article in *The Saturday Review* for February 28, 1948, John told how, in an attempt to help his son Preston, then about eleven, with his stamp collection, he wrote to his mother in Kentucky and asked her to look in her attic and see if there were any old letters with interesting stamps on them. The result was far beyond any possible expectations: Mrs. Stone turned up eleven letters to her grandfather, Captain Miller, from no less a personage than General William Tecumseh Sherman, then in north Georgia preparing for his attack on Atlanta and subsequent march to the sea. John Mason Brown published these letters in the *Saturday Review* article just mentioned. They consist largely of thanks for various favors Captain Miller had bestowed upon the General: cigars, whiskey, even a horse by the name of Duke. It would be interesting to know just how these gifts were delivered, especially since, in one of Sherman's letters, he speaks of the difficulties of transportation: the disruption of the railroads, and the curious fact that even those railroads still running were built on different gauges.

* One who has had the privilege of working at the Filson Club and receiving the patient and knowledgeable help of its staff would not put it past the abilities of this organization to trace them all, even unto the fourth generation. Otherwise it is only royalty who keep the records so scrupulously.

In the *Saturday Review* article (most unfortunately, never reprinted in any of John Mason Brown's books) * the author calls Miller "a business man, a Republican, strongly pro-Union." In one of his letters, Sherman told Miller to tell the ladies of Louisville that Kentucky was not going to be raided by Morgan (General John Hunt Morgan, the "gray ghost" of the Confederate Army, who, born in Alabama, spent much of his youth in Kentucky).†

Silas Miller died February 4, 1902, the year of the great sleet. Miller, having been a vestryman and senior warden of Grace Episcopal Church, was buried from there. City wagons had to spread sawdust on the streets to make the cortège possible.

The first Fergusons of Carrie's line to come to this country were Adam (b. 1730) and John (b. 1736), sons of Peter Ferguson, who had fought in the Scots Greys under the Duke of Marlborough against the forces of Louis XIV. The brothers had a profitable snuff mill and tobacco business in Rhode Island. John's third wife, Anne, gave birth to no fewer than ten children, of whom Carrie's great-grandfather was the eighth.

His son John, who had to be satisfied with only two wives, first married Mary Hammett of Newport, moved to Whately, Massachusetts, became ordained as pastor of the First Congregational Church in Attleboro in 1822, and has left behind a reputation for having denounced sin as vigorously as any Aberdonian Calvinist. This may be why his son, the third John, moved to Louisville at the age of fourteen. He went on to Nashville, thence to New Orleans, where he went into the tobacco business and was successful. At the time of the Mexican War he returned to Louisville and became a leading citizen. In January 1849 he married

* Although four of his books were drawn entirely from his *Saturday Review* column, "Seeing Things," and so were considerable parts of others.

† In January 1953 John wrote another piece about Sherman for *The Saturday Review* (issue of January 17), defending his reputation on the ground that he destroyed property rather than lives. It was about this time that John was heard to refer to the South as "the land of Catton," after Bruce Catton, the Civil War historian.

Sarah Moore of Louisville, who promptly in November produced the fourth John, John Moore Ferguson, eldest of nine children. He attended Washington and Lee College, and in 1875 married Mary Johnson Miller, born in 1854 in New Albany, Indiana, just across the river from Louisville. She was the daughter of Silas Miller and the mother of Carrie (Carolyn Carroll), our John's mother, born in 1877.*

John the fourth and Mary Miller—need it be pointed out that her granddaughter was her namesake?—separated early. In appearance, Carrie was a Ferguson. Her father had three brothers and three sisters; the four brothers all had a predilection for bourbon. According to Mrs. Wood, "John had a dramatic story of his grandfather's coming one night to the house on Park Avenue . . . and banging on the door. Mrs. Ferguson told him to leave at once, as he was drunk and she did not wish to see him anyway. . . . John was always amused by great-uncle Edwin Ferguson's handsome French Renaissance house (near our old houses) being now a 'mortuary' (horrible word)!"

In a diary kept for a few months immediately after his graduation from Harvard, John has left a picture of his grandmother seeing him off at the railway station. It was in August 1923, and she was sixty-seven. "She was standing tall and erect in the L. and N. [Louisville & Nashville] station—her regal dignity, her beaming sweetness dominating the platform. It really cut very deep when the thought of another year ahead without seeing her came stinging the mind."

Although it was Mary Miller Ferguson who brought him up, the closest relations John maintained throughout his life were with his father's sister and brother, Aunt Mary and Uncle Preston. Aunt Mary was born in Lexington in 1875; she was graduated from Bryn Mawr in 1896, and she married Henry M. Waite in 1914. She was as much like John Mason Brown as it is possible for an aunt and nephew to be alike: in appearance, especially

---

* The author is indebted for the Ferguson annals to Mrs. Frances Starks Heyburn, a second cousin of John's, sent via Ellen Barret Wood.

the vivid red hair, and in personality—witty, charming, loqua-
cious. Unfortunately she was like him in another way—people
remember her qualities without remembering their manifesta-
tions, especially in regard to her wit. She has left an atmosphere
from which the particles have not precipitated. The same is true
of John, except that more of his contemporaries are living—and
of course he left almost twenty books. Her letters are pretty much
of family interest only. There are a few characteristic anecdotes.
Notably her remark when her nephew took up his career as a
lecturer: "What! A Brown *paid* for talking?" She and her husband lived in Cincinnati for some years; Mr. Waite was in business there. Later he joined the Department of the Interior, under
the redoubtable Harold L. Ickes, during the Roosevelt Administration in the 1930s. John saw her in New York in August 1923,
soon after leaving his grandmother at the station in Louisville.
Another aunt, Margaret Brown, had died in July. John wrote in
his diary for August 29: "I found Aunt Mary brave—heroic with
Aunt Marge's death so near. Two of the world's most perfect
creations, they were, as well as the two sisters nearest and dearest to each other I have known. It was a joy to see Aunt Mary
again, to talk to her for hours at a stretch, to feel the sympathy
of her great spirit, to hear the crackle of her endless wit. If Oscar
Wilde or Congreve had only possessed a dictaphone to catch her
conversation permanently—hours of epigram hunting would not
have been wasted, and the results (especially in Wilde's case)
would not have smelt of polished straining and revision."

That was years before John was married. Of course they saw
each other—as individuals and later as families—for the rest of
her life. One other remark of Aunt Mary's has survived; in a certain club which had just put new chintz covers on the furniture—
"If only they could slipcover the membership." Like her sister-in-
law, she became an invalid, being taken care of temporarily in
clubs to which she belonged. Her last three years were spent in a
hospital on Martha's Vineyard, where she died. In a letter to his
London friend, the drama critic Alan Dent, John wrote on Sep-

tember 17, 1963: "Aunt Mary—remember your Betsy Trotwood from Kentucky?—died last week, having been a poor vegetable for four years of anguish."

Uncle Preston has left a much clearer trail. He was, needless to say, named for his Confederate grandfather. He was born in Lexington on January 2, 1872, and was graduated from Yale in the Class of 1892. The Thirty-Five Year Record of that class discloses that he joined the Regular Army of the United States on September 1, 1894, "and therein found his life service. On February 8, 1905, at Wilkes-Barre, Pa., he married Susan Ford Dorrance, a graduate of Miss Porter's School at Farmington, Conn." They had a son, born in 1905, whom his father survived.

Preston Brown's military career was highly distinguished. He wrote for the Thirty-Five Year Record that he was

commissioned 2d Lieutenant, 2d U.S. Infantry, March 2, 1897; promoted through grades to Major General, December 10, 1925. Served during the campaign of Santiago de Cuba with the 2d Infantry, and later on throughout the Philippine Insurrection with the same regiment. . . . Became Chief of Staff, 2d Division near Verdun, at Château-Thierry, Soissons and St. Mihiel, April–Sept. 1918; Chief of Staff, 4th Army Corps in front of Metz, September, 1918; Commanding General, 3d Division, Battle of Meuse-Argonne, October, 1918; Assistant Chief of Staff, A.E.F., at Advanced General Headquarters in occupied German territory, November, 1918; instructor, director, and acting commandant, Army War College, Washington, D.C., 1919–1921.

Awarded Distinguished Service Medal "for exceptionally meritorious and distinguished service." The citation reads:—

"As chief of staff of the 2d Division he directed the details of the battles near Château-Thierry, Soissons, and at the St. Mihiel salient with great credit. Later, in command of the Argonne-Meuse offensive, at a most critical time, by his splendid judgment and energetic action, his division was able to carry to a successful conclusion the operations at Claire-Chênes and at Hill 294." —G.O. No. 12, W. D., 1919.

Other honors were to follow, and the Thirty-Five Year Record includes an account by Colonel A. K. Conger of General Brown's service in World War I, giving colorful details of the actions referred to in the citation just quoted. He adroitly and forcibly managed to keep his troops out of the French Command, and he did indeed direct the fighting with exceptional skill. Colonel Conger writes:

The [French] 6th Army Chief of Staff, to whom Preston Brown—as Division Chief of Staff—reported, tried to scatter the [American] Second Division all along the Army front, bits here and there to strengthen this, that and the other French division. Brown spoke French—fluently at times, vehemently always—there[fore] it fell to him to negotiate. It was a battle of wits and character; Brown won it.

General Brown went to Washington in March 1930 to assume his new duties as Deputy Chief of Staff; he had been for four years in command of the First Corps Area, with headquarters at Boston.

The General and his wife—Uncle Preston and Aunt Susan—had a summer place on Martha's Vineyard, where John and his growing family were often to visit them. It was a long and very close relationship. John wrote an article about his Uncle Preston, which appeared in *The Saturday Review* for July 26, 1947 *—his uncle was to die in June 1948. The article was largely an account of the difference between John and his uncle, essentially that Uncle Preston threw away everything and was tidy; John kept everything and his study was messy. "As a man of action, my uncle distrusts words. He is, however, no enemy of literature, at least of what he recognizes as literature. Only a few novels can be found on his shelves. . . . The annals of campaigns or the lives of generals are not unnaturally his specialty. History he cherishes, even if by his incessant discarding he sets an example which, if universally followed, would make the writing of history impossible."

A better picture of General Brown is in a letter of John's, dated April 6, 1964, to Edward M. Coffman, Professor of Military History at the University of Wisconsin, who was preparing a book on

---

* This article is reprinted as a chapter in his book *Seeing More Things* under the title "Two Other Races of Men."

America's part in World War I.* "My uncle, Preston Brown . . . was, as you have guessed, one of the wittiest and most colorful of men, a thunderer when it came to demanding discipline of his officers but kindhearted and tender beneath all the bluster. I remember as a boy staying with him for a week in Washington when he was heading the War College. One of his favorite tricks there, and I believe in WWI, was to give orders in terms of Biblical references. In his writing he was imprisoned by facts and the accuracy of his mind; in his conversation he was all color and invention. He was greatly loved and greatly hated, and I discovered when I was in the Navy in World War II that those who hated him were usually lax soldiers, and those who loved him were usually good ones. General Bradley was among the latter." Aunt Susan was still alive at that time, but eighty-nine and an invalid.

It remains to be said that, when Preston Brown was in the Philippines, he dealt firmly with a Filipino who was his bearer, and whom Brown saw making for the bushes with the burden he carried. Brown shot him.

---

* Professor Coffman's book is *The War to End All Wars: The American Military Experience in World War I* (Oxford, 1968). It includes several references to General Brown, including the following: "In early June, Preston Brown's criticism of the French was so vocal and continuous that it came to Pershing's attention. Although the 'C-in-C' was not noted for his affection for the French, he was concerned enough with good relations to clamp down sharply on Brown."

# Chapter Three

# Harvard

Since John had not passed all the entrance examinations on his first try, he had recourse to a cramming establishment: the "Widow" Nolen's, on Harvard Square, as famous an institution in its day as the second-hand clothing emporium operated by Max Keezer. On April 13, 1960, John was to write to J. Donald Adams, in a letter of congratulation on Adams's biography of Professor Charles Townsend Copeland: "As one of those who had to use the 'Widow' Nolen, to get into Harvard, I was grateful to have him included" (in Mr. Adams's book).* The so-called "Widow," by the way, was a male.

At Harvard John's principal activities were theatrical, both in the Dramatic Club and as an acting member of Professor George Pierce Baker's "47 Workshop," so called because the course which it represented was called English 47. Following World War I and the reactivation of the Workshop, Mr. Baker wrote in the preface to *Workshop Plays, Second Series* (1919) that the new policy of the 47 Workshop was to produce original plays by students at Harvard and Radcliffe (most of them were graduate students who had come to Cambridge—or remained there after their un-

---

* J. Donald Adams, Harvard '13, was a former editor of *The New York Times Book Review*. Mr. Copeland, who taught at Harvard until 1928, when he was sixty-eight, and lived to be over ninety, conducted a composition course like Dean Briggs's English 5, but on much more unconventional lines. (He finally succeeded to Dean Briggs's Chair.) He was the source of many legends, some of them true, and he started many a successful writer on his merry way. John did not take his course.

dergraduate years—for the specific purpose of studying with Baker). The Dramatic Club, largely an undergraduate organization, would produce worthy plays of foreign origin unlikely to be produced commercially.

John was elected to the Dramatic Club at the end of his freshman year, having already played in at least two of its productions. In May 1920 the Dramatic Club presented *The Governor's Wife*, a comedy by Jacinto Benavente, in Cambridge, Boston, and Wellesley; John had the part of a picador. H. T. Parker, the celebrated H.T.P. of the *Boston Transcript*, critic of drama and music, encouraged the Dramatic Club by customarily reviewing their productions, but he said what he thought; while he was an admirer of the play, he thought it beyond the capacities of the Dramatic Club. He called it "[a] task for a most expert producer, for a plastic, resilient, mutually practised company of comedians." Philip Hale in the *Boston Herald* was kinder to the production; so was Joseph Auslander, '17, in the *Harvard Crimson*. At least one of the actresses in the play, Miss Dorothy Sands, went on to achieve considerable success in the theatre. She also became a lifelong friend of John's.

One of the survivors of the Dramatic Club of that year thinks that it must have been at the Wellesley production of *The Governor's Wife*, on a warm evening in late May, that the male members of the company, after the final curtain, went off skinny-dipping in Lake Waban, adjoining the campus. While they were refreshing themselves, the lake was approached by a man who, whatever he was called then, would now be known as a "security officer." The boys were obliged to tread water as silently as possible, with only the tips of their noses exposed to the air, until he went away. As Uncle Remus says, that's as far as the tale goes, so any questions about the young men's clothes, where they were and why the campus guard did not spot them, must remain unanswered.

John's scrapbook also includes a notice of what was presumably a short play, presented the following week, called "A Spanish

Pickle, or Eleven up, and One to Go (to be followed by a banquet)." John had the part of La Eddyendeth (P.H.), whatever that may have meant, and the program notes that "the action takes place in Immortality, capital of Anyplace." Anyone who has seen an undergraduate romp can imagine what this may have been like.

It was at this banquet that John and sixteen others were elected to membership in the Dramatic Club. The *Crimson* reported that "on account of the depletion of the membership during the war an unusually large number of men was taken on this year, putting the club back on its full peacetime basis."

During the early summer of 1920 John evidently wrote to Lee Simonson of the Theatre Guild inquiring about the possibility of being employed by a stock company. There is a letter from Simonson dated June 8, from which one deduces that he had given a talk at Harvard, and this encouraged John to inquire as to possibilities. Simonson's letter was gracious and considerate, but not particularly helpful, though he offered to investigate further if John would say exactly what he had in mind.

In December 1920 the Dramatic Club produced *The Dragon* by Lady Gregory. This time the production won higher praise—though with a reservation or two—from H.T.P. John took the part of the dragon—years later, in 1954, he was to write to Alan Dent in London that he was an offstage voice. The cast included, as "Foreign Men Bringing in Food," two young men who were not to pursue careers on the stage, but were to become lifelong friends of John's: Marshall Ayres Best and Henry Cabot Lodge (grandson of the senator who had opposed the Treaty of Versailles). The scenery, although designed by another hand, was painted under the direction of Donald M. Oenslager, who was to become John's closest friend as well as one of the most gifted and illustrious scene designers in the American theatre of his generation, with many brilliant successes to his credit over several decades.

In that same month of December 1920 John made his first appearance as a member of the acting company of the 47 Work-shop, playing a character called John in a one-act play, *Mis' Mercy,* by Louise Whitefield Bray. Although he had only three speeches and many long silences, the author wrote him a note of congratulation on his performance, saying that because of the silences Robert Edmond Jones would call it an ideal part. More than forty years later, in March 1961, she recalled this to him in a letter enclosing a copy of the current *Radcliffe Quarterly,* which contained an article by her about George Pierce Baker. John wrote on April 3 to thank her:

"I was touched to see that photograph of *Mis' Mercy.* It was my first Workshop play. I remember the play and the performances vividly. I remember rehearsing and rehearsing the trip I was sup-posed to make for my entrance and having my roommate say, after the show, 'Too bad you tripped up but you covered it very well.' I also recall the consternation I caused by being the one member of a New England seafaring family with an unmistakably Southern voice. When I said, 'Where's Hannah?' with a drawl, several of my friends thought that my mother in the play must have had an affair with some itinerant Dixiecrat."

In March 1921 John appeared in Philip Barry's full-length play, *O, Promise Me,* previously entitled *A Punch for Judy.* Ac-cording to George Oppenheimer, then a member of the 47 Work-shop and now the drama critic of *Newsday,* in his autobiography, *The View from the Sixties:* "It concerned a breach of promise suit and a faked trial that a young lawyer engineered in an at-tempt to regain his former fiancée. John Brown played one of the leads along with Dorothy Sands. . . . I was cast as the Italian foreman of a rigged jury. I had only one line: 'I finda for plaintiff one hundert tousand dollar and a costa.' The night of the open-ing performance I delivered the line with such resonance that I blew off a florid moustache. I got quite a laugh, but I also in-curred the wrath of Barry, who thought I was trying to pad my part."

The 47 Workshop went that spring on tour, visiting Worcester,

New York, Utica, Buffalo, and Cleveland during the week of April 18–23. (This would have been spring vacation week at Harvard, which in those days centered on Patriot's Day, April 19, the anniversary of Paul Revere's ride.) They presented *O, Promise Me* and three one-act plays: *Mis' Mercy; Torches* by Kenneth Raisbeck, '21, who was to become Baker's assistant; and *Cooks and Cardinals* by Norman F. Lindau, a graduate student.

It had originally been tentatively planned to produce on this tour a play by Thomas Wolfe called *The Mountains.* John's essay "Thomas Wolfe as a Dramatist," which originally appeared in 1938, the year of Wolfe's death, and is reprinted in *Dramatis Personae,* made this observation:

> Tom carried the mountains with him to the Workshop. The first of his plays Mr. Baker produced was an utterly conventional little one-act, known accurately enough as *The Mountains.* Although it might almost have served as a mountain play to end all mountain plays, unfortunately it did not. Its hero, as is the custom in hillbilly scripts, was an unhappy fellow, anxious to get away from the mountains. As I remember, the curtain had not been up two minutes before he walked to a window and shook his fists vehemently at an inoffensive peak painted on the backdrop, crying, "Goddamn you, Baldpate [for that was the mountain's name], yuh hemmin' me in!"

In at least one production of *The Mountains* John played a mountain doctor, but another program lists a different actor in this part.

That same spring of 1921 the Dramatic Club planned to present Chekhov's *The Sea Gull,* but changed its plans upon making the discovery that *The Sea Gull* had been performed by the Washington Square Players of New York; the policy of the club was to give only foreign plays never before presented in this country. Instead they announced three one-act plays: *Wurzel Flummery,* a comedy by A. A. Milne; *Hagorama,* a Japanese fantasy; and *A Good Woman,* a farce by Arnold Bennett. *A Good Woman* was replaced by Maeterlinck's *The Blind.* H.T.P. reviewed these in his customary thoughtful manner, finding much to admire in *The*

*Blind.* John does not appear in the program of these plays, but it includes the statement that the "Scenery was designed and painted by D. M. Oenslager, '23," and it was praised by H.T.P. (Meanwhile, a month earlier, H.T.P. had written a favorable review of *O, Promise Me*—favorable on the whole, not without calling attention to the shortcomings, as he saw them, of both the play and the production. Mr. Parker did not mention John's performance.)

Incidentally, the Dramatic Club invariably sent complimentary tickets to its performances to President and Mrs. A. Lawrence Lowell, who invariably gave them to members of their domestic staff. Mr. Lowell is remembered as being not only indifferent, but hostile, to the theatre. This was a compelling reason for Baker's later move to Yale.

Evidently the blood of the Puritans who closed the theatres in Cromwell's time ran in Mr. Lowell's veins with undiminished force. Two stories survive. The first may be apocryphal: it is said that one fine day, walking across the Yard, Mr. Lowell saw George Pierce Baker at his customary location in Massachusetts Hall. Finding the window open, Mr. Lowell is supposed to have said: "Baker, I hear that you want Harvard to give you a theatre. *I* would not ask Harvard University for so much as a lead pencil." The second story comes from a very reliable source. Some time in the early twenties a group of theatrical personages offered Mr. Baker the money for a theatre at Harvard, or at least offered to raise it. Mr. Baker took the project to Mr. Lowell, who turned it down.

There survives a telegram from Mr. Baker to John dated June 15, 1921, advising him not to expect summer work "here"—presumably in connection with Mr. Baker's activities. His report for 1920–21 discloses that he received A in two half-courses, B in two, and C in two; in full courses, one B and one C. This entitled him to inclusion in Group 3, those who gained distinction, but not such high distinction as those in Groups 1 and 2. Early in September Mr. Baker wrote to John from his summer place in

New Hampshire regretting that he had been unable to have him for a visit, owing to illness in the family.

With nothing else to occupy him, John had gone home for the summer of 1920, and had got a job, through Arthur Krock, as a reporter on the *Courier-Journal*. His stories include a report on the Letter Carriers Association; on a soldier who, while AWOL, hijacked a local farmer's automobile only to have a blowout after five miles and get caught; and various other events. He also reported on an unfortunate girl who had been drowned; there is a note by John on the clipping of his story reading, "coroner explained enlivening details to me." His first night on the police court assignment yielded three suicides. He reported several sermons, also miscellaneous news items. He covered a number of Chautauqua lectures. And he telephoned in a portion of the story which appeared under the head "Man Spurned by Wife Found Dead."

In addition, the *Courier-Journal* printed a number of his reviews of books and plays, the latter sent from Boston or New York. Already, in December 1919, it had published his article on "The Craftsmanship of Robert Edmond Jones," and in January 1920 a very favorable review of John Drinkwater's *Lincoln*. His piece on Jones particularly mentioned Jones's work on Tolstoy's *Redemption* and Sem Benelli's *The Jest,* in which the Barrymore brothers appeared. He found another treatment of Lincoln, this one in *A Man of the People* by Thomas Dixon—whose previous book, *The Clansman*, had inspired D. W. Griffith to make *The Birth of a Nation*—mediocre and cheap. In November 1921, in what may have been the first of his many reviews of plays by Eugene O'Neill, he reported that *Anna Christie* was "a bold and absorbing play." To anticipate, two later reviews may be mentioned: his old *bête noire,* Robert B. Mantell, by now fourteen years older than when John had seen him as King Lear in Louisville, had the temerity to appear in *Richelieu* before an audience including John, who gave him a royal panning in the *Harvard Crimson;* and in 1923 he wrote an unfavorable review for the *Courier-Journal* of Maugham's *East of Suez*. He wrote numerous other reviews for the *Crimson*, chiefly of books on the theatre. He also contributed occasionally to the *Harvard Lampoon* and the college's literary magazine, *The Harvard Advocate*.

Meanwhile, in October 1921, John was elected president of the Dramatic Club, a post he was to keep for his remaining two years as an undergraduate and in which he was to distinguish himself by his firm opinions and unshakable authority, qualities vividly remembered now by some of his surviving associates, notably Donald Oenslager and Bertram K. Little, the latter elected vice-president of the club when John was elected president. A disagreement arose when John announced that he thought all productions of the Dramatic Club should be screened through Professor Baker and the Workshop; Bertram Little took issue with him emphatically; Oenslager, a born man of peace, acted as intermediary, and he recalls that a compromise was effected at a Chinese restaurant.

It was in this same October that the 47 Workshop presented *The Mountains* by Thomas Wolfe. This was followed by two other one-act plays, one of them, *The Other One* by Arthur Ketchum, with scenery by Oenslager. At the same time the Dramatic Club was preparing *The Witches' Mountain,* a play of the Argentine by Julio Sanchez Gardel, and *The Violins of Cremona* by François Coppée. John had a part in the latter, which was the curtain-raiser. This time the review in the *Transcript* was unsigned; it was written by Brooks Atkinson, later to become one of the most distinguished of drama critics, occupying that post for *The New York Times* for several decades. He was also to become a close friend of John Mason Brown. There were only four parts in the play: one actress and one actor (not John) were singled out for praise; "the others sputtered and spurted." Both plays were designed by Oenslager.

Perhaps it was in his junior year that John began to turn his hand to playwriting. One play, called *His Place in the Family*, in one act, exists in manuscript in the Theatre Collection at Harvard; almost certainly it was never produced, for it is difficult to conceive of a more inept piece of work. It concerns a lower-middle-class family living outside Louisville, consisting of the father, his wife, and two sons in their twenties: Jack, the elder, strong, fit, responsible; Tom, the younger, a cripple from birth, and a disappointment to his father. He reads all the time. His mother tries to reconcile the father to Tom. Jack has a date with a girl; his father tries to persuade him to break it; Tom encourages him to go. Jack does go, only to be killed by an interurban trolley as a result of failing to look both ways before crossing the tracks. The news comes by telephone. The father holds Tom responsible, and the curtain falls to general misery. A totally unconvincing melodrama; a soap opera but no soap.

He was to improve upon this. Meanwhile, somewhere along the line, Mr. Baker undoubtedly discouraged John from the pursuit of a career on the stage. Possibly Brooks Atkinson's review of *The Violins of Cremona* contributed to this discouragement. Incidentally, John's recollection of this review was not quite accurate, or perhaps he was making a good story even better, when he came to write about it in a *Saturday Review* essay published August 11, 1951.* John wrote that Atkinson had praised *three* of the four undergraduate actors; "the rest of the cast, he concluded, 'sputtered and spurted.' As I happened to be the rest of the cast, I have been reading Mr. Atkinson with increasing pleasure ever since." But John actually had a companion to sputter and spurt.

Even so, his acting career was not quite at an end. Aside from the frivolity of playing the comedian (opposite Bert Little's comedienne) in the Hasty Pudding Show of spring 1923 (the Hasty Pudding Club puts on a musical comedy, written, acted, and produced by undergraduates, every year), John acted during his senior year in the 47 Workshop production of *Catskill Dutch* by Roscoe W. Brink. This was unveiled in Cambridge on Febru-

---

* Called "Manhattan's Thoreau," it was an essay review of Atkinson's book *Once Around the Sun.* It is reprinted in John's book *As They Appear,* published by McGraw-Hill the following year.

ary 19, 1923. It was a three-act play, and it was taken seriously. John played the part of Cobby, "a Negro, a one-time slave." It would be interesting to know whether he wore a towel around his head; his own hair, at that time red, curly, and luxuriant, could have served as a model for Harpo Marx's wig. The Theatre Collection at Harvard preserved a letter from Mr. Baker to John, thanking John for his assistance in making the "outside" performances of *Catskill Dutch* successful. Just what John did besides portray Cobby is not mentioned; however, the word "outside" suggests that the opening of *Catskill Dutch* in Cambridge was immediately followed by other performances elsewhere—Boston and Wellesley, perhaps.

The program of *Catskill Dutch* contains the following paragraph:

The 47 Workshop of Harvard University started as a place where promising plays written by men and women students taking the playwriting courses, English 47 and English 47A, might be tried out. Slowly this laboratory theatre has grown until now The 47 Workshop, under the direction of Professor George Pierce Baker, in putting on its four to six annual productions, gives to actors, scene-designers and stage-force connected with it, an opportunity to co-operate in placing before the playwright a sympathetic and careful presentation of his play. An audience of some four hundred persons interested in the arts of the theatre see the result, and within a week after each production, make a written comment on any or all parts of it. [The names of the writers were removed before the criticisms were shown to the playwright.] From a careful study of these with Professor Baker, the author revises or rewrites his play.

The program also lists an Undergraduate Advisory Committee, fourteen in all, including Don Oenslager, Bert Little, and John. In his senior year John was no longer confined to the acting company of the Workshop, but was enrolled as a student of playwriting in English 47. He wrote a one-act curtain-raiser, *The First Day,* which was produced in March 1923 along with *The Trap* by Lydia Gansser. *The First Day* was a light-hearted comedy, no doubt autobiographical in inspiration, about a young man who wants to leave home and try his fortune in the theatre. John carefully preserved all the critiques of the audience—with the names of the writers removed, as aforesaid—and one of the critics called the play "a rollicking comedy that didn't rollick." * John himself played the lead.

In May, apparently, *The First Day* was given as the curtain-raiser to Thomas Wolfe's new play, *Welcome to Our City*. This play is as great an improvement over *The Mountains* as *The First Day* is over *His Place in the Family*. *Welcome to Our City* is concerned with unscrupulous politics in the South (Wolfe—need it be said?—came from Asheville). To quote again from John's essay of 1938, the year of Wolfe's death:

In May, 1923, Mr. Baker staged the first of Tom's plays to bear signs, however faint, of his genius. It was *Welcome to Our City*, a long, occasionally expressionistic drama in ten scenes. It was not a good play. Although it was as undisciplined as you would have expected a play by Thomas Wolfe to be, it contained some promising writing. It boasted, moreover, one hilarious satiric scene, written in dumb show (amazingly enough). In this episode a phony Carolina governor (played by Leon Pearson) was shown up in all his phoniness by the simple act of permitting the audience to watch him undress. He had retired alone to his hotel bedroom, full of political pomposity. First he surveyed himself in a mirror, making fine oratorical gestures. Then little by little he shed both his clothing and his dignity. First he removed his padded coat. Then his layer-after-layer of vests. Then he took  off his toupee. Finally, just as he was getting into bed he slipped his false teeth in a tumbler. Before this scene was over more than the body of this governor was unclothed. His character was naked.

Tom must have been amused as he watched the Cambridge performances of *Welcome to Our City*. His play was deeply concerned, among other things, with the way in which a proud young Southern aristocrat seduces a pretty young mulatto. In choosing his actors Mr. Baker could never have been accused of type-casting. New England was conscripted, much to its surprise. It was Cambridge's Dorothy Sands who assumed a sweet-potato voice to impersonate the wronged mulatto.

* Much later, John credited that *bon mot* to the author of this biography, who is honored but must disclaim it. This author liked the play, has examined all the critiques, and identified his own, which is favorable but, with the confidence and vanity of youth, somewhat patronizing.

And it was the elder Senator Henry Cabot Lodge's grandson, John . . . who played the rebel seducer.

John went on to say that Wolfe submitted the play to the Neighborhood Playhouse in New York, which expressed considerable interest, but when they suggested some revisions, he exploded in Biblical wrath and withdrew the script. Wolfe himself went on to write at least one more play—if it can be called one play—named *Mannerhouse,* recalled by an acquaintance of Wolfe's, to whom Wolfe spent an entire night in Paris reading it aloud, as a nine-act epic of a southern family from the Civil War to the 1920s. This may, after fifty years, be inaccurate. (In Wolfe's *Letters to His Mother,* he tells how this play was rewritten at white heat after the original script had been lost on Wolfe's first night in Paris.) In any event, Wolfe was to achieve his celebrity as a novelist, with *Look Homeward, Angel* first, and then with *Of Time and the River,* which contains a somewhat unflattering portrait of the 47 Workshop, its professor, whom he calls Hatcher, and his assistant, whom he calls Starwick. (Professor Baker's assistant was actually Kenneth Raisbeck, who will be recalled as the author of *Torches,* one of the plays the Workshop had taken on tour in the spring of 1921. Baker gave Raisbeck this assignment after Raisbeck's graduation that year.) Wolfe wrote directly from life, and his characters are easily identifiable; but many of his contemporaries considered his portraits grossly unfair.* When he became a novelist he overcame his objections to being edited; it became well known, through Wolfe's short book *The Story of a Novel,* written in the midthirties, that Maxwell E. Perkins of Scribners—editor also of

---

* "Tom was beyond good and evil," Maxwell Perkins once said to the present author. George Oppenheimer, in his book previously quoted, recalls Wolfe's description of "Professor Hatcher's celebrated school of dramatists," as well as the following: "False, trivial, glib, dishonest, empty, without substance, lacking faith—is it any wonder that among Professor Hatcher's young men few birds sang?" Mr. Oppenheimer names a considerable number of Mr. Baker's alumni who went on to high distinction.

Hemingway and Fitzgerald, and generally considered the most distinguished book editor of his time—was indefatigable and invaluable in helping Wolfe to give form to the thousands of pages that had come shapeless from his pen.

George Oppenheimer, though he defended Baker against Thomas Wolfe (see preceding footnote) had a criticism of his own:

Good as Baker was as a teacher (his history of the drama was a liberal education in itself), he was not an ideal producer. His choice of plays was erratic and their production often beset with accidents. [Look who's talking: the man who blew off his moustache in Philip Barry's play.] Kenneth Raisbeck, one of his more promising students, was now his assistant, an effete young man with a penchant for purple prose. His one-act play about the Renaissance, *Torches,* was a Baker favorite. Raisbeck's tragic end some years later was as baroque as his play. He was found dead in a Connecticut graveyard. At first murder was suspected, then an autopsy revealed that he had been the victim of a meningitis attack. Later still there was evidence of strangulation. The police never ascertained what he was doing in the graveyard. He might well have been searching out a theme for a new play.

John ended his presidency of the Dramatic Club in a blaze of glory. This consisted of the presentation, most appropriately in Harvard's Germanic Museum, of two miracle plays under John's directions: *The Lutterworth Christmas Play* and *The Pageant of the Shearmen and the Taylors.* The latter was done in John's version—rather his adaptation of the original sixteenth-century Coventry mystery play.

The play, in twelve brief scenes, begins with a prologue by Isaiah, followed by the Annunciation uttered by the angel Gabriel. Joseph is skeptical of his wife's virginity, but Gabriel convinces him. Next come the shepherds and the star, followed by the Nativity. Mary talks with the shepherds. The fifth scene introduces Herod, a buffoon. The three kings appear, to be welcomed by Herod—but privately he intends to kill them. There is a scene of the kings with the Holy Family, then Gabriel advises the kings to go home before Herod finds them. Herod then decrees the slaughter of the innocents, and in the final scene Gabriel tells Joseph and Mary to go to Egypt.

John's version preserves the unsophisticated charm of the original (one supposes), and if the four-square, singsong rhythm of the verse occasionally suggests that the Nativity took place on the shores of Gitche Gumee, he was probably preserving the original rhythm. His version rhymes alternate lines.

John and his friend Donald Oenslager were particularly fortunate at Harvard in being included in the circle that gathered on Sunday evenings at Shady Hill, the home of Professor Paul J. Sachs and his family—Mrs. Sachs and three daughters. (Shady Hill had formerly been the home of Charles Eliot Norton.) Mr. Sachs had come to Harvard following a distinguished and successful career in banking, as a partner in Goldman, Sachs & Company of Wall Street. At the invitation of Edward Forbes, director of the Fogg Museum of Art at Harvard, he came to Cambridge in 1915 to act as assistant director of the Fogg— "without precedent, without specific duties, and without salary." Two years later he became an assistant professor in the Department of Fine Arts, a full professor in 1927, and chairman of the department in 1933.

On Sunday evenings a dozen or more students, mostly undergraduates, came to Shady Hill for an evening of conversation and charades. One of Mr. Sachs's daughters, herself considerably younger than John and Don, remembers them as spark plugs of the Sunday evenings. The Sachses had a chest full of old costumes that were appropriate for charades. As for conversation, John must have done much of the talking. Mrs. Sachs was especially interested in the theatre. It was Don who took Mr. Sachs's courses —Don being the visual man, John the verbal man, which is not to say that Don has ever been inarticulate. The point is that these evenings contributed greatly to their college experience. It is unfortunate that more college professors and their families do not mingle with the students as the Sachses did.

Aside from the Dramatic Club, John's undergraduate friendships centered in the Signet Society, a (more or less) intellectual club, intellectual indeed when compared with those clubs which were symbols of status for their members. (Harvard did not, and does not, have chapters of national fraternities.) At his inauguration into the Signet membership, John was asked his opinion of a possible marriage between the United States and Great Britain. He replied without hesitation that he could not imagine a marriage between Uncle Sam and John Bull.

In John's day the Signet membership included David McCord, '21, and Roy Larsen of the same class; from 1922 Myles Baker (son of G.P.B.), Edward A. Weeks, and R. Keith Kane; and, from his own class Donald Oenslager, Garrison Norton, Joseph Sill Clark (later to serve two terms as United States Senator from Pennsylvania); Bertram Little, Marshall Best, and Theodore Morrison. From '24, Henry Cabot Lodge, also to become a U.S. Senator; and from '25, John Lodge and George Pierce Baker, Jr. Many of these men were to become distinguished, some of them eminent; and several were close friends of John's for life.

The recollections of the surviving members do not agree in all details. Apparently the club invited faculty members, and sometimes well-known writers, to lunch; on one such occasion the guest was Heywood Broun of the *New York World*. There was a dish of marmalade in the middle of the table, intended to be shared by one and all. Broun, thinking it was his dessert, pulled the plate to him and ate all the marmalade with a spoon. The other version is that Broun was a supper guest, and ate the marmalade because the Spartan fare left him hungry. One of the members, Edward A. Weeks, later for several decades editor of *The Atlantic Monthly*, has written of the Signet in the first volume of his autobiography; he told the present author that the supper menu usually consisted of Shredded Wheat with brown sugar, but one could get shirred eggs by applying persuasion. Lunch was the principal meal.

Everyone agrees that John was a constantly witty and charming ornament of the membership; very few can remember any-thing in particular that he said, aside from the remark at his inauguration. But there is no question that he left an impression. The Signet was noted for good conversation, often led by John, whose talent for spontaneous punning had already come to flower. He could be simultaneously vulgar and elegant. In 1956 the Signet gave an award to John. The citation, written by David McCord, reads as follows:

THE SIGNET SOCIETY MEDAL
FOR ACHIEVEMENT IN THE ARTS
AWARDED TO
JOHN MASON BROWN
CLASS OF 1923

JOHN MASON BROWN: Dramatic critic and dialectic essayist with the superior gift of wit. Like Shaw, whom he admires, he knows whether to run the lawnmower through a bed of tulips or use the brush of a Chiang Yee with spare and exquisite effect. He is second to none among his contemporaries in love and understanding of the theatre. A mili-tant humanist in war and peace, he is thrice versatile as teacher, lec-turer, and reporter. The world is his revolving stage, and early green-room thoughts in a green shade have led him lately to examine in pure sunlight contemporary figures on the national and political landscape. As when Q says that "Prospero was not conjuring by halves," so the author of *Seeing Things* has an eye to see them whole; and not even Prospero could begin to conjure with him in the realm of childhood. We honor the man who remembers the Signet as "Harvard's conversa-tional paradise," and not in small part because he helped to make it so.

HARVARD UNIVERSITY
3 MARCH 1956

In a letter of John's following that occasion, he wrote: "What an oasis the Signet truly is."

Professor Baker accepted an invitation to transfer to Yale in 1925. Yale was ready to give him a theatre to work in, as Harvard, under the domination of President A. Lawrence Lowell, was not. Mr. Baker's move was by no means the end of his relations with John. Meanwhile, a fitting conclusion to this chapter is a summary of John's essay on Baker, published a few years after Baker's death in 1935.* John writes of four Bakers: first, "the formal classroom Baker whose business it was to teach the history of the drama. . . . This classroom Baker . . . was the most professorial of the four Bakers, and, for that very reason, of later years the least important of the lot.

"For some years he was a slightly bored and tired man.† . . . [However,] even in his weariness he managed to give the impression that the desk behind which he was lecturing was surrounded by footnotes." The essay goes on to tell how Mr. Baker, "abandoning his professorial calm, began to make his points as an actor." He skillfully imitated certain favorite characters through whom he "would expose the virtues or the follies of a type of playwriting."

The "second of the four Bakers was beholden to no notes. . . . This Professor Baker who dared to teach such an unteachable subject as playwriting was the least dogmatic of men. . . . There was nothing oracular about his methods in these seminars. . . . His program for his beginners was as similar each year as the results were different. Invariably the course would start off with a one-act dramatization of a short story. . . . Next came an original one-act play, and, finally, by spring, a long play. . . . A sure test of the merits of a play was Mr. Baker's reading of it. He was an exceptional reader. . . . The wonder was he never succumbed to the temptation of making fun of the stuff he was reading. He could spoof the classics, real and pseudo, in his his-

---

* This essay was published, together with essays by Donald M. Oenslager, Sidney Howard, and Allardyce Nicoll, also a telegram and a letter of condolence to Mrs. Baker from Eugene O'Neill, by the Dramatists Play Service of New York, in a small book entitled *George Pierce Baker: A Memorial* (1939).

† A classmate of John's who took Baker's half-course in the history of the drama disagrees with this impression, having found Mr. Baker's presentation of the subject maintaining a high level of interest; but then this classmate did not have the other Bakers to compare with this one. However, he saw enough of Mr. Baker to be impressed by him as a warm and friendly man; indeed, somewhat afraid of impressing students from the South (including John, Wolfe, and John's classmate) as being cold and remote.

tory courses, yet he never made sport of his young playwrights' work. He was on their side. He was fully aware that their fellow students would tear them limb from limb when the time for comment came. Accordingly he acted as their defender. . . .

"The third of the four Bakers known to his Cambridge students was the tireless Baker." This was the one who, after a full day and a hastily eaten dinner, came to direct the rehearsals of the plays chosen for production. "His hope was that his playwrights would learn by having had a real production before a selected audience. . . . With his actors, as with his playwrights, his patience knew no bounds." The essay goes on to describe how Mr. Baker, "sparing, almost stingy, with praise," got young men and women to work night after night on every aspect of the production.

"This Baker, who inspired more active loyalty than any other teacher at Harvard (not excepting the great 'Copey' himself) was the fourth of the four Bakers. This man Baker, with his extraordinary personality, was the keystone upon which everything else rested. He may have put people off. His seeming coldness may have terrified some and antagonized others. Yet everyone who actually worked for him, and hence knew him—because he was the kind of man who revealed himself only in his work—felt affectionately toward him." *

There is a program in John's files dated January 19, 1925— a program of the 47 Workshop for a production called *The Last Act.* The chairman for the evening was Dean Briggs; the speakers included Dorothy Sands, Robert Edmond Jones, John Mason Brown, and Mr. Baker himself. It was a farewell to the man leaving for New Haven. (The event was celebrated at the time by

* John reprinted his essay twice—in *Broadway in Review* and again in *Dramatis Personae.* He does not say in this essay, but he did in one of the Serrell Hillman interviews, that Mr. Baker had no enthusiasm for Shaw, preferring the well-made plays of Pinero and Henry Arthur Jones. In the same interview he spoke of Mr. Baker's "passionate interest in the work of others." As to Mr. Baker's range of interest, the present writer recalls his excitement at the time when Pirandello's *Six Characters in Search of an Author,* a genuine and interesting novelty, was produced.

a headline—in the *Yale News?*—"Yale 47, Harvard 0." In one of the Serrell Hillman interviews, John attributes this remark to Heywood Broun.)

From evidence supplied by the memories of two of John's oldest and best friends, it seems conclusive that Mr. Baker told John, presumably at the beginning or middle of his senior year, that he had no talent for acting; * and that by the end of that year he had also—in spite of having produced *The First Day*—discouraged him as a playwright. Much more to the point was his positive advice: that John prepare himself for a career in criticism. Which he did.

---

* Mr. Baker had no way of knowing that John's considerable talent for acting was to be expressed on the lecture platform.

# Chapter Four

# Europe—with Interludes

After graduating *cum laude* in June 1923—John received his degree *in absentia,* being in too much of a hurry to get to his summer job to stay in Cambridge for commencement—he set out for the University of Montana at Missoula, where he had a teaching assignment. Professor Harold G. Merriam, then chairman of the Department of English at the university—later chairman of the Division of the Humanities—engaged him to teach in the summer session. John gave courses in Shakespeare, Elementary Public Speaking, and Dramatic Presentation; he also produced a few plays with his students, including *Torches.* Mr. Merriam had consulted George Pierce Baker, with whom he had taken a graduate course at Harvard in world drama: "Incidentally," writes Mr. Merriam, "the best course I ever had with any professor, and I was a graduate from Oxford University. Professor Baker highly recommended John."

In another letter Mr. Merriam wrote:

John came thinking he was to enter a primitive region where culture was in a crude state. When he found, for instance, that Mrs. Merriam and I knew a good deal about drama on Broadway and about what was going on in the world he was amazed. We enjoyed a delightful summer with him. He was in our home almost every day. Although John was never an outdoor man and therefore did not explore the wonderful country about Missoula . . . the Merriam love of Glacier Park would not allow him to miss seeing it.

John later visited Montana with his wife, and both of them (according to Mr. Merriam) suffered the effects of horseback riding with insufficient experience. Later he was to take his son Meredith to Glacier Park.

John always made warm friends whenever he was with us. . . . At that time we had "ice cream parlors" in Missoula. He loved to take friends after lectures and plays to one of them [perhaps recalling his banana splits as a boy in Louisville]; on those occasions we had bubbling witty, happy hours. . . .
The Merriam family was in New York during 1925–26 when I was working for the doctorate at Columbia University. During that time he took Mrs. Merriam to the opening of at least a dozen plays while I took care of our two children, of whom he was fond, and studied. This was wonderful satisfaction for her, for she had a keen interest in drama, as I too had.

John was to return to Missoula for the summer sessions of 1929 and 1931; in 1929 he gave courses in the History of the Theatre and Contemporary Theatre; in 1931, courses in Shakespeare and World Drama Since World War I. He also lectured at the Writers' Conference. The summer sessions lasted six weeks.*

In 1942, when he returned to the University of Montana to receive the honorary degree of Doctor of Letters and to deliver the commencement address, John made a statement, probably for the campus paper. Mr. Merriam has supplied a copy of it:

"It was here in Missoula, on this campus, that the first magnolias were not plucked but blown from my hair. Here I learned to sense the wonder of this country as a whole; to have deep respect for its regional differences, and to know that, when Kipling chattered about the cleavages between East and West, he may

---

* For a newspaperman's picture of Missoula in the summer of 1923, see *One Man's Montana* by John K. Hutchens (Lippincott, 1964), then between his freshman and sophomore years at Hamilton College, and working for his father (editor of the *Missoulian*) as a full-time staff writer. Hutchens later became a distinguished critic of drama and books on the *Boston Transcript, The New York Times,* and the *New York Herald-Tribune;* still later, a fellow member of John Mason Brown's on the board of judges of the Book-of-the-Month Club. Mr. Hutchens reviewed John's production of one-act plays at the University in 1923 for the *Missoulian.*

have been telling the truth for the decades of imperialism, but he was telling a lie so far as this nation and the future of the world are concerned. Here I learned much more than I was ever able to teach, and here I found friendships which over the years have been among the most valued and sustaining I have been privileged to enjoy."

His friendship with Mr. and Mrs. Merriam never flagged; they corresponded often, and their friendship lasted until the end of John's life.

No doubt at Missoula in the summer of 1923 John earned enough to start him on his way to Europe—he also had a traveling fellowship from Harvard—for a wide tour of European theatres, a tour that was to make it possible, on his return, for him to begin his career as a drama critic. Earlier, however, there had been another European trip, more frivolous in purpose and in nature. Mary Miller and John had come into a small legacy, and they had decided to blow it all on a trip to Europe in 1922— the summer following John's junior year at Harvard.

The Brown siblings traveled on the *Noordam* of the Holland-America line, and were fortunate to have as fellow passengers Justice Learned Hand of the Court of Appeals of New York, the highest court of the state, and his family, including three daughters. The Hands and the Browns saw a great deal of one another on board. John was particularly taken with Mary Hand—she liked him also—and one evening he asked her to join him for a crème de menthe. Since she was only sixteen, five years younger than John, the Hand family went into conference and decided that she might go, but should be chaperoned.

Unfortunately there survives little or no record from the Browns themselves; whatever letters they may have sent home are irretrievable. This lack is more than compensated for by several anecdotes in *Our Hearts Were Young and Gay* by Cornelia Otis Skinner and Emily Kimbrough. First, there was the *pension* with the bedbugs. Miss Skinner and Miss Kimbrough had moved from a fashionable hotel in Paris, because it was too full

of Americans, to a *pension* near the Étoile. The very first night—
it rarely takes longer when the little creatures are present—they
were attacked by *les punaises*. Rather surprisingly, instead of
moving out, they took a taxi to the American drug store, where
they met a friend of Miss Skinner's mother. When this lady had
taken in the situation, she marched into the store and ordered a
gallon of Lysol solution and some large brushes. She then departed, leaving the girls to find Mr. and Mrs. Otis Skinner back
at the France et Choiseul. Mr. Skinner took the Lysol and the
brushes, set off for the *pension,* and began to lay about him; he
did a thorough job of extermination.

In spite of this drawback, Mary Miller and John came to take
rooms at this *pension.* They arrived separately; Mary Miller had
a date for dinner "with the cutest man you ever *saw."* So she
dashed off. Soon John arrived—Miss Kimbrough knew Mary
Miller but neither she nor Miss Skinner had met John—with
another lady from Kentucky. The owner of the *pension,* appropriately named Mme. Griffe, took them for husband and wife,
and since she spoke no English and they knew very little French,
some confusion resulted.

Mme. Griffe was looking at [John] in bewilderment as he made abortive attempts to explain something to her in a French which had a high
flavor of blue-grass. From a nearby bedroom came a girl's voice, loud
and mad, and also from the land of Man-o'-War.

"Listen to me, John Brown," it said. "Ah've grown up with you, an'
gone to Sunday school with you, but Ah've never gone to bed with you
an' Ah'm not startin' now. You tell that woman to stop showing us
rooms with bigger beds in them and get me a room with a bed to myself. Go on, now, tell her!"

The owner of the voice stepped out of Mme. Griffe's most seductive
double room. It was a girl named Anne Camden, another product of
Miss Wright's [the school where Miss Kimbrough had known Mary
Miller]. Mme. Griffe stood shrugging and making despairing gestures,
unable to fathom the behaviour of this eccentric couple.

But John Mason Brown, the future eminent critic, author and lecturer, . . . met the crisis with the ingenuity and charm with which he
now [1942] overpowers every woman's club from the Atlantic to the
Pacific.

"Madame!" he cried, and the blood of a long line of Kentucky Colonels was evident in his bearing. "Elle," and he pointed to Anne, "Mademoiselle Camden! Je!" and at this point he beat his own breast, "Monsieur Brown.* Pas un ensemble! Pas at all ensemble! Je veux coucher tout seul!"

There is one more episode involving John, which must be quoted—paraphrase would take the edge off.

Dear knows why we thought that one of the chief high spots in a girl's life was to go to the Ritz bar. Certainly it was the smokiest hole of Calcutta ever conjured up out of an old coat closet. But we stepped across its threshold experiencing a pleasant series of those nervous thrills the French call *frissons.* . . . We . . . sat down uncertainly at a dim corner table. The bar, I think, was across the hall. There wasn't one in the room. We leaned back against the wall and ate overflowing handfuls of peanuts while we tried to think of what to order. . . . Everyone in the small room stared at us and we were fairly harassed until Providence stepped in in the person of Mary Miller. She was exhausted after a three hours' fitting at Doucet's and needed reviving. She flopped down at our table and we cried gaily, "What'll you have?" which sounded, we felt, sophisticated. It also sounded alarmingly liberal and we had not counted on such additional expense, but Mary Miller was kudos worthy paying for.

"An Alexander," she said, and we all, even Mme. Venuat [chaperone and French teacher] said that was just what we were about to order. To be sure, none of us had the faintest notion, outside of a conqueror, what an Alexander was.

The things arrived and it was either a comment on the lack of development of our palates or a proof of our abstemious habits that we tasted that rich, sweet concoction of brandy, crème de cacao and straight cream and found it delicious. We sipped with delight and kept on shoveling in handfuls of peanuts.

In the midst of the epicurean debauch, John Mason Brown arrived, rather suddenly. I don't believe he was much in the habit of patronizing the Ritz bar alone, for he seemed inordinately relieved and pleased to see someone he knew. After his first inrush, he strolled over to us, very casual and handsome and Harvard.

"What are you all having?" he asked and we said "Alexanders" as nonchalantly as we could, only in chorus. So he beckoned a waiter with his cane, an impressive gesture. I realize now, it must have been because he had forgotten to check it.

---

* Anticipating the famous line, "Me Tarzan—you Jane."

"Alexanders all around," he said. "Et un de plus pour moi."

We hastened to say NO, that we didn't want another. I wasn't sure that I wanted the one I had. But John was firm and lordly. He wanted to "treat" and he was going to "treat." Moreover, the waiter had gone off to fill the order. We became indignant and a little alarmed, for we'd "begun to feel" the first Alexander, and to risk a second after several pecks of peanuts, was playing with fire. We were firm and said no *sir*, we weren't going to have any more. And our stubbornness made him mad.

"Very well," he said with hauteur, "if you all won't accept my hospitality, I shall treat myself and drink them all!"

That scared the living daylights out of us and we begged him not to do anything so crazy. But he wouldn't listen. The cocktails arrived, and, with injured dignity, he picked up the first and downed it. Then, without pausing, he drained off a second. With awful fascination, and in pin-dropping silence we watched him top off five of the sickening mixtures, one right after another. Then we waited. But not for long. He had hardly finished the last drop before he stood up. His face was a malarial green, his eyes bulged and his cheeks blew out like an allegorical drawing of Aeolus. From afar, he groped for the check, but to lower his head and focus his eyes on it, seemed too difficult, so he handed it over to Mary Miller, together with his cane. He forced himself to give us a dreadful grin, and a dying swan wave of the hand. Then he pulled himself to attention and, in a wan imitation of a West Point cadet on parade, marched from the room and disappeared around the corner.

We sat for a few minutes in stunned speculation. Mme. Venuat said poor young man, it was the fault of American Prohibition. Mary Miller wanted to be furious at him, but she was too frightened. When we could speak, we thought we had better go see what had happened to him, so we pulled ourselves together and divided up the bill. By this time Emily and I were past caring what we were spending. We tried to saunter out of the room, but our gait was more of a scuttle. At the threshold, we paused and peered apprehensively around the corner. We thought we might find his body there. But the hallway was empty and it was not until we were out on the street that we saw John again. He was lying back in a taxi which was parked just outside the rue Cambon entrance. The greenish tinge of his face had faded to alabaster white, and his eyes were closed. As we watched, they opened, and with difficulty fixed themselves on the taxi meter. He tried to say something to the driver, but the effort was apparently too great, so he shook a fist at him, after which he collapsed again. We thought this behavior the most alarming we'd seen yet, especially since the driver had turned around in his seat and was looking on with the most sympathetic watchfulness. In a moment, however, things became more clear. For at the first droop of John's eyes, the sympathetic driver seized the flag of the meter and spun it round and round with a rapturous smile. Every turn rang a little bell, and every ting of the bell marked an *up* in the fare. It was this sound which would rouse John, near death as he was, to such righteous protest as he could muster.

We were afraid to interfere, and anyway, Mary Miller said she'd take charge of things. So we left them there in front of the Ritz, the cab still quite stationary. But by the reckoning of the meter, John was far, far beyond the outskirts of Paris.

We have only one record of John's theatrical interest during that European trip, but it is a good one. That was when he went to see the Passion Play at Oberammergau, produced for the first time since World War I; from May to September 1922. He published his opinion of the Passion Play in the spring of 1923; his short article appeared in the issue of April 7 for that year of *The Harvard Advocate,* the undergraduate literary magazine. (Incidentally, John published two other articles in the *Advocate* that spring: "Grease Paint and Puritans" in the issue of March 1, an account of Harvard men who had made their mark in the theatre, whether as playwrights, designers, actors, or critics—one hopes President Lowell read it; and in the issue of June 19, "The Drama That Was," a piece about old-fashioned melodramas like *East Lynne.*)

Since John's was a minority report, and since it is one of his early pieces of published criticism, it is worth quoting at some length.

This is no attempt to under-rate the beauty of portions of the Passion Play, or to doubt the sincerity of any part of it. This is no attempt at slander for slander's sake. But the nice things have been said in bunches, obscuring the less nice things that were part and parcel of the production. Consideration of the play as a religious ritual has blinded consideration of it as a dramatic performance. . . .

After a passage comparing the auditorium to Boston's South Station, and the scenery to the Scenic Railway at Revere Beach, not to mention the discomfort of the audience, John continued:

It is not to detract from Anton Lang's Christus to call attention to some of the stage tricks employed in the Crucifixion scene. . . . The sight of Lang when he came on the stage for the Crucifixion must have caused no little wonder to the spectators. The two thieves were stripped to the waist, but Lang's chest had an unreal, opaque, pinkish quality. . . . He was wearing flesh-colored tights. . . . In their pink midst was concealed a bladder . . . a stage bladder . . . full of red ink. . . .

The Crucifixion . . . was actually performed on the stage. One had the sense of being present at an execution in a dress-suit. The cross was laid down on the stage, and Lang stretched on it. The feeling of revulsion, the shudder of horror, when the soldiers drove the nails through his hands is still vivid. Of course, nails such as one buys at a trick shop were most probably used, but still the thud of the hammers, the mildly twisting body of Lang was hideously realistic. . . . The two thieves, their arms tied over the bars of their crosses, with their bodies hanging limp, were unpleasant. But a feeling of downright nausea grew as their arms became blue, then black from the stoppage of circulation. . . . But the worst artistic blow of all came when a Roman soldier crossed over to the Christus and jabbed the bladder beneath those pink tights. . . . The auditorium was breathless. With a sickening rush the red ink spilled and splattered on the stage some twelve feet below. It did not start slowly, as blood would. It gushed forth with a great thud, sounding like a paper bag filled with water when it hits the sidewalk after a four-story fall. . . .

If Hollywood produced a Passion Play, with simplicity and without scandal, how many Americans would travel across the continent to see it? How many of them, even if they did make the pilgrimage, would lose their critical faculties, and sit meekly for eight hours? Oberammergau is in Europe; Hollywood in California. Therein lies a great difference and also an explanation.

The year in Europe that followed the summer at Missoula was altogether serious. From Montana he went to Louisville, and then for almost two weeks to New York—that was when his grandmother saw him off at the station, as described in Chapter Two. He was in New York longer than he had planned to be because his traveling companion, Donald Oenslager, was delayed in his home town of Harrisburg, Pennsylvania, by the removal of his appendix. They changed their sailing from September 1 to September 8.

John made good use of his time in New York. Meanwhile, he

had stopped in Harrisburg for a day, to find Don "in fine shape—a bit weakened and quiet from his puncture, but still the same Don—the joyous, lanky artist—the playful, invigorating being that he always is.* Don's sister Betty had met John at the station, and he takes the occasion to mention that "she is a pretty, charming girl with a fine Greek head." Pretty girls never failed to catch John's eye.

He saw Aunt Mary in New York, as previously reported. He had already made arrangements to send articles from Europe to the *Courier-Journal,* and H.T.P. had promised him space in the *Transcript* for reviews of important productions he was to see in Europe. Armed by these encouragements, he set out to call on editors in New York. First, overestimating the interest of the American public in the theatre, he went to see the president of the Bell Syndicate, John N. Wheeler, who promptly discouraged him. "No sale in newspapers," he muttered. "Try magazines." Next he went to see Laurence Stallings at the *New York World* —this at the suggestion of Mr. Stone, who had met him. This was the year before Stallings and Anderson's *What Price Glory?*

"Why the hell do you want to go into the theatre? It's an awful game." he said.

"I told him I just couldn't help it," John noted; "I had no illusions as to a paradise on earth—but the excitement of it all was inescapable—tugging."

Stallings echoed Wheeler's advice: try magazines, not newspapers. At once Stallings typed a letter of introduction for John to Arthur Hornblow, editor of *Theatre* magazine (generally so called, though its correct title was *The Theatre*). Stallings said that he would also give John a letter to Frank Crowninshield, editor of *Vanity Fair,* "but we've just had a little disagreement." John went to see Mr. Hornblow, slightly uncomfortable in his mind because he had used articles in *The Theatre* for purposes of adverse criticism in Missoula. Hornblow, who did not know

* This and other quotations from John, unless noted otherwise, come from a diary he kept from August 1923 to February 1924.

this and who was an admirer of George Pierce Baker, was friendly and receptive, promised to consider any pieces John might send him, but regretted that he could not commission them in advance. (Mr. Hornblow also wanted to ask Baker for an article, and disillusioned John by asking not only for Baker's address, but for his full name, having known of him only as "Professor Baker." "A new light," John comments, "was thrown on the editor of America's *Theatre* magazine—or was the Missoula conception reaffirmed—though softened by personal contacts?")

Next John went to see Frederick Lewis Allen, whom he was to know very closely years later; Allen was defined as "a reader and literary scout for *Harper's,* and formerly in charge of publicity for Harvard." (Allen was later to become editor of *Harper's,* and a member of Harvard's Board of Overseers.) Allen made the same encouraging but indefinite promise as Hornblow had done.

The weekend of August 31–September 2 John spent in Boston and Cambridge, much of the time as the guest of his Signet friend Henry Cabot Lodge and his family at Nahant. "The whole weekend was an unprecedented pleasure. It contained talk—talk—talk, endless talk. Talk that with Cab, John [Lodge], Helena, and Mrs. Lodge all actively engaged was charming and instructive. . . .

"Wilson, the League—events—futures—dreams—ideals were all part and parcel of the discussions. Mrs. Lodge was afraid that Cab was overstrong in his arguments, too positive, too sure for his age, too vehement in his stands. But not for me at least—though we disagree violently about almost all political issues—he, backing his stand with reason and facts; I trying to back mine with instinct and much talking—his mind is a joy."

Sunday John was taken to lunch at Senator Lodge's. (John calls it dinner and luncheon interchangeably, but it took place about one o'clock.) The talk was mostly of local affairs and people, then Cabot the Younger began asking questions about the Navy; he wanted to write an article on the subject for the *Transcript.*

Later John was left alone with the Senator. "I was dying to ask him what he really thought of Wilson—the question was burning my tongue, but I managed to keep it back, and ask a more polite—and less exciting one. 'How do you find time to write so much when you're so busy?' The reply was rather noncommittal. 'The Senator's life is a life of interruptions,' said Lodge." As John was leaving, the Senator mentioned that he had known John's grandfather, and thought highly of him as an authority on Kentucky history.

(In a marginal note, John mentions that he defined tragedy to Mrs. Lodge as "an impoverishment of potentialities.")

Before the weekend at Nahant, John had gone to Cambridge to look up his old friends, most of whom were in New Hampshire, at Professor Baker's, rehearsing a new play for the 47 Workshop. He did run into Kenneth Raisbeck while crossing the Yard, and went to Raisbeck's room with him and another friend. "Kenneth gave me the blues badly. He was immaculately dressed—but the room in 508 Fairfax was in an upheaval. Formerly it had always been spick and span. Now it was hopelessly untidy. Books were upside down in the bookcases, no rug was on the floor, with ashes everywhere. . . . He was courageous and hopeful, but depressed by his outlook for the next year of assistant's work to Mr. Baker, with so much academic drudgery to perform that he would have no time to write. . . .

"What a pity that this person—who could write *Torches,* one of the best of American one-acts—can find no pleasant or fair working conditions. As usual, his talk on the theatre was illuminating and penetrating. I took him to the Touraine for luncheon. He asked me if I'd ever be willing to stay in Boston. I replied, 'No, it would be like riding on a merry-go-round when it was right beside a race course.' "

Back in New York, John went to see Jeanne Eagels in *Rain,* one of the most successful plays then running, both with the critics and the public. Based on a story by W. Somerset Maugham, it concerned a missionary on the island of Pago Pago who fell in love with a prostitute. John did not share the prevailing opinion. "The play was obvious and melodramatic, irritating because it shirked its greatest possibilities and took the easiest way." After telling off the missionary, both in characterization and in performance, he continued: "Sadie Thompson, herself, was not the most subtle prostitute—with her great love of color—her drooping plume, her stock-in-trade repartee and age-worn repentance mood. . . . No—no—Anna Christie is still my favorite prostitute."

John met the sculptor Frederick W. MacMonnies at dinner with Aunt Mary and Uncle Henry Waite. (John does not comment on the coincidence of his meeting the sculptor of "Civic Virtue" immediately after seeing *Rain*.) MacMonnies gave him a letter of introduction to Frank Crowninshield at *Vanity Fair,* probably as influential a taste-maker as existed in New York at that time. John was ushered into the office while Crowninshield was dictating: "a genial, dudish person, with a charming Anglo-American voice—that most people would have considered affected, but which struck me as thoroughly natural." After being quite warmly greeted, John "was expecting the usual 'I would be glad to see anything you write.' That, however, was not to be the case.

" 'Of course, you see, Mr. Brown,' he said, 'it's different with you and Mr. Oenslager. When Jones and Macgowan went over I knew their work, and could just turn them loose. . . . Now I don't know you. I might make a find or be disappointed.' "

John offered to submit articles for Crowninshield's acceptance or rejection. But—" 'No, that wouldn't be fair,' he continued. 'It isn't fair to ask you to go to the trouble of writing them if I'm not sure I can use them. I tell you what you do. Have you thought of any possible subjects? Suppose you write them down.'

"So I did—I mentioned 'The Abbey Theatre Since the War,' 'The English Repertory System Compared to Our Little Theatre Movement,' 'Expressionism in Germany,' 'The Commedia dell'Arte in Russia—a New Form,' and 'The Moscow Art Theatre at Home.' " Crowninshield picked the last two, told John how he wanted them treated, and offered ninety dollars each for the two articles. Then he took John to lunch at the Coffee House, where John was impressed by the celebrity of the members and the interest of the general conversation.

Cornelia Otis Skinner was playing in *Tweedles,* a comedy by Booth Tarkington. John went to the matinée, then backstage to renew his friendship with Miss Skinner. They went to her apartment, where her parents joined them. This meeting led John to tell in his diary of an occasion in Memphis, when a large theatre party had been taken backstage to meet Mr. Skinner who was playing in *The Liars* by Henry Arthur Jones:

"One girl said, 'Oh, Mr. Skinner, I loved the play—but I couldn't hear all you said.'

" 'That's funny,' Otis Skinner replied. 'I heard everything you said.' . . .

"He asked me what I thought of the play and I told him without mincing.

" 'I think you have to see it three times to get everything out of it. At least that was my experience. And you know Tarkington is much more sensitive about his plays than anything else. You can say anything you want to about his novels and he never objects. Say one word about his plays and he will write you long protests. He wrote several about *Mister Antonio.* Kenneth Macgowan got one. And in Boston Philip Hale came around and said, "I've got a 24-page letter from Tarkington. And I haven't the time to read it. What shall I do?" I told him I didn't have, either.' "

The next afternoon John sharpened his critical faculties against the current production of *The Devil's Disciple,* with Basil Sydney as Dick Dudgeon and Roland Young as General Burgoyne. He thought well of Young, poorly of Sydney, who in his opinion lost most of the comedy.

Don Oenslager arrived on September 7. They visited the publisher Samuel French with an idea of selling him "The First

Day"; when French mentioned a possible outright purchase for twenty-five dollars, John was deflated. They called on Mrs. Edith J. R. Isaacs at the offices of *Theatre Arts* magazine, and she invited them to tea. They had lunch with Kenneth Macgowan and Robert Edmond Jones. "Jones was thrilling. He sat us down and gave us a lecture on our duties in the theatre. He talked rapidly, excitedly, earnestly with an unusual flow and brilliance. He objected to plays like *You and I,* and begged for an expression of a dominant note of our times—the expression of the inexpressible things driving us all on." Then Jones wrote a page or so, developing his ideas, and gave it to John and Don on condition they they were not to read it until they were at sea. It is a bit nebulous, perhaps, but one can understand the excitement with which the boys opened and read it. Its topic sentence, and a good sample of the style: "The theatre of the present offers to the creative artist an undreamed-of opportunity, if he can grasp it, to discover the movements of the titanic forces that urge and guide his own time and to reveal them to his fellow men in the flux and flow of life on his stage." At tea, Mrs. Isaacs asked them to send contributions for her magazine, which she had recently acquired and was changing from a quarterly into a monthly.

They sailed on September 8, and nothing noteworthy seems to have occurred on the voyage, since the reader of the diary now comes upon four blank pages. In fact the diary skips the voyage altogether, and also skips England, but John and Don spent some weeks in London, and John sent reviews of several plays to the *Courier-Journal:* he did a piece on Shakespeare at the Old Vic, and one on several current plays, including *Our Betters, At Mrs. Beam's,* and *The Green Goddess.* (He was to send from Germany articles to the *Courier-Journal* similar to those he sent to the *Transcript.*) Don Oenslager remembers that they traveled in England, visiting Newcastle, among other places; presumably it was from Newcastle that they sailed for Sweden. The next date in the diary is October 11: "After a perfectly hectic passage on the canoe called the *Baldric* we landed today in Gothenburg."

Meanwhile John had sent at least one review from London to the *Transcript*—a review of James Elroy Flecker's *Hassan,* which he found "a strangely beautiful and compelling composition." (Would a reader or theatre-goer today find its poetry pretentious, its plot obsessively sadistic?) However that may be, it should be said now that the *Transcript* must have had space to burn, for John's reviews were likely to run as long as two thousand to twenty-five hundred words.

In Gothenburg they "splurged for one night." It was evidently their habit to spend the first night in a new city at the best hotel, then move to a place they could more easily afford. There was an exposition at Gothenburg which they visited several times; John, with the aid of Kenneth Macgowan, wrote an article about it. In Gothenburg they saw *Madame Butterfly* in Swedish—the language "did not more than once or twice get in the way of Puccini."

On to Stockholm, where they saw *Die Walküre*—John preferred the production he had seen by the Chicago Opera Company. Also from Stockholm John reviewed a production of *Carmen*—"opera as it should be given." John was to review several operas on this trip, and opera would naturally be the form in which a man born to the theatre liked music best. (One friend of his remembers a violent discussion in which John maintained, contrary to fact and reason, that the hackneyed march in Elgar's *Pomp and Circumstance* is written in a minor key.) Also in Stockholm they saw John's "favorite prostitute," but he was disappointed in the production of *Anna Christie*—the director had missed the subtleties of O'Neill's drama and especially of his characterizations. John made the most of his presence in Stockholm by reading as much of Strindberg as he could get his hands on, and comments perceptively on Strindberg's *Inferno,* and later on *The Growth of a Soul.* Also in Stockholm they saw *Butterfly* again, and *Carmen,* which John liked at the Royal Opera even more than in Gothenburg. He discusses it for several pages in the diary.

Early in November to Copenhagen, which seems to have been a disappointment, and after a few days there, on to Berlin. From Berlin John sent several reviews to the *Transcript.* Whatever language difficulty there might otherwise have been—evidently Don Oenslager's German was better than John's—was obviated by John's knowledge of the plays in English translation: he had gone prepared. He praised the work of Leopold Jessner as a director: "the most prominent figure of the Berlin stage today." He reviewed Schiller's *Fresco;* pronounced excellent the production he saw of *Faust,* and "ordinary" that of *Wilhelm Tell.* Ibsen's *Enemy of the People* he saw in "an exceptionally good realistic production." In his diary he discusses a production of *Peer Gynt,* which he considered superior to the New York production with Joseph Schildkraut. (The diary also discusses at length *Fresco* and *Faust.*)

In Berlin they lived with an architect's family, opposite Gordon Craig's studio. Berlin was in the most miserable depths of its inflationary period. "Berlin is a depressing place at present. Thousands are out of work. They crowd the streets, wandering up and down without aim, or forming into little groups and talking excitedly. . . . Tension can be felt. The rumors of the return of the Crown Prince were again denied this morning. The entente, according to a newspaper, won't hear of it. . . . The older people are resigned—the young ones (below war age) are rebellious. But both are united in feeling a hatred for France which they can never forget. It all means another war within a generation." That was written on November 7, 1923. The diary continues:

"Berlin is depressing. Food is scarce. So is light at night. . . . Taxis are to be seen—but private cars are very scarce. The preposterous rate of the mark makes eating more of an inconvenience than an expense. Tonight at the theatre we saw people bring their own food (chocolate and sandwiches) into the foyer. And the food stores are guarded by iron frameworks over the windows." However, as he was to write to the *Transcript,* "Berlin is overwhelmed by defeat, yet the theatres are crowded." Although food was scarce, the future uncertain, inflation incredible, still Ibsen, Shaw, Schiller, Strindberg, Georg Kaiser, and Goethe were drawing crowds. On November 14 he saw Kaiser's *Nebeneinander.* "It was interesting to see because of *From Morn till Midnight*—and also because of itself. [*From Morn till Midnight,* Kaiser's expressionist drama, had been produced in New York in 1922.] If I had not read *From Morn till Midnight* I would have been lost. As it was it was the hardest play to understand without knowing the language that I have ever seen."

Two days later he saw *Figaro*—Beaumarchais, without benefit of Da Ponte or Mozart—and wrote a highly favorable review which the *Transcript* published a month later.\* All this time he was reading, writing (including a long article for *Theatre Arts*), taking long walks with Don, and corresponding with his family. For instance, though the correspondence is in the reverse direction, and he seems to have paid no immediate attention to it: "Thursday—November 22—Got a letter from Mother in which she asked me to come straight home because of my bills!" He "heard also from Cab—and that the Merriams' son had arrived." That evening he heard *The Magic Flute,* which he greatly enjoyed. He compared the music, "in its lighter moments," to the songs in *The Beggar's Opera.* "It has infinite wit and dash."

After *Candida,* where John was interested in the audience, which laughed but shushed the laughing in order not to miss a line, and *Götterdämmerung,* where the Rhine maidens looked "like Vassar graduates doing stunts at their twentieth reunion," they went on to Leipzig for a day, then to Frankfurt, where they saw Aeschylus in German: *Agamemnon, The Libation Bearers,*

---

\* In reading John's diary along with his reviews, it is difficult to remember that in 1923 transatlantic air mail did not exist. The *Transcript,* in any event, was seldom in a hurry.

and part of *The Furies*. Also *Macbeth,* of which John gives a long account. Then to Mainz and Darmstadt, where they saw *Der Rosenkavalier*. In Stuttgart to the opera—*Oberon* by Weber; John speaks of Gustav Mahler's new scenery. (Evidently the designer was not related to the celebrated Viennese composer—a coincidence of names only.) After a tour of the theatres—"The Stuttgart State theatres are the best and most complete plants I have seen—*Othello* and *Tannhäuser*."

To Munich on December 12; very long critical account of a production of *Hamlet* there; "write an article on the provinces for H.T.P." Long discussion of a production of *Macbeth,* comparing it to the production he had seen in Frankfurt. The *Transcript* was to publish a report of John's from Munich: "Munich in spite of everything is still active in the theatre. With the Bavarian yearning for independence growing daily, with the Revolution of some weeks ago [no doubt the reference is to the Beer-Hall Putsch] and the possibility of another to come still in everyone's mind, the theatres remain open and crowded. Dr. Albert has taken Stresemann's place, the trial of Hitler impends, but still the Bavarian theatres remain undaunted."

To Nuremberg and Halle, then to Dresden, where the entry for December 25 reads, "A wonderful Christmas. . . ." Presents in the morning, then: "Luncheon in our room—soup, fish, goose, ice cream, our own supply of cheese—and coffee. But there was more. A bottle of champagne—Rhine wine—curaçao—and another liqueur. We were at the table until six—many toasts—friendlier and friendlier—then both of us sound asleep by 6:30." The next morning they took a walk, and by afternoon were in the mood for a sleigh ride.

Good news in Dresden: checks from the *Transcript* and the *Courier-Journal;* "letters from Mother retracting the Berlin ultimatum. . . . A cable from beloved, blessed, much-suffering grandmother saying she would send money." Many letters from friends. At a performance of *Boris Godunov,* which on the whole John admired, he found the crowd in the coronation scene "smelling strongly of *The National Geographic*." Another long account of another production of *Macbeth*. Then *Twelfth Night* at the Staats Theater. "It was fascinating—particularly when it came after the *Macbeth*. The overstraining was gone. Instead quiet—calm—brilliant ensemble playing—much less of horseplay than Sothern permits in his Sir Toby crew. It was by far the best all around performance of Shakespeare or anything else we have seen." Altogether John's accounts give a good idea of Shakespeare in Germany at that time.

They had hoped to go to Russia, but news that their visas would be delayed sent them to Prague and Vienna instead. An article sent from Prague to the *Courier-Journal* mentioned several Czech plays. "The Czechs crowd to see Shakespeare." He thought *East of Suez* was Maugham at his worst. Much more detail in the diary: worth noting is a paragraph about a meeting with Karel Čapek: "unassuming, modest, and intensely agreeable. . . . Greatly interested in American literature—knew O'Neill and admired his works, but wanted especially to know our modernist poets and novelists. I made out a hurried list." One wishes John had included his list in the diary: "modernist" in a period dominated by Sinclair Lewis and Willa Cather, Frost, Sandburg, and Vachel Lindsay?

To Vienna, January 17 (1924). More sightseeing, theatre-going, writing. Also "the best symphony concert I've ever heard. . . . Mozart's *Jupiter* I loved—Haydn's cello concerto with Emanuel Feuermann as soloist—and most thrilling of all—Beethoven's Seventh—the most soul-twisting symphony I've ever heard. And all three beautifully conducted by Hans Knappertsbusch." He sent a review to the *Transcript* of a "mundane performance" of *Cyrano*, a similar judgment of a Viennese production of *Antony and Cleopatra;* but he praised Molnár's *The Swan*.

John had evidently expected to meet Cabot Lodge early in February in Trieste, but on the fifth he "heard from Cab that he couldn't get to Trieste until the eleventh so I made up my mind to find him at any trouble. Cook's refused to take back my tickets—I was feeling worn down and tired—so I left tonight for Trieste." He left Trieste at once for Venice, then he took the night train for Florence, had a disappointing first day there, but February 7 was "a morning of discovery! I refused to use Baedeker. I wanted to find out for myself, to have the pleasure of exploring unguided. Trusting to luck while waiting for the sun to rise, I reached the Arno just as it did—and I reveled in the beauty—the startling shimmering beauty of the Duomo and Cathedral [Baptistery?] uncertain in the mist—gaining color slowly. Four times I went to mass—there—and in three other churches I have forgotten. Finally I reached the Piazzo [Palazzo?] Vecchio—passed by the Uffizi to the Arno—saw the Ponte Vecchio—scenery-like, with green and pink splotches melting into gray."

Then came the search for Lodge, who was supposed to be staying with some friends named Otis. John tried several hotels, Cook's, the American Express, and the police—no trace of Lodge or the Otises. However, a lady overheard him asking about the Otises, and supplied the information that there were some people of that name living nearby. Finally he met Gray Otis; "loose-jointed, Boston-English," who said that Lodge was expected that evening. Actually he got in from Rome at 4:00 a.m., and was asleep when John called in the morning. He waked up—that is, John awakened him—and they were ready for a nonstop conversation about everything.

They had a fine time together in Florence, riding about and addressing passers-by with high spirits and bonhomie. John was to recall all this when he was in Florence in 1960; he sent Lodge a postcard on May 14: "I have been thinking of you even more than usual. And why not? You are all over Florence for me—laughing, singing, waving to a befuddled populace from a fiacre, with Gray Otis and yours truly in your court. It was fun to be young, wasn't it? It's fun to be older, too, isn't it?"

John went back to Vienna, Lodge with him, and they rejoined Don there. At this point John's diary comes abruptly to an end.

Don recalls that he and John, leaving Lodge in Vienna, went to Constanṭa, on the Black Sea, en route to Istanbul. Again there was a mix-up about tickets; they had been sold reservations on a summer schedule, and here it was February. But they found an uncomfortable passage to Istanbul, presumably via Budapest, for John reported to the *Transcript* on a production of *The Comedy of Errors:* "seems childish and naïve when one sees it fresh from the more sophisticated manners of the German Theatre." Then from Istanbul to Athens, where they saw theatres but no theatre, the weather being too cold for outdoor performances. Eventually they went to Florence, where they separated (to Don's everlasting indignation, since he was left alone with a miserable ailment, the flu perhaps, while John set out for Paris with Stanley McCandless, architect and expert on stage lighting).

In Paris John put up at the Hotel Récamier and began to think seriously about what he was going to do when he returned to the United States. His letters to Don tell what he was doing, and what was on his mind. One, dated April 31, 1924—a date that goes April Fool's Day one better—refers to an offer from George Pierce Baker, who was uncertain whether to take his sabbatical the following year. "The trouble," wrote John, "evidently was that he wanted me to get all excited—and I have been." This letter had begun with John's writing: "I have been up in the air and still am about next winter. Funny, but the only complication is G.P. I am perfectly willing to go back. In fact I am hankering to but so far the news has not been encouraging to a thrilling extent. I got here to find a letter from G.P. It was a very brusque business letter, which was all right, and I would not have objected at all to its style if it had only said what I wanted it to say. But it didn't at all."

Mr. Baker had offered John a full-time job as his assistant—succeeding Kenneth Raisbeck—at $1500 a year, without allowing him to take his playwriting course, English 47A, as a graduate student; or alternatively, half-time as assistant plus 47A, but at a salary of only $750, which was not enough for John to live on.

Meanwhile he had an offer from Northwestern University for half-time work at $1600. "That has been tempting me sorely, because G.P. said I could have nothing to do with the [Dramatic Club] and evidently nothing to do with the *Transcript*. And I was counting on both as helping out financially.

"I would not consider [the Northwestern offer] at all if it were not a question of having to make money. I just can't offer myself on a silver platter to Daddy for another year's keeping. It's immoral to be kept . . . and especially immoral at my age, and probably most immoral of all if you are kept by your own family."

In the same letter he wrote: "You have missed a great deal by not coming to Paris as far as theatre goes. . . . Copeau's work is more than interesting. It is magnificent. I don't think I have ever been to a theatre that is quite so evocative of thrills that belong to all the artists concerned. Its simple Greek-fashioned background is adjustable to any change . . . and most of the settings suggested by vital properties do carry illusion. The acting is superlative. Copeau is extraordinary . . . and so is Tessier, his leading woman. *The Mistress of the Inn* is the most brilliant acting performance I have ever seen . . . and *The S.S. Tenacity* is not far behind it. I saw *R.U.R.* directed by Komisarjevsky. Very interesting and well set. His direction of *The Dover Road* for the Dramahouse Players' premiere was mediocre and some of the playing would not have been tolerated by the Radcliffe Idler. The Comédie is as odious as ever. *The Cid* almost killed me because I promptly became convulsed with the giggles and they lasted for five ranting acts. Molière and *Le Médecin Malgré Lui* helped to put me square again. . . .

"I had a long talk with Copeau, which was thrilling in a friendly way, and his daughter, who speaks excellent English, showed me all over papa's theatre. I liked that, I did."

Some time later, he reported to the *Transcript*—no doubt considerably later, for the report was not printed until October 11— as follows on Jean Cocteau's *Romeo and Juliet:* "One of the strangest Shakespearean productions on record, if it could be called a production of Shakespeare at all." He continued that Cocteau's theory of rhythmic movement might work applied to another play, but *Romeo and Juliet* is "a play massacred and a theory unrealized."

On May 16 he wrote Don another long letter from Paris. "Since you have deserted me, I have formed a new habit. To disperse loneliness I have taken to birds. I have two little things . . . I don't [know] what . . . chirping in a cage, and a paraqueet [*sic*]. Daily I close the windows and the doors and then turn them loose. But for little birds they can do the biggest things and they have absolutely no sense of decency." (Don says that in the course of time the birds escaped through an open window, presumably to be devoured by a predator.)

The letter continues: "Listen . . . you . . . come on to Paris soon. The most wonderful season is just about to start. Copeau is through, yes, but Pitoëff is still going. Then at La Cigale they are going to start tomorrow for a month's season of highly expressionistic things. Picasso is doing the settings for *Romeo and Juliet* [Cocteau's production?] . . . as well as some of the settings for the Diaghilev season . . . with Stravinsky's ballets, and Stravinsky directing.

"About next year. I am even further in the clouds now than when I last wrote. To begin with a most wonderful and unexpected thing happened. Two days ago I got a letter from Mrs. Isaacs in which she asked me to come to New York and to be an assistant on *Theatre Arts*. She said I would get a bread if not a butter salary. Of course, as she pointed out, I would have to start in a small way, but think of the chances! She said she would have asked me sooner but she had seen G.P. and he had told her he was trying to get me back to Harvard, so she said she would do nothing until he had written. Then Macgowan and Stark Young told her she was not acting square to me, that I ought to be able to choose as I wanted. So she wrote . . . and of course it's all very confidential now.

"I do think G.P should have mentioned it in his letter and advised me, don't you? . . . I think I will go to N.Y. instead of going back to Cambridge. It means so much . . . this chance . . . that I am afraid to let it go by. It might mean holding the prompt book at the Provincetown Theatre too.*

"G.P.'s letter put so many restrictions on me, and meant that I would have so little time for outside writing, that I must say it dampened my enthusiasm. If I go back for half-time work to take 47A it means that I make so little money that I [might] just as well not assist at all. If I go back for full-time work, it means that I will have no time to do anything on the outside." (Although his letter does not say so, surely John was thinking of the predicament in which he had found Raisbeck when he called on him in Cambridge late in the previous summer.)

"Isn't it hell . . . trying to decide things like this. I adore G.P. . . . I adore the Workshop . . . I get veritably sick when I think of being a year away from you and the bunch. New York is the harder decision to make . . . it is the hardest I've ever made . . . but I think it's the wise one. Please write me what you think." Don advised him to join Mrs. Isaacs.

The next available letter to Don is dated August 2, and it makes clear that by now John had accepted Mrs. Isaacs's offer. "The book is progressing. To the chapters finished I have added the Gemier *Merchant,* the Cocteau *Romeo and Juliet,* and the Hevesi-Hungarian Shakespeare, Kvapil and Hiltar, and rewritten the Comédie Française chapter. . . .

"I had a letter from Bill Wells † a day or two ago in which he said that even if Appleton should decide to publish it, he did not think they or any other publisher could make a Christmas

* The Provincetown Theatre, which had started on Cape Cod under the auspices of George Cram Cook and Susan Glaspell, had moved to New York, and was producing new plays by the most promising American playwrights, Eugene O'Neill among others.

† William H. Wells, a Harvard classmate and fellow member of the Dramatic Club; at that time, a member of the staff of D. Appleton & Company, book publishers, in New York.

book out of it. Furthermore there was not time for that. That was rather a blow. Then he felt the essay form of unrelated chapters was bad business as a book and wanted us to extract some thesis idea around which to sting our pearls. That is, of course, exactly what I don't want to do. I don't want to whip it arbitrarily into a book arranged like a textbook or subdivided according to the chief divisions of the stage. The first is repulsive and untrue, as I see it. And the second has been done to death from Moderwell down. . . .

"Mrs. I.'s objection to printing the book is that, though I have had an excellent year of experience in the theatre, my text is bound to be lacking in critical background due to my youth, ignorance, and inexperience in life, the theatre, etc. . . . There is a great deal in that, of course.

"I like Mrs. I. a lot and I like the prospects of next year. She is extremely kind and sympathetic and really inspiring. I can understand fully what she has meant to Macgowan, Young, and Jones. I hope she'll do us the same good! [Throughout this letter the use of the first person plural is puzzling.] I am to learn the mechanics of arranging the magazine at first, write articles and go to the theatre at night, and all that kind of thing. Furthermore she wants me to speak, whenever invited, on the theatre." (Prophetic words.)

Later in August Don was evidently in Paris, and John had departed. The final letter of this series was written on board the R.M.S. *Mauretania*, and comments that the passengers are "dumb and uninteresting . . . with the exceptions of the *big six* on board. . . . And I'm one of the big six if not the biggest. Mrs. Isaacs I love more every day. I don't know when I've ever seen a more genuinely sympathetic person in my life. Mr. Isaacs I've grown to like, too. He's interesting about most things but especially about music. The other three in the big six are Joseph and Mrs. Urban, and Rollin Kirby, the cartoonist of the *World*. Urban is one of the kindest, simplest, most winning people alive— with his funny ungrammatical German English which is more to the point than most English. And Kirby is a peach, too, sensitive and screamingly funny." There is a final paragraph about Don's new sketches, and Mrs. Isaacs's enthusiasm for his evidence of development.

And so to New York and the new job.

## Chapter Five

# Portrait of the Critic as a Young Man

John was to be on the staff of *Theatre Arts* from 1924 to 1928 as associate editor and drama critic. Mrs. Isaacs had taken over the magazine from its previous publisher, Shelden Cheney of the Theatre Committee of the Society of Arts and Crafts of Detroit, who had issued the magazine as a quarterly. He had made himself unpopular for publishing a picture of a German theatre during World War I and saying good things about it.* Mrs. Isaacs brought the magazine to New York and made it a monthly. As John's letters have shown, she attracted distinguished associates in Stark Young and Kenneth Macgowan, and equally distinguished contributors like Robert Edmond Jones. She was a good businesswoman as well as a brilliant editor. She had an instinct for discovering artists and writers before they were generally recognized—Donald Oenslager and John Mason Brown, for example. She produced an annual issue on the so-called "tributary theatre," college theatres, community theatres, and so on, "springs which lead to the river of Broadway"—although the professionals of Broadway looked down on amateurs. John, whose letters have demonstrated his esteem for Mrs. Isaacs and his devotion to her, was later to remark that she had a "marshmallow heart." Rosamond Gilder was her right hand on the editorial staff, and eventually became editor of the magazine. She

* Mr. Cheney remains the distinguished author of many books on the theatre and other arts.

also became a lifelong friend of John's.

By the spring of 1925—perhaps even earlier—John was writing regularly for the magazine; many, if not most, issues were to contain essay-reviews by him. Meanwhile he had written for the *Transcript* a summing-up piece—the article previously referred to, published in October. He also wrote an article for the *Harvard Alumni Bulletin* on European and New York Theatres, 1923–25.

Naturally a monthly magazine gives scope for thoughtful criticism which the pace of reviewing for a daily newspaper precludes. In May 1925 in a review of the season which he had found "disheartening," he singled out for comment a production of *The Wild Duck:* "The greatest acting difficulty in *The Wild Duck* exists in the part of Hialmar Ekdal, which in the writing takes on the quality of a satire of a satire."

"A ghost of Ibsen, tinctured and modified by Freud, is James Joyce's *Exiles.*"

Of course, snippets like these can give no idea of the quality of John's criticism or of his writing at that time. But they can preserve some of his wit. In 1951 he wrote for *The Saturday Review* a substantial article called "The Theatre of the Twenties," in which he summarized his reminiscences and opinions. After a brief discussion of the important productions of that decade, as he remembered them, he concluded: "In the theatre things hummed in the twenties. . . . This is not to claim that every production made then was a masterpiece. . . . Nor is it to say the theatre is dying today. . . . There is a difference, however, between then and now. Our theatre is sadly shrunken. What is perhaps most alarming about it is the extent to which it depends even now for its life upon those who made it so interestingly alive in the twenties." *

* "The Theatre of the Twenties" is preserved in *Dramatis Personae.* Unfortunately his *Theatre Arts* articles are not available in book form, except what he used from them in *Upstage.* The articles in *Theatre Arts* were often more caustic than the tone of the reminiscences set down in 1951. In one of the

To continue with the quotations from *Theatre Arts:* of Michael Arlen's *The Green Hat* he wrote, "His story of the Constant Nymphomaniac throbs but briefly behind the footlights."

"*Arms and the Man* stands up badly against time. . . . It seems made for 'The Chocolate Soldier.' "

In December he reviewed *Craig's Wife* by George Kelly (which has been mentioned in another context); Molnár's *The Glass Slipper; Hamlet* with Walter Hampden and Ethel Barrymore; *Hamlet* in modern dress with Basil Sydney: "In spite of its scenes of power, the modern *Hamlet* was a disappointment." It was the season of Sidney Howard's *Lucky Sam McCarver,* of John Van Druten's *Young Woodley,* of *Androcles and the Lion* with settings by Miguel Covarrubias.

In 1926 came O'Neill's *The Great God Brown,* a play in which the characters wore masks to signify the different aspects of their natures and emotions: "Uneven and unedited, and in spite of containing passages of sheer rant, it contains, as well, some of the most haunting lines and soliloquies which have come from O'Neill's pen."

In the issue published on Shaw's birthday, July 26, he wrote of Shakespeare: "To achieve immortality is one thing, to survive it another, and Shakespeare is one of the few playwrights who have succeeded at both." After a discussion of the mayhem inflicted on Shakespeare by Garrick and others, he concluded that the new movement is dominated by the director who "permits a Shakespearian play to reach the stage as a play and not as a vehicle." But all such directors were in Europe.

The autumn of 1926 was the season of melodrama, wit, and wisecracks, of *Broadway* by Philip Dunning and George Abbott, of *Loose Ankles* by Sam Janney—and the season of three excellent comic actors: Lee Tracy, Osgood Perkins, and Charles D. Brown. Tracy and Perkins were later to star in *The Front Page* by Ben Hecht and Charles MacArthur.

---

Hillman interviews, John called the theatre of the twenties "a revolt against the literal."

1927 brought *The Silver Cord* by Sidney Howard, "one of the most arresting plays of the season," John wrote at the time, and remembered vividly in 1951, "Laura Hope Crews in *The Silver Cord* when, as that appalling example of Momism at its worst, she opened the door of her married son's bedroom to coo, 'It's only Mother.'" That year Sacha Guitry and Yvonne Printemps brought a repertory, "as French in spirit and felicity as their own playing is in lightness and precision."

The year 1927 also brought Robert E. Sherwood's first play, *The Road to Rome,* and it is amusing to read what John wrote of it, considering the amount of time he was to devote to Sherwood's biography: "One of those modern comedies in ancient dress that cries for the cerebral onslaught of a Shaw. . . . In the hands of Robert Sherwood it is a fairly amusing satire on modern habits and a pretty stinging indictment of war, that never completely clicks in either purpose, but that offers an entertaining evening in the theatre for all that." By 1951 his opinion had mellowed somewhat; he recalled the play as "that antique romp in modern terms in which Philip Merrivale was a most romantic Hannibal and Jane Cowl delightful as the Roman lady who conquered him for a night." Later Sherwood wrote other anti-war plays, notably *Idiot's Delight* and *There Shall Be No Night.*

Of the first of S. N. Behrman's plays to be produced, *The Second Man,* John wrote: "a comedy that aims at being very *haut-monde* but that somehow does not admit its characters beyond the vestibule of authentic sophistication." However, he found it enjoyable.

In 1928 there were Shakespearean revivals and the Irish Players, who opened their season with two plays by Sean O'Casey, *The Plough and the Stars* and *Juno and the Paycock.* "These two plays have been carried to New York by actors who belong to Sean O'Casey's Dublin. . . . The merits and excesses of their acting are the merits and excesses of his plays, and in the case of each the merits more than redeem the excesses."

Of one of O'Neill's less memorable works he wrote: "It is not fair to dismiss *Marco [Millions]* as a one-finger exercise rendered heroically by a symphony orchestra." And of the new play by his old acquaintance at the 47 Workshop, he wrote: "In *Paris Bound* Philip Barry puts promise behind him and writes one of the most adult and engaging comedies yet to come from the pen of an American." Of *The Royal Family,* a *drame à clef* by Edna Ferber and George S. Kaufman, it was "not played with the drive with which it is written. Probably only its prototypes could do it that final justice." In "The Theatre of the Twenties" he added that it was a play "in which such a theatrical clan as the Barrymores were lovingly shown with all their eccentricities and virtues."

Finally, back to O'Neill, this time in one of his more memorable plays, *Strange Interlude,* which interspersed the dialogue with soliloquies in which the characters would speak their unconscious minds, supposedly unheard by the others. "This flux in the meaning that each of his characters has for the others gives *Strange Interlude* an interest that is as unusual as it is subtle and unflagging." He added that O'Neill's "story is so intrinsically melodramatic . . . time and again in the telling of it, when he has done a fine thing, he has marred it by a breach of taste and lack of subtlety."

Most of this time John was sharing an apartment with Don Oenslager. Later they were joined by Marshall Best. (Don moved to New Haven for a year following his appointment to the Yale faculty.) At first, and for some years, they lived in a flat in Greenwich Village. Their friends have vivid memories of what would now be called their life-style. When friends came to dinner, the boys pretended that the gin from which the cocktails were made was kept in a chamber pot—not an inappropriate receptacle for the gin that was drunk in the years of Prohibition. Their dinner guests included Mrs. August Belmont, Mary Churchill from Louisville, and on one occasion Lawrence Langner and Theresa Helburn of the Theatre Guild, who came on the evening of a Guild opening; their car was stuck in the snow, there were no cabs, and these distinguished personages were obliged to go to the theatre by subway. Obviously this contretemps appealed to John's and Don's senses of humor rather than to their sympathies.

John and his roommates later moved to an apartment on East 78th Street. Presently Marshall—for reasons of comfort, or the reverse; he had been sleeping in a cold passageway—moved out, and his place was taken by Henry Hazen Reed, known as Bud, a lawyer, and another '23 alumnus of Harvard. They had a maid (those were the days when people had maids), shared with Aunt Mary. Her name was Ethel Snow; she called John "Old Massa," Don "the Professor," and Bud "the Judge." Many years later (November 1958) John wrote to Alan Dent, who had edited the Shaw-Campbell letters and was now embarking on his biography of Mrs. Pat Campbell (published in 1961):

"Once upon a time, in 1932 I believe, Donald Oenslager and I had a luncheon party for Mrs. Pat. The guests were Otis and Mrs. Skinner and Mrs. August Belmont. We had a Nova Scotian cook-maid with the sweetest, most innocent and scrubbed face I think I've ever seen. Her name was Ethel. Once, when she had gone to the pantry, the talk at the table turned to *Macbeth.* I wish you could have seen Ethel's amazed expression when she re-entered the dining room and heard Mrs. Pat in her great voice and with great gestures boom, "I have given suck and know how tender 'tis to love the babe that milks me.' Mrs. Pat at this same luncheon said that, when she played Lady Macbeth to Hackett's Thane, she went up to him at the end of a performance and said, 'I wish by all that's holy, sir, you would have your catarrh during your own speeches, not mine, or when you are off-stage.' "

John had a small female dog named Mitzi; at this distance in time it is difficult to say whether she was a Yorkshire terrier or a mongrel. In any case, she looked like the business end of a mop, and Don and Bud detested her. She was, nevertheless, the apple of John's eye. Once he took her to his bank where he went to cash a check, and she committed a nuisance in the lobby. "I just brought her in," John announced to no one in particular, "to leave a small deposit."

After the move uptown, the center of their social life was Sunday breakfast—what came later to be called brunch. They invited a dozen or even up to twenty people for scrambled eggs or whatever. Almost if not quite invariably the breakfast would conclude with John reading aloud his latest article. (For that matter, he used to call up friends, even as late as midnight, to read what he had just written.) In 1949 he wrote an article for *The Saturday Review* called "Pleasant Agony," * about the pains and tribulations which beset him in the act of composition, but in those days he must have enjoyed it. John was extremely active in the preparation of the breakfasts—he was one of the most impatient men ever to draw breath, and he hated to leave to others what he thought he could do better himself. However, he did want a show of cooperation. One Sunday morning, while John was trotting around getting the provisions ready, one of his roommates came into the living room, clad in pajamas, yawning and stretching, and said, "Has anybody seen the Sunday paper?" "If you don't get out of here," said John, "I will kill you with this kitchen knife." (That story was told to the author by John himself, and although it is now denied by the prospective victim, it is confirmed by one of the other roommates, who says, however, that it was an ice pick, not a kitchen knife.)

However great his zeal in the kitchen, John had occasional disputes with his roommates over money; they maintained that he was not paying his share of the commune's expenses, and he would remark loftily, "I can't be bothered with tradesmen." Later in their association, perhaps owing to the legal training of Bud Reed, they cracked down on him and made him put up his share of the household expenses. Brooks Atkinson wrote a letter, ostensibly to Reed, which turned up in John's papers.

* Reprinted in *Dramatis Personae*.

It is dated October 16, 1931, by which time John had published at least two books and was established as the drama critic of the *New York Evening Post*. It reads in part as follows:

> Your client [John] drinks too much, encourages his dog to commit major nuisances on the scattered sheets of a family newspaper, shouts perfidious maledictions at innocent young ladies on the street, gives presents recklessly and his conversation is criminally revolting. As further proof of his insanity let me point to his extraordinary instinct for the stage.

The letter refers to John as Judd Mason Gray, after a recently executed corset salesman, Judd Gray, who, together with Ruth Snyder (also executed) had murdered Mr. Snyder in order to pursue happiness together. The trial was a sensation of the sensational twenties, when New York had no less than three tabloid newspapers eager to exploit sensations. Of course Atkinson, drama critic of *The New York Times,* was a close friend of John's, as is demonstrated by an account in Atkinson's journal dated April 4, 1931, which he came across by serendipity in 1967 and sent on to John, with a covering note saying, "I had completely forgotten it. But I have copied it out this morning, thinking that it might interest you and recall a time when we were all full of beans." The passage follows:

> Last night John Mason Brown was here to dinner and stayed all evening. Sometime I should write a long account of him. He is an extraordinary man and about the best friend I have in New York. Being a Southerner he is about as unlike me, a Yankee, as anyone can be. He is honest and open and spirited and of high character. When he, Oriana [Mrs. Atkinson] and I are together we rush the conversation like people possessed and turn ourselves and each other inside out. We get to the bottom of everything. It is so exhilarating and heady that I cannot sleep or sleep so lightly that I keep up the same line of argument in my dreams. John is no sedative. He is a rare being with many accomplishments and traits of character that are beyond me. I bank on him.

A word must be said about John's numerous courtships during his years at *Theatre Arts.* According to a woman friend with whom he was closely associated at that time, the girls John knew found him very attractive; he was certainly fun to be with, and he began each courtship by making the girl think he was serious. In one or two instances he even went so far as to buy an engagement ring. But the girls always cooled him off before things got too serious. The situation could not be better described than in a passage from P. G. Wodehouse:

Yes, it's curious about Freddie, said the Crumpet, sipping a thoughtful martini. He rarely fails to click, but he never seems able to go on clicking. A whale at the Boy Meets Girl stuff, he is unfortunately equally unerring at the Boy Loses Girl.*

When Cornelia Otis Skinner was married, in 1928—the wedding took place in Paris—John cabled her: CONGRATULATIONS HOPE THE BABY HAS RED HAIR. And previously, when Ellen Barret in Louisville became engaged to Thomas J. Wood, he took on in the most extraordinary way, seeming to think—and to take it for granted she also thought—that because they had grown up together they were inevitably destined for each other, and that she was supposed to wait until he got ready to propose to her. The circumstance that she had become engaged on his birthday, July 3, 1926, was particularly mortifying and hard to bear. He did everything he could to make her change her mind, but evidently with so possessive an approach that it had the effect opposite to the one intended—not that she was going to change her mind in any case. She spent a week in New York before her wedding, and he made her life miserable; later, when she was back in Louisville and the wedding day approached, he peppered her with telegrams asking her to let him come and plead his cause before it was too late. She stood firm, and was married before the year was out.

Meanwhile, in September, John's Aunt Mary took part, and most usefully. She wrote to Ellen on the thirteenth:

* From "Bramley Is So Bracing," in *Nothing Serious* by P. G. Wodehouse (Doubleday, 1951).

You may have wondered that I did not insist to John that his trip to Louisville would be as useless as it would be in bad taste. I tried him out by asking ironically if he was in love with a situation or a person. . . . He presented the argument that he did not for one instant presume to question your decision, if only he might be given his chance to speak. . . . There was no vain sense that you would alter your decision because of his persuasiveness . . . but there was an intolerable ache that *life* had denied him a hearing. . . . That is a grown up pain and John in the last week or so has emotionally become a grown up person. Intellectually he is so sophisticated and emotionally so immature until now.

Ellen and John remained good friends until John's death. But even as late as the summer of 1932, part of which he spent in northern Michigan near Ellen and her husband, he continued to bedevil Ellen—apparently just for the hell of it; he knew she was happily married and he liked her husband. Just as, when Ellen last saw him, a few months before his death, he once more brought up the ten-cent-store diamond ring which she had haughtily rejected more than fifty years earlier. The whole story illustrates a characteristic of John's, previously mentioned: the ability to believe something and pretend to believe it—or to feel an emotion and pretend to feel it—simultaneously. In any event, it was not until the summer of 1932 that he was at last ready for the real thing.

During his *Theatre Arts* period, John was a staff lecturer at the American Laboratory Theatre, which had been founded in New York in 1925 by Richard Boleslavsky and Maria Ouspenskaya. Richard Aldrich, who had known John at Harvard and was to become his lifelong friend, took over as manager of the Laboratory Theatre in 1925, after two seasons as manager of the Jitney Players.* He supplies the information that the Laboratory Theatre was principally an acting school; Boleslavsky, a director, who had been with the Moscow Art Theatre, thought he could train any one to become an actor. As part of the training

* The Jitney Players were mostly Equity members finding summer employment by touring Long Island and New England, before the days of summer theatres. They traveled in Ford trucks, sometimes using the truck for a stage.

of the students, the theatre put on productions from time to time. Aldrich recalls that the theatre had its first location, consisting of one large room, at the corner of Sixth Avenue and 58th Street; it later moved to East 58th between Lexington and Third Avenues, the premises here being a beer garden and a large stage. The students, about twenty in number, ranged from grubby kids to debutantes. During the last years the emphasis was more on theatrical production, less on teaching; and the location had moved, once more, to an abandoned brewery on East 59th Street. In 1930 the American Laboratory Theatre succumbed to the Depression.

John began in 1926 to give a course on the history of the drama—three lectures a week for which he received ten dollars a lecture. Among his other contributions to the American Laboratory Theatre, there crops up among his papers a document of four single-spaced typewritten pages, untitled and undated. It is obviously by John, for corrections on an earlier draft as well as on the final version are made in his handwriting. One of his colleagues at the "Lab" believes it was written in the spring of 1928 and delivered as a talk to the members.

He begins with an apology for his impertinence at making suggestions at all; excuses himself by his enthusiastic belief in the "Lab"; and concludes his preamble as follows: "To my mind the next season will be the most decisive year in the history of the Laboratory Theatre. For during the coming winter it must make itself felt very definitely as a theatre that stands on its own merits. I, as you know, do not feel that the present organization is in any sense of the word a theatre that stands on its own merits. It is instead a theatre backed by a fine and contagious devotion, but I do not believe that the devotion is enough."

He went on to suggest that the standard of performance be raised to a level "that is so excellent and self-reliant that it will attract both audiences and playwrights to its doors"—this before deciding on a policy regarding the plays, or school of playwrights, to be produced. As to the present company, "the Laboratory Theatre now pays a salary list of five hundred dollars to some thirty actors. If you do not mind my saying it I will have to admit that I think that practically twenty-eight of the thirty actors are extravagantly overpaid."

He suggested engaging four first-class actors at a better salary, letting minor parts be filled by members of the acting school. Next, he thought Boleslavsky should direct no more than three of the five annual productions. Third, open the door to more scene designers. Fourth, include a dance pantomime in next year's repertory. Fifth, special attention to publicity. Sixth, suggestion of several plays to be produced, notably *Troilus and Cressida*. "It seems to me an ageless satire on war should, if you made the actors resemble the equivalent of Paris and Achilles, etc., in the last war, dressed them in contemporary dress, and played the whole play over the rhythm of machine guns, prove very exciting." * The seventh suggestion more or less repeats and elaborates upon the first; it is followed by two more in illegible handwriting.

In 1929 John joined the *New York Evening Post* as drama critic. Meanwhile he had made two more trips to Europe. In 1928 he went, again to see the European theatres, with his friend Eliot Cabot, the actor who had played the part of the young man in *The Silver Cord* whose bedroom was invaded. This trip, which included a visit to Russia, led—combined with his previous experiences—to his first book, *The Modern Theatre in Revolt*.† This book may be said to have solidified his reputation and led to his job as drama critic of the *New York Evening Post;* it also represents about the only record we have of the trip. Not that the book is in any way a travelogue; it begins with a long historical section, centered chiefly in the French Theatre; it is only in the final section, "Russia's Theatre of Social Revolt," that he

---

* But John's enthusiasm for *Troilus and Cressida* did not last forever (see page 205).
† W. W. Norton & Co., 1929. (Reprinted in full in *Dramatis Personae*.) Evidently the book he had discussed with William H. Wells had fallen through.

tries to give the kind of picture of a place that he had given throughout his diary four years earlier. In 1928 America had not recognized the U.S.S.R.; American travelers to Moscow were few and far between; we had no idea of what Stalin was going to prove himself capable. Accordingly, while John was by no means wearing rose-colored glasses, he did take into consideration that Russia was still in the early stage of the new regime, and that if the Russian people were not enjoying freedom, they were accustomed to tyranny under the czars.

The Moscow Art Theatre had visited America successfully; so had the Musical Studio, the Habima, and Balaieff with *The Chauve-Souris*.

But the vivid propagandist theatre of the Revolution, unlike the theatre forms which have originated in artistic protest alone, can never survive transplanting. . . .

It is the drama of the streets, however, and particularly of the streets of Moscow, which is an essential background to the shrill turbulence of the Soviet theatres. . . . For melodramatic contrasts Moscow is without an equal. The most flagrant of these is, of course, the ever-present paradox of a crumbling, malodorous Oriental capital, at least two hundred years behind the rest of the world when judged by all the usual tokens of enlightenment, boldly striking out to realize a Marxian Utopia by methods no other nation would dare to try even if it wanted to. . . . The Revolution seems still to be fought in the streets, waged now with a melancholy irony instead of shrapnel, between the old buildings and the new purposes they serve and the new people they house.

That it is a new people is affirmed by every minute spent in the streets, the stores, hotels, restaurants, trams, and stations—a new people in command, as new to Moscow as they are to the rest of the world. It is when this drab proletarian army is seen, and then alone, that the propagandist theatre which feeds it becomes explicable. . . .

Crude, infantile, noisy, obstreperous, cheap, confused, and formless as it is, it has, however, a thrilling quality of life that has made it magnificently successful in being what it set out to be—a propagandist theatre.

That is the gist of the section on Russia, which is worth reading in full even after forty-five years—especially after forty-five years. A pity that no letters—and John must have written many

—seem to have survived. John's old friend Theodore Morrison, then on the staff of the *Atlantic Monthly,* asked to see what John had written on the Russian theatre, for possible use in the magazine before book publication, but after three months the editor, Ellery Sedgwick, declined it.

Although this comes out of chronological order, it is convenient to record here John's last trip to Europe as a bachelor, which was made in the early summer of 1932—a walking tour of England and Scotland with his old friend Dorothy Sands, preceded by a couple of weeks in London. Fortunately Miss Sands's letters home have been preserved.

[Arrival in London, June 27.] Coming into London there are many nurseries . . . sheets of vivid color. The tower of the Abbey and Parliament, and Paddington Station where John was standing on the platform looking dreadfully pale . . . he had been sick with a grippe cold and still coughs and wheezes—but is better after the week-end. He had reserved a "bed-sitting room" at Mayfair Court Hotel for me with a bath. . . . John has more elaborate quarters, a bed-room and a sitting room where he can work and have people for lunch. . . .

I find John loves to sight-see. Of course this is his fourth visit to London so he knows it fairly well and is steeped in all the historical background that he needs to write out of.

They walked to Trafalgar Square, then to Westminster School; visited the Poets' Corner at the Abbey; back by way of Whitehall, Buckingham Palace, St. James's Park and Palace. Next day John's old friend and college roommate Curry Watson called for them, with his wife, and they had a day at Hampton Court, which John had never seen. The Watsons had taken "a beautiful estate" at Adelstone.

This morning the gardener cut me flowers, and my room is decorated with glorious larkspur, blue and purple, a bunch of roses and white carnations. John groaned at the idea of my carrying flowers back, but I noticed he was very pleased when I took some up to his room. He is lunching with P. P. Howe, Shaw's biographer. He has had numerous letters of introduction that he is getting answered this week. Tonight Cornelia Otis Skinner Blodget and her husband are taking me to the theatre to see Lilian Braithwaite, then to a night club. John meets us after the show. Cornelia is playing at the Haymarket for two weeks, losing money, but considering it an advertising investment for American prestige.

[June 29.] Wilella * arrived late Monday. John met the boat train at eleven. . . . Cornelia had a farewell tea at their hotel, the Connaught, yesterday—she looking very gorgeous in a white brocaded medieval-cut tea-gown, and Wilella, John, and I had dinner here. Then John left to go to the theatre again with the Blodgets.

I would have hoped John would have seen all his important people, but his letters of introduction are just coming back this week and he has been tied up each day with engagements. Today it is E. V. Lucas, Lamb's biographer, and Friday he has been invited to lunch with George Bernard Shaw! That will be the day of days. . . .

[July 5.] Shaw lives at Whitehall Court rather near-by, so after walking over to 10 Downing Street . . . we went in search of Whitehall Court. . . . Being ten minutes early we walked the block several times. It seems to be my fate to lead my friends to their great shrine—and depart. I well remember an identical performance with Rachel Field, who had a long-cherished desire to meet Barrie. . . .

John's luncheon was somewhat disappointing—as all long-awaited moments are apt to be—in that, having been introduced by a letter from [Maurice] Hindus, the writer on Russia, Shaw had thought him a Communist. [Hindus was not a Communist.] Clare Sheridan, the sculptress, and her son were the other guests, and the talk was all of Russia. As it's a subject John doesn't respect Shaw too much on he didn't get much kick out of it. But he was keen about the man himself, the brilliant quality of his mind and his amazing gift to talk. He never got to ask him the questions he wanted to about his critical days. Fortunately John had been to Russia.

[On July 10 they went to Salisbury.] Then to Winterslowe, an old Inn where Hazlitt wrote, which was the particular reason for John's pilgrimage.

[Back to London, a late dinner in Soho, then to Stratford.] The Memorial Theatre . . . is very wrong for this place. It should be the National Theatre in London. They should have had a perfect Elizabethan theatre here—this is far too modern.

After Stratford, Kenilworth; then north to Scotland. Any letters written from there seem not to have been preserved—only a series of beautiful picture postcards which define their itinerary.

* Wilella Waldorf, of the drama department of the *New York Evening Post*, a friend and colleague of John's.

But from Kenilworth Miss Sands wrote a charming paragraph. After criticizing their fellow tourists ("Kenilworth was filled with such dreadful people . . .") she continues:

When we went into the dining room for lunch there were Edward Massey and his mother! I'm sure John had a fit. He really is a most conventionally minded person for all his scandalous talk and I'm sure gets quite nervous over this particular trip. He tried to get rooms on different decks on the *Laconia,* which struck me as too ridiculous.

A word has been said about John's financial difficulties. Evidently he did not come to the end of them until he married and settled down, early in 1933, by which time, in addition to his salary from the *Evening Post,* he was becoming established as a highly popular lecturer. His career had begun while he was on the staff of *Theatre Arts,* with a lecture arranged for him by Rosamond Gilder, at the Cosmopolitan Club in New York. Ellen Barret gave him his first opportunity to lecture outside of New York and its vicinity. He wrote her that he would like to lecture in Louisville; he wanted to pay his home town a visit, and a lecture would pay his expenses. Ellen's mother was a friend of the president of the Women's Club, who remembered John, and persuaded the drama committee to have him, in spite of the natural skepticism with which a prophet is confronted in his own country. John gave his talk in December 1925 and was enthusiastically received; he also had a good visit with his family and friends. So began the career of the man who was to supplant William Lyon Phelps—of whom he had spoken disparagingly, in private—as the favorite of the Women's Clubs of America.

The final notes on his financial affairs come in 1932. Early that year he was posted at the Harvard Club of New York, but soon paid his bill and cleared his good name—possibly the delay had been caused by his election in 1931 to the Century Association, and the consequent necessity to pay both the dues and the initiation fee there. Also, this was the depth of the Depression, the next to last year of Hoover's administration. Then, in August, from Wequetonsing, Michigan, where John had spent many boyhood summers (his grandmother still had a cottage there, and Mary Miller, then Mrs. Pelham Turner, had one next door), John wrote to Dorothy Sands that he and Bud Reed—Don Oenslager was away on a trip—had agreed to split up, owing to the constant arguments over money, and Bud suggested that when Don came back, he could choose between them. "I assured [Bud] that the Judgment of Paris had already been written into the records as a cause of discord, that under the circumstances (as I was the erring member) there was nothing for me to do but to get out, and that as fond as I was of the boys get out I would.

"Due to Buddie's extreme kindness, and in spite of his justified indignation, the whole matter shaped itself up in the most amicable and satisfactory way." He goes on to say that he has "all but taken a two-room flat at 157 East 72nd Street. . . .

"In other words—and due largely to your influence—I am going to try to face the facts of financing next winter. You once said to me this summer, when I was as usual whining to you about my deficiencies, that though I was thoroughly aware of my faults, I never did anything about them.

"That was so true that it hurt."

This letter was written only six months before John's wedding, so the matter of the apartment made little difference after all.

One of the acting students who attended John's lectures at the Laboratory Theatre was Catherine Meredith of Harrisburg, who of course knew Don Oenslager, from the same home town. In the course of one lecture John asked the class to identify the phrase, "my salad days." No one else volunteering, Miss Meredith —hereinafter known as Cassie—raised her hand and said, "Shakespeare."

"Shakespeare!" John exploded. "What an answer! Anybody knows that much!"

Cassie, thus encouraged, proceeded to recite enough of Cleopatra's speech to show that she was familiar with it. John saw her after the lecture and invited her to an opening that evening. She accepted the invitation, but nothing developed then and there. Cassie, whom Richard Aldrich considers to have been talented as an actress, did go from the Laboratory Theatre School on to the stage; she played a season of stock in Richmond, another at Virginia Beach, and in late 1930 and 1931 was a member of the road company of *Lysistrata* while the successful revival, which opened in New York in June 1930 with Violet Kemble-Cooper, Miriam Hopkins, and Ernest Truex, played over 250 performances.

But in the autumn of 1932 she was back in New York, and she and John began seeing each other: going together to openings. By this time, as we have noted from John's low spirits during the summer of that year, after returning from his walking tour with Dorothy Sands, John was ready for love, marriage, and responsibility. At Christmas time he telephoned Cassie in Harrisburg and told her that he had a break in his lecture schedule in early February, and said that the eleventh of that month would be a good date for them to be married. Cassie said she wanted to speak to her parents. No, said John, he couldn't wait. So she accepted him, and they were married in Harrisburg on February 11, 1933: bridesmaids, ushers, reception, and all.

# Chapter Six

# Two on the Aisle

John's own books are the best records of his work at the *New York Evening Post,* but they are highly selective; it is surprising to find that, of the five books he produced between 1930 and 1940 (inclusive), only two consist of reprints of selected *Post* reviews. The first—and the first to follow *The Modern Theatre in Revolt*—is *Upstage* (1930), and it does, to be sure, largely consist of John's selected writings from his earlier days; he credits, besides the *Post,* the *Boston Transcript* and *Theatre Arts,* but does not identify the origin of each piece, as was to be his custom later. Since the book must have gone to press soon after John took the *Post* job, it presumably contains little from that source; most of the chapters are as long as his *Theatre Arts* pieces. He took the trouble to make a book out of what might have been a collection. The subtitle is "The American Theatre in Performance," and the preface begins by disclaiming any intention to write "a book of backstage personality sketches." There is a section on the American playwrights whom the author considered the most important of the period: Barry, Kelly, O'Neill, Sidney Howard, Paul Green. Then a section on actors, one on scenic artists, one on directors (Belasco, Ames, Hopkins), one on reviewers (Woollcott, Nathan, Stark Young), one on theatre buildings, and finally one on the audience. Although the subject matter was briefly summarized in John's later essay, "The Theatre of the Twenties" (1951), the book still is worth reading either for the awakening of reminiscence or for the enlightenment of later generations. It remains to add that *Upstage* is dedicated to Aunt Mary.

The next book of essays, *The Art of Playgoing* (1936), taken out of chronological order for convenience of discussion, contains no credits in the front matter or elsewhere for previous publication, and while it may have picked up passages here and there from magazine and newspaper articles, it is a book and not a compendium. The ten chapters are thoughtfully written, and they are connected in that they contribute coherently to the same theme, which is expressed by the title: what should the audience —including the critics—bring to the theatre so that there will be a symbiotic relationship between them, each enriching the other? *The Art of Playgoing* has a density unusual in books on the theatre. The section of poetic drama in the chapter called "The Dramatist's Ear" foreshadows John's later reviews of T. S. Eliot's attempts at writing poetic plays on modern themes: *The Cocktail Party* and *The Confidential Clerk*. While paying due respect to *Murder in the Cathedral* (Eliot's first poetic play, about the martyrdom of Thomas à Becket, of which he wrote: "Slow in starting as it was, it rose to moments of high beauty, became dramatic almost in spite of itself, and brought poetry back to a prosaic stage"), John was quite unbluffable by Eliot's reputation when he was discussing the two later pieces. Not that the opinions expressed are uniformly unfavorable; John finds much to say for *The Cocktail Party* and a few things in favor of *The Confidential Clerk,* but he certainly expressed a minority opinion among his colleagues in the presence of the poet whose idolators had made him the sacred cow of the sacred wood.

Possibly the best book of this period, like *The Art of Playgoing* in being all criticism and no reviewing, is *Letters from Greenroom Ghosts* (1934). This is a short book, consisting of five imaginary letters from theatrical personages of the past to their counterparts of the present, preceded by a brief prefatory letter from the author to his colleague Stark Young. The long letters are from Sarah Siddons to Katharine Cornell; from Peg Woffington to Ina Claire; from Christopher Marlowe to Eugene O'Neill; from Richard Brinsley Sheridan to Noel Coward (this one is reprinted in *Dramatis Personae*); and from Inigo Jones to Robert Edmond Jones. This book is no less brilliant for being a *tour de force*. The author succeeded in placing himself inside the personalities and points of view of those figures of the past—ghosts for whom he was acting as ghost writer—and at the same time pronouncing valuable critical opinions on his contemporaries, the recipients of the letters.

It is tempting to quote at length from *Letters from Greenroom Ghosts,* but we must be content with the example of a single paragraph, from Mrs. Siddons's letter to Katharine Cornell.

You are a symbol as I was a symbol, but where I stood for abstract woes or represented the divinities on earth, you speak for personal griefs and represent the devil in women. I was a solemn force from heaven, where you are a primitive instinct in man. I spoke for the gods, where you speak for what men have come to identify as the glands. I was an eagle; you are a cobra. You are the embodiment of what mortals must conquer in themselves; I was the bodily incarnation of the supernatural forces that control the destinies of men. Where I was florid, you are repressed; where I blazed, you glow.

This was written at a time when John, in the person of Mrs. Siddons, thought that Miss Cornell had chosen parts not good enough for her abilities—perhaps her genius; this in spite of her having appeared in *Candida, The Barretts of Wimpole Street,* and Sidney Howard's *Alien Corn.* "Remember, too," ran a later sentence in the same letter, "that the great parts of the past and present still await you—Lady Macbeth, Cleopatra, Hedda, Madame Ranevsky and a score of others. They need your illumination as much as you need theirs."

Parenthetically, *Letters from Greenroom Ghosts* was probably written before John had met Katharine Cornell, who, with her husband, Guthrie McClintic, was later to become a very good friend of the Browns. At that time, however, John tried to avoid meeting actors and actresses, thinking that it might impair the independence of his position when he had to write reviews of their performances. Mrs. August Belmont, who—it will be recalled—knew John in the Greenwich Village days, tried several times to introduce him to Miss Cornell, but he declined for the reason given. Neither his hesitancy nor Mrs. Siddons's opinions affected the warmth of their long friendship later.

The other two books of this period, *Two on the Aisle* (1938) and *Broadway in Review* (1940), were reprints of his reviews, coherently arranged. "Two on the Aisle" was the title of his newspaper column. No doubt the most famous—or notorious—of all John's reviews was that of Tallulah Bankhead in *Antony and Cleopatra* (November 11, 1937), which began: "Tallulah Bankhead barged down the Nile last night as Cleopatra—and sank." In her memoirs fifteen years later, Miss Bankhead was to recall this without any sign of acrimony. She also quoted unfavorable opinions by George Jean Nathan and Brooks Atkinson, as well as the remark of Richard Watts, Jr., in the *Herald-Tribune;* he called her "the serpent of the Swanee." In March 1939 John was to give high praise to Miss Bankhead's performance in *The Little Foxes* by Lillian Hellman:

> The faults of her Cleopatra have long since slipped into ancient history and been forgotten. Even at their worst they had nothing to do with Miss Bankhead's extraordinary powers as a realist. For some years, in such insufficient scripts as *Dark Victory, Forsaking All Others, Something Gay,* and *Reflected Glory,* she has been giving tantalizing glimpses of these powers. . . . Fortunately for all of us, *The Little Foxes* brings Miss Bankhead her long-awaited opportunity.

It is regrettable that John never wrote a comprehensive essay on the thirties as he was to do in "The Theatre of the Twenties." (He came near doing this in a long section in *Broadway in Review* called "Background.") There is another section in *Two on the Aisle* called "Sing Me a Song with Social Significance" (this was the title of a song in *Pins and Needles,* a revue presented by the International Ladies' Garment Workers' Union). The section consists of several reviews, reprinted out of chronological order for the purpose of making his points. It begins with a review of an Elizabethan play, Dekker's *The Shoemaker's Holiday,* which in Orson Welles's revival struck him as an important ancestor of the American plays of social revolt; *We, the People* by Elmer Rice; *Both Your Houses* by Maxwell Anderson; *They Shall Not Die* by John Wexley; *Stevedore* by Peters and Sklar; three plays by Clifford Odets—*Waiting for Lefty, Awake and Sing!* and *Golden Boy;* the productions by a government agency, the Works Progress Administration, called *The Living Newspapers;* and finally *Pins and Needles.* Of that revue he wrote: "It is class-conscious enough to satisfy the most avid propagandist. Yet it manages to say serious things lightly and to indict with a song and a smile. By so doing it makes its point twice as effectively as it would have done had it followed the sober routine methods of agit-prop drama in this country."

John wrote a preface to this section in which he recalled some of the pre-Depression propagandist plays. Whatever the shortcomings of these plays, both of the twenties and of the thirties, "all of them have given a new vitality to our theatre. Their significance cannot be overstressed." He concluded: "For extending my horizons by having widened the theatre's, and for having opened my eyes and quickened my conscience, I feel grateful to the hatred and violence, and the bad art of even the sorriest and most sullen specimens in the lot, with the overstated opinions of which I still disagree, and abhor."

It may be that because the decade of the thirties is remembered as the decade of the Depression, the theatre of the thirties is remembered as the theatre of revolt. But *Two on the Aisle* and *Broadway in Review* demonstrate that the theatre of that decade had other things in abundance. Maurice Evans in *Richard II;* Katharine Cornell's *Romeo and Juliet;* John Gielgud's *Hamlet;* the Lunts' *Taming of the Shrew.* And such other distinguished revivals as *Electra* with Blanche Yurka, Lillian Gish as Camille, Eva Le Gallienne's *Hedda Gabler;* Nazimova in *The Cherry Orchard*. O'Neill was represented—hardly the *mot juste*—by *Mourning Becomes Electra* and later by his nostalgic and uncharacteristic comedy, *Ah, Wilderness!* Plays by Philip Barry and Robert E. Sherwood; Eliot's *Murder in the Cathedral,* produced by the WPA and reviewed at regular length (March 30, 1936) but in the terms well summarized in the quotation previously given. Thornton Wilder's *Our Town* and the musical satire which was a smash hit and Pulitzer Prize winner, Kaufman and Ryskind's *Of Thee I Sing,* with some of George Gershwin's best music. An impression of extraordinary richness is left of the period.

One other piece must be mentioned: a combination of two reviews of *Abe Lincoln in Illinois* by Robert E. Sherwood (October 17 and 25, 1939)—interesting not only for what John had to say at the time, but in retrospect, because he was to devote so much of his last years to Sherwood's biography. His review begins by listing Sherwood's unnamed collaborators: the audience, which came to the play knowing the chief character and the events in advance; Lincoln himself; even John Wilkes Booth. Of these, Lincoln was by far the most important:

Just as surely as Mr. Hart and Mr. Kaufman worked together, so have the Messrs. Sherwood and Lincoln emerged as a playwriting team in which Mr. Sherwood on the whole functions as the silent partner. . . . The best scene in Mr. Sherwood's play is ghost-written by a ghost who haunts all Americans and is the chiefest glory of our dream. This scene is the episode in which Mr. Massey [Raymond Massey, who took the part of Lincoln in the production] faces Douglas on a public platform to speak some of the fine, free words Lincoln himself delivered during the course of these historic debates. . . . Timely, reverent, and ultimately impressive as it becomes, Mr. Sherwood's play is not so much written as it is assembled in the best manner of Detroit. . . .

In his biography of Sherwood John was, rather like Shaw's *Saint Joan,* at least partially to recant and then to recant his recantation. He tells how on opening night Mr. and Mrs. Sherwood went to Elmer Rice's apartment to wait for the reviews:

The raves in the *Times* and *Tribune* put an end to the agony. By the next afternoon all the daily notices were in, and Sherwood summarized them in his diary by saying, *Times, Tribune, World-Telegram*—fine. *Mirror, News, Sun, Journal*—fair. *Post* (John Mason Brown)—rotten."

I was rotten [continues Sherwood's biographer] and wrong, though not entirely so. I had some points to make which were not without their validity, though they now [1965] seem to me academic, ungrateful, and carping. One of these was that, if Sherwood had taken a curtain call, he would in all honesty have had to lead Abe on stage with him as his collaborator. . . . I was decidedly in the minority with almost everyone against me, certainly everyone whose opinion I respected. I have come to know from his diary that what I challenged in *Abe* was what in part bothered Sherwood in his despairing moments while writing it. This was too much reading, too much homework, and too little playwriting by Sherwood himself.

Which brings us back to 1939. One other piece reprinted in *Broadway in Review* has a personal application: "The Dodie Bird" (January 1939). This was a brief survey of the work of the English playwright Dodie Smith, author of *Autumn Crocus, Call It a Day,* and *Dear Octopus.* John's review was patronizing but not unfair. "As a dramatist Miss Smith is the theatre's cricket on the hearth. What she chirps is a song of domesticity. . . . She even dares to write affectionately about what, in some quarters, is such an unmentionable subject as a happy family. This is the boldest thing about her. It makes her placid mediocrity appear revolutionary." However, he concluded: "Even when we roast her, she does manage to make marshmallows of us all."

It was unusual for John to write a piece about the plays of an author whose work he considered negligible. A conjecture may be offered as to how this came about. During the run of *Call It a Day,* a friend of John's, without malice aforethought, happened to mention that he liked the play. John erupted. "The trouble with you," he declared, "is that you hate the theatre. You may love books, but you hate the theatre!" This was another example of John's meaning what he said and pretending to mean it at the same time. It led to a friendly running argument between the two men, neither of whom would budge. But—to complete the conjecture—did John feel called upon to do some justice in print to Dodie Smith, whom he had denounced so lavishly by word of mouth? Parenthetically, it may be said that John had, in spite of his parents' divorce, lived a happy family life in Louisville, and by 1939 he was living another one in New York. He and Cassie spent many evenings at theatre openings; from 1933 on she was, of course, the constant occupant of one of the aisle seats. They often spent other evenings at dinner with friends. The present writer recalls many such evenings with one particular, beloved, and distinguished friend, Amy Loveman of *The Saturday Review of Literature* and the Book-of-the-Month Club—evenings filled with opinionated discussions (except that Amy was always firm without ever seeming opinionated, as the rest of us often did) of books and plays and absent friends, evenings usually made hilarious by John's witty effervescence. John's family life was interrupted by his frequent lecture trips, but when he was on the road he wrote to Cassie at least once daily. And by 1939 their first son, Preston, was going on three years old—with Meredith to come a year later.

Brooks Atkinson says that John was—at least up to that time—the only drama critic who had deliberately prepared himself for the job. His trips abroad, and his decision to go with Mrs. Isaacs rather than with G. P. Baker, bear this out. One who has not lived the life of a daily theatrical reviewer is not in a position to describe the effect it has upon the reviewer: the constant succession of first nights; the early deadline, necessitating—even for a critic of an evening paper—the preparation of the review as soon as he gets home (John once said to H. G. Merriam, "If I can get the first line of a review I am all set"). Then the wait for the messenger, and the afterthoughts, the second guesses, after the copy has irrevocably gone. This last feeling John has described in his essay "Pleasant Agony" (1949), reprinted in *Dramatis Personae*. Presumably they get used to it. John customarily caught up on his sleep with naps in the afternoon. He could be a rather difficult companion at lunch, eating his own meal with alarming rapidity and then calling upon his companion to do the same—no doubt because he was anxious to go home and snooze. But John gave every appearance of thriving on this life, at least throughout the thirties; and this in addition to his demanding lecture schedule.

John's colleagues recall some anecdotes. Brooks Atkinson, John Mason Brown, John Anderson of the *Journal,* and Gilbert Gabriel of the *American* got together a few times a year—calling their informal association, rather coyly perhaps, "The Girls' Friendly." During the long intermission at the premiere of *Mourning Becomes Electra*—since O'Neill's tragedy consisted of four full-length plays, it was necessary to make the intermission long enough for dinner—several of the reviewers ganged up on John Anderson, pretending that they were going to roast the play. What effect this may have had on Anderson's review is not disclosed—probably none, for he was an honest man. In any event, the praise in the next day's papers was universal. Once Atkinson and John went together to the *Brooklyn Eagle* to urge the reinstatement of Arthur Pollock, who had been dropped as drama critic because—the two missionaries believed—Pollock had been promoting the Newspaper Guild. The mission was at best partially successful; Pollock stayed on the paper, but not in his old job.

Mrs. Burns Mantle, wife of the drama critic of the *Daily News,* is reported to have remarked that Cassie—long established as the other member of "Two on the Aisle"—came to the theatre with John in such an advanced stage of pregnancy that Mrs. Mantle thought of bringing a basket. This could have happened only at the beginning of the seasons of 1936–37 and 1940–41, for both the Brown boys were born in October, Preston in 1936 and Meredith in 1940. In any event, it seems altogether sensible for a woman in an advanced state of pregnancy to have her husband on hand to call a taxi and conduct her to the hospital. No melodrama occurred in Mrs. Brown's case—cases—whatever the proceedings onstage may have been like.

John was spontaneous, witty, effervescent; almost everybody thought he had that quality known as charm. Not quite everybody, perhaps. Richard Lockridge, drama critic of the *Sun,* once remarked to a friend that John reminded him of a puppy. The remark was intended to be off the record, but like most secrets, which seem to be incorrigibly fluid, it leaked. Not long afterwards Lockridge, sitting in his aisle seat waiting for the curtain to rise, found John at his side squatting in the aisle, bouncing up and down and saying "Woof."

For years *Variety,* New York's daily newspaper written in original and imaginative English and devoted to show business and other forms of entertainment, ran an annual "box score" rating the critics by correlating their favorable opinions of plays with hits, and their unfavorable opinions with flops. Then the critics were listed by percentages of accurate predictions. John was at the top of the list several times, first in his first year on the *Post.* Years later—in 1958—he wrote to a correspondent: "One thing I violently object to in the *Twentieth Century Authors* sketch [of himself] is that last paragraph about the correctness of my *Variety* predictions. I never meant to be a prophet of flops or hits. I hated the whole process of such irrelevant and tawdry distinction. The only reason I won the box score (since abandoned as misleading by joint request of the members of the New York Critics Circle) was that in my redheaded youth on the *New York* [*Evening*] *Post* for four years I wrote more unfavorable reviews than any other daily reviewer. Since the failures always outnumbered the successes, this inevitably upped my chances to win a laurel wreath which was poison ivy as far as I and my colleagues were concerned."

This brings us to the Critics Circle, of which John was president four years. Surviving members of the Circle of John's day report that it was by no means a mutual admiration society; it was difficult to get many of the critics to agree on anything; and John was the only one who could hold the group together. Meanwhile, the *Post* had changed hands, and "Two on the Aisle," along with its conductor, had moved in 1941 to the *World-Tele-gram,* where he was to remain until he joined the Navy in October 1942.

The Critics Circle is best described by a passage in *Broadway* by Brooks Atkinson (Macmillan).

The definitive and continuing New York Drama Critics Circle was founded in 1935, because a press agent supplied the enterprise. She was Helen Deutsch, at that time a press representative of Maxwell Anderson's "Winterset." She was a dynamic and personable young lady who did not stand in awe of egotists or custom. She shared a general dissatisfaction with the Pulitzer Prizes, some of which had no theater significance. The Pulitzer Prize for the previous season was a case in point. The significant plays of that season were Lillian Hellman's "The Children's Hour," Robert E. Sherwood's "The Petrified Forest," Maxwell Anderson's "Valley Forge," and Clifford Odets' "Awake and Sing." But the Pulitzer Prize went to Zoe Akins' sentimental dramatization of Edith Wharton's "The Old Maid."

Mr. Atkinson goes on to say that Miss Deutsch called up a couple of critics and started the ball rolling; then got all of them together for a meeting at the Algonquin, where Frank Case, the manager and one of the celebrities of his day, provided a room and free drinks. So the Circle was organized, with the rule that no prize would be awarded unless at least three-quarters of the members agreed on the choice—this in order to protect dissenters. The first two Critics Circle Awards went to plays by Maxwell Anderson: *Winterset* and *High Tor.* To quote further from *Broadway:*

Since the taste of human beings is fallible, it is better to have two theater awards than one. But committees frequently go to pieces when they make art awards, and many of the Circle and Pulitzer awards look hackneyed in retrospect. In 1935, it seemed likely that professional theatergoers would be more discerning than the Pulitzer newspapermen, but it has not turned out that way. The average taste of the Critics Circle is no more discerning than the average taste of the Pulitzer judges. Neither the Circle nor the Pulitzer prizes can be intimidated by genius; both of them have on occasion preferred commonplace plays to classics. [Mr. Atkinson had previously pointed out that in 1938 the

Circle awarded the prize to John Steinbeck's *Of Mice and Men,* and Thornton Wilder's *Our Town* won the Pulitzer Prize.] "Of Mice and Men" became a statistic; "Our Town" became a classic.

Wolcott Gibbs was drama critic of *The New Yorker* in 1946; his remarks were taken from the April 13 issue of that year. The Critics Circle had awarded no prize for the best American play of that season. Two plays that, in the words of Mr. Gibbs,

survived to contend in what might be called the finals—"State of the Union" and "Born Yesterday"—had been at least temperately praised by the dissenters, so that there was no question of damning them as wholly worthless. The objection therefore was based on the theory that neither one of them was a work of art by the high, inflexible standards of classical criticism. In the course of the meeting, Mr. John Mason Brown, who presided with a curious and charming blend of Boss Tweed and Santayana, remarked that the membership was gathered to choose not the best play since Aeschylus but merely the best play of one year in the life of the New York stage. It strikes me as a sensible point of view.

Louis Kronenberger, the distinguished author of *Kings and Desperate Men, Company Manners,* and other books on history and culture, was drama critic of *Time* during one of John's administrations. When he joined the Critics Circle and came to his first meeting, John, who had never met Kronenberger before, said to him, "Come and sit at the amusing end of the table." It was the beginning of a friendship that lasted the rest of John's life.

John's files are crammed with letters, most of them to budding playwrights but some to producers, declining to read the scripts of unproduced plays. In a letter of December 11, 1944, he wrote to his good friend, the producer Alfred de Liagre, Jr., returning unread the script of a play: "Nathan has always been happy to read plays in advance. JMB has never done so; and won't do so now. . . . I still believe the critic's job, except in the case of revivals, is to review the produced play from the audience's point of view."

The phrase "from the audience's point of view" is perhaps not strictly accurate; John had neither the ability nor the desire to subordinate his own point of view to that of others, least of all to conceal it; what he meant was that *as a reviewer for a daily newspaper,* his job was to tell his own readers enough about the play to give them a basis to decide whether to see it or not. We have already seen his opinion of the *Variety* "box score." If not from time immemorial, certainly for several decades there has flourished a public argument as to whether a few drama reviewers wield a power out of proportion to their intelligence and abilities—an argument that has become more intense as the number of newspapers in New York has so precipitously declined. (Most of this decline has taken place since John's days with "Two on the Aisle.") The question has repeatedly come up—frequently from producers who believe, often rightly, that a few reviewers have the power of life or death over their productions—whether justice would not be served by counterbalancing the reviewers' opinions with opinions from random members of the audience, taken down on opening night by an inquiring reporter. In 1966 John wrote to a correspondent about this.

"I am flattered, of course, that you want my opinions on the equal-time proposal in the field of dramatic criticism. I'm afraid it is one of those ideas that sounds fine on paper but would never work out in practice. The authority exerted over the stage by a few drama critics seems, even to many critics, unfair. These critics, however, do not seek that authority. It is given them by the tyranny of print. No panel, no matter how well intentioned or distinguished, is going to produce the ideal critic.

"Theatrical openings are news and, as such, have to be covered by newspapers. If only the public would learn how to read criticism (and some of the critics to write it), it would all be simpler. By learning how to read criticism I mean reading it to see how well an opinion is justified. In other words, is it as well presented as a brief should be? As for the practicing critics, isn't it fair to consider them a jury of five (instead of twelve)? . . .

"P.S. When I was a critic on the *New York Post* from 1929 to 1941, we did try for about two years to have a reporter present at openings, interviewing the audience at random so that the public reaction was stated as well as the personal, critical one. The idea, however well intentioned, did not work out at all. The trouble was that the reporter did not know who the people he was interviewing were. Some of the most favorable comments were made invariably by those who were angels of the show or friends of the cast or playwright. The devastating comments came from rival dramatists, actors who hated other actors, or theatrical people who were hostile to the management. But we did try."

A final Critics Circle anecdote is taken, not from one of John's books on the theatre, but from his light-hearted account of his experiences as a lecturer, *Accustomed As I Am*. But it manifestly belongs here:

Although I know after-dinner speaking is a special art in which Chauncey Depew in his day was the acknowledged Homer and Shakespeare of witty triviality, and although I have listened with pleasure to many excellent addresses of the kind in my own time, I must admit the most eloquent after-dinner speech I have ever been privileged to hear was delivered at a dinner which was not public at all. Nor was it meant to be a speech. It was spoken by a man who was a newcomer to the hated ranks of New York's drama critics. He was attending what was for him the first of those intimate dinners with which the Critics Circle each year at Mr. Woollcott's Christmas season sweetly celebrates the Yuletide. He was a shy novitiate, this newcomer; a little awed, as all of us are who follow the craft of Aristotle, by being so near George Jean Nathan and Kelcey Allen.

He stood quietly at the bar and drank when drinks and oysters were being downed and Brooks Atkinson was discoursing learnedly on the home life of the heron. His silence was no less respectful as, while he continued his drinking, he heard John Anderson talking at one moment like Horace about his Sabine farm, and the next like Shaw about Mrs. Patrick Campbell. He was mute but manually active when the wine came, and Richard Watts held forth contrapuntally on the charm of the Irish drama and the charms of some maiden he had spied once in the lobby of a hotel in far-off Java.

Only the wine crossed his lips as he heard Louis Kronenberger, Wolcott Gibbs, Joseph Wood Krutch, Walter Winchell, Sidney Whipple, Richard Lockridge and Stark Young vary their tussles with the match game with discussions of Duse, Jimmy Durante, S. N. Behrman, and

Lillian Hellman. For three hours after dinner, in spite of sipping one encouraging highball after another, he sat like Caspar Milquetoast between Mr. Nathan and Burns Mantle. Little by little his face whitened as he listened to Mr. Nathan when he appraised Schnitzler, Sean O'Casey, and O'Neill; to Mr. Mantle when he described John Drew and the Federal Theatre; and to Robert Benchley, across the table, as he released that glorious laugh of his and told droll stories Balzac could not have equaled.

Finally, this novitiate could stand it no longer. Suddenly he arose and banged the table with a Jovian hand. "Listen to me, you bastards," he cried in a great voice, and, catapulting through the air, he passed completely out of the picture and from view.

For brevity, though not necessarily for accuracy, this has always struck me as being a model speech of its kind.*

It must be added that in the roster of Critics Circle members given in the third paragraph of the selection quoted, John—like his fellow Kentuckian, with malice toward none—tactfully included the name of the after-dinner speaker among those who were supposedly his audience.

* From *Accustomed As I Am* by John Mason Brown (W. W. Norton & Co.)

# Chapter Seven

# One on the Platform

John's book about his experiences as a lecturer, *Accustomed As I Am,* was published in 1942. It is too humorous and lighthearted to be taken as anything approaching a literal account; the emphasis is on the absurdities of the lecture platform: the irrelevant questions; the presidents of women's clubs throughout America, their appearances, personalities, sometimes their husbands; the indistinguishable meals consumed as a compulsory part of the proceedings; the introductions, either too long or in some cases leading up to the announcement of some other name than John Mason Brown, which naturally came as a surprise. As to the women's clubs, they—and John's lectures—were immortalized by Helen Hokinson's famous cartoon in *The New Yorker* late in the 1930s: a woman of ample girth standing on a platform, announcing, "Next week, our intellectual cocktail—John Mason Brown." *
As to the introductions, John tells of one occasion when the chairman, after an elaborate build-up, introduced the speaker as Heywood Broun. On another occasion, the chairman apologized for the absence of several distinguished personages who had been invited earlier than John but who had been unable to appear, concluding with a man of medicine who had been expected to come and deliver a talk on syphilis. John, in his first sentence, made the unseemly comment that he regretted being only a scab.

* The caption, as with many of Miss Hokinson's cartoons, was supplied by James Reid Parker.

John's career as a lecturer began, as we have seen, at the Cosmopolitan Club in New York, followed by the appearance in Louisville. By the thirties he was a full-fledged, hard-working, widely traveling professional lecturer. (Aunt Mary's comment is worth repeating: "What! A Brown paid for talking?") In addition to his lecture tours, there were several summer teaching engagements, following the session in 1923 at the University of Montana; there were two more summers there, four at Harvard, and various engagements at other colleges.

In 1931–32 John gave a course at Yale on the history of theatrical criticism. This of course was under George Pierce Baker's auspices; a letter from Mr. Baker, in John's files, dated September 15, 1931, agrees to pay him $1200 and expenses for a weekly lecture of one hour. John had never lost touch with Baker, from the time in 1924 when he decided to go to *Theatre Arts* instead of back to Harvard. If he had decided to go with Baker he would have followed him to Yale; he had written Baker, on April 20, 1925: "It was a terrible temptation not to go with you to Yale. I don't know whether I was right or wrong. I can only hope that I was right, but I do know that a large part of my heart will find itself, strangely enough, in New Haven next winter." *

They continued to correspond through the following years. The letters discuss contributions to *Theatre Arts;* a request from Baker that John see a couple of plays and report on them to him; then, on January 19, 1926, Baker wrote that he was coming to New York to see O'Neill's new play, *The Great God Brown,*† and asked if John could put him up for the night. John replied on the twentieth: "Delighted to have you Saturday night and Sunday night, too. I wish I could go with you to O'Neill's play in my honor, but I have to go to it on Friday so as to get it in the next review. . . . The magazine will be out the twentieth of

---

* It is possible that this letter may refer to a repetition of Baker's offer, made when Baker went to Yale, but the author has found no evidence of this in the correspondence.

† Revived as recently as late 1972.

next month (I mean the one with 'The Theatre Goes to Yale' in it)."

In April Baker wrote John to express appreciation of "the article by your distinguished new contributor [G.P.B. himself] on the work of the Department of Drama. Will you convey to him, please, my deep appreciation of his understanding, right emphasis, and cordial spirit?"

A few days later (April 16, 1926) John wrote Baker about a summer issue of the magazine to be devoted to Shakespeare. Donald Oenslager, who had begun in 1925 to teach a course in scene design at Yale,* had shown him in New Haven "a really marvelous collection of Shakespearean models made in the class. With Don's dramatic instinct, he lighted each one of the models by fugitive matches, and looking through the front door of The Swan and The Globe was really an almost unbelievable sensation in that kind of light." John asked for photographs of the models.

On December 13, 1927, John wrote Baker that he was going west on a lecture tour for the magazine, and asked for something that could be quoted in the announcements. Baker graciously complied, remarking that the angels, when they read it, would say he had just kissed the Blarney Stone. His words of praise read, "John Mason Brown, an enthusiastic student of the theatre for some years, has had unusual opportunities to study both in this country and in Europe. Audiences show keen appreciation of his lectures because he is not only well grounded in his subject but also an entertaining speaker." The circular, issued by John's lecture agent, James B. Pond, listed his subjects: "What the Moderns Are Doing to Shakespeare"; "The Pioneer Theatre"; "The New Movement in the Theatre"; "Contemporary American Playwrights"; "The Amateur Impulse" (the little theatre movement); and "Broadway in Review."

On April 15, 1929, John wrote Baker to remind him not to forget the dinner of the 47 Workshop Association on the twenty-

* He later became a full professor and taught the course until his retirement in 1970.

eighth; Baker replied, teasing John for having addressed the envelope to Harvard rather than to Yale. Walter Prichard Eaton, who was to join the Yale faculty in 1933 as an instructor in playwriting (later professor of playwriting), presided; John reported that the speeches were good. Later he wrote Baker proposing that the association issue a monthly mimeographed bulletin to report the doings of its members; Baker replied, May 30, that he thought a quarterly bulletin would suffice.

In a letter dated only June 6 (to which has been added, in pencil, 1931, but it must have been 1932, since it followed the year of John's Yale lectures, and announced his departure for Europe —surely the excursion with Dorothy Sands): "I can't go without telling you how thoroughly I've enjoyed my year at Yale. It's been the happiest feature of a very happy year. Also I must thank you for your kind and flattering offer about next year [unspecified in available correspondence]. You can't imagine how pleased I was by it—and how tempted."

On March 2 (to which has been correctly added the year 1933) John wrote to thank Baker for his wedding present, John Jenest's *History of the Stage,* and alludes to Baker's approaching retirement. (The letter is on the stationery of the *New York Evening Post.*) "I'm anxous to have Catherine meet you and Mrs. Baker and equally anxious to have you all meet her. . . . I'm tremendously happy. As a hardened old reviewer I want to go on record as endorsing marriage. It's a swell show (Post)."

John was unable to go to New Haven to pay homage to Baker on the occasion of his retirement. He wrote on May 29, 1933: "I'm heartbroken about tomorrow. There's nothing I want to do more than come up to New Haven. Catherine and I have both been hoping and hoping that we could make it . . . but I'm afraid we can't. We've just had a solemn financial conference with our checkbook, which blushes so easily, and we've been forced to come to the conclusion that, unless we grow wings by tomorrow morning (as we may yet from just wanting them so) we can't get up. . . .

"Here's to you for tomorrow, with thanks . . . for all you have meant and mean to me."

Finally, on April 5, 1936 (the year after Baker's death), John wrote to Mrs. Baker: "I'm delighted to hear that Harvard plans through its Theatre Collection to pay tardy homage to Mr. Baker." The plans included an exhibition of photographs of Baker's former students; John suggested a list of names.

During the years 1937–40, inclusive, John gave courses at the Harvard Summer School on the modern theatre, playwriting, and the history of dramatic criticism. The students were not necessarily undergraduates or graduates; some of them, especially in the course on playwriting, were well-known novelists wishing to expand their scope. An associate of John's at the time recalls that at one lecture a woman in the front row went to sleep; John had books on his desk, which he arranged in a pile in front of the sleeping beauty, then accidentally on purpose knocked them over to the floor directly in front of her. It is not recorded, but there is no doubt that after the session he made soothing remarks to the lady.

John was designated in the Summer School catalogue as Visiting Instructor and as Drama Critic, *New York Evening Post.* In 1937 he gave two courses, meeting five days a week for sessions of an hour each, and running from July 6 to August 14. Here they are, with their descriptions.

*English SA-4   Playwriting*
  A detailed study of such essentials of a play as plot, dialogue, characterization, action, climax, and "flavor." A consideration of the various forms of tragedy and comedy. The principles of dramatic technique as they show themselves in universal, period, and personal ways. Round-table discussion and criticism of the plays written by members of the class.

*English S53b   The History of the Modern Theatre*
  The end of Romanticism and the coming of Naturalism. The contribution of Charles Kean, Wagner, the Meiningen Players, Antoine, and Stanislavsky to contemporary standards of acting and production. The influence of Ibsen, Chekhov, Strindberg, and Shaw on the play-

wrights who have followed them. The advent of the "Free Theatres," and so-called New Movement, inaugurated by Appia and Craig. The growth of Expressionism, and a study of the theory and practice of the major dramatists, designers, directors, and critics, both in Europe and America, since the turn of the century.

John taught these courses again in 1938, from July 5 to August 13, and in 1939 repeated (for about the same period of time) the History of the Modern Theatre. Instead of Playwriting, his second course was English S85c, The Theatre As Seen by Its Critics:

This course traces the history of the theatre from the Greeks to the present time in terms of what its outstanding critics have had to say about its practice or theory in each of the major periods. From Aristotle through the writings of Horace, Scaliger, Castelvetro, Dryden, Rymer, Diderot, Lessing, Schiller, Goethe, Schlegel, Victor Hugo, Coleridge, Hazlitt, Leigh Hunt and Lamb, the history of dramatic criticism (and of the theatre it reflects) will be followed down to the time of Shaw, Archer, Walkley, Brunetière, Sarcey, and such contemporary reviewers as James Agate, St. John Ervine, Alexander Woollcott, Stark Young, George Jean Nathan, Joseph Wood Krutch and Brooks Atkinson.

These courses were repeated in the summer of 1940. John had compiled a book in collaboration with Montrose J. Moses in 1934, *The American Theatre As Seen by Its Critics: 1752–1934*. It is a useful compendium, representing critics from Washington Irving and Poe to John and his contemporaries; and playwrights from Royall Tyler to Robert E. Sherwood. But this kind of book is self-defeating if not periodically revised and enlarged.

For two or three summers in the mid-thirties John was on the staff of the Bread Loaf Writers' Conference, a two-weeks' session at Bread Loaf, Vermont, sponsored by Middlebury College. The members of the Conference fell into three groups: the staff, consisting of professional writers and editors; the fellows, promising young writers who had published a book or two or at least had a work in progress; and the paying customers, who hopefully brought along manuscripts to be criticised, preferably with the kind of constructive criticism that would lead to publication. Each of the staff members was expected to give several lectures.

John's were superb: witty, knowledgeable, informative. As a teacher hoping to see some promising work, he was slightly dismayed to find that he was expected to deal with a short play by a midwestern schoolteacher, written for performance by schoolchildren, called "The Germs in Billy Smith's Mouth," in which all the characters were either teeth or germs: the dialogue began with a germ exclaiming, "Goody, goody! Billy Smith forgot to brush his teeth this morning!"

That particular summer one of John's fellow staff members was the late Robert Hillyer, best known as a poet, who had recently published a novel called *Riverhead*. John had done his homework by reading it in advance, and was utterly delighted to find that it concludes with a scene in which an act of sexual intercourse takes place in a canoe. Since this may be difficult to believe, a brief quotation from *Riverhead* is herewith presented:

> So, like all lovers new to rapture, they accomplished their love in both anguish and delight and, happy at last in fulfillment, they lay side by side on the floor of the canoe, neither daring to speak.

Throughout the two weeks of the session John let no opportunity pass to tease Hillyer about this. Though the teasing began with the innocent question as to how the feat was accomplished without tipping the canoe over, it became rougher as time went on, and presently, every time Hillyer came into the dining room, John—if he were there first, as he usually was; his compulsive promptness has been mentioned—would say nothing but go through the unmistakable motions of wielding a paddle.

Another episode, both unique and characteristic, took place on the day of Don Oenslager's wedding in March 1937. John was best man. He had a morning lecture engagement in Scarsdale, in Westchester County, twenty miles or so from New York, where the wedding was to take place in the afternoon. After the lecture John returned to New York in a taxi, and adroitly contrived to change into his morning clothes, which he had brought in a suitcase, while the taxi was getting him to the church on time.

Don's bride was Mary Osborn Polak, of a distinguished Brooklyn family. She has always been called Zorka, a Polish nickname bestowed upon her by her nurse. The Browns and the Oenslagers, as families, continued the close friendship the two men had enjoyed as bachelors, but owing to their proximity in New York, they had little occasion to correspond. Don was one of Meredith Brown's godfathers. Zorka is delightfully gifted with a touch of Mrs. Malaprop; John used to tease her unmercifully, not at all to her consternation. He was an inveterate tease, and said whatever came into his head; but his teasing was so humorous and affectionate as to leave no scars. (Once, at a picnic, he told the wife of another close friend—she was placidly sitting under a tree —that she looked like a cow chewing a buttercup.)

A picture of John's life on the road is provided by excerpts from letters to Cassie. (Incidentally, during his second summer at Bread Loaf, when she was pregnant and stayed at home, he wrote to her at least twice a day.) The excerpts which follow are from the early 1940s.

From Evansville, Indiana, February 25, 1940: "I'm waiting in a sun-filled room (at last!) for the Judas Ram to arrive and lead me to the slaughter."

From Chicago, three days later: "Just think, this is the last chapter. I feel as relieved as old Leo himself must have when he reached the epilogue to *War and Peace*. These thirty-five days, the Cassie-less days and nights, have for me added up to an eternity. At home—with you—weeks gallop by. They race by in such clouds of happy dust that I am alarmed at their very speed. Time, however, as Mann knows, is variable. What he, poor fellow, does not know is how eagle-like is its flight *with* you; and how snail-like is its crawl *without* you."

From Cleveland, January 29, 1941: "Check off the Cleveland lecture! . . . The audience, though large, is not intimate or responsive. Several elderly ladies left for 12:10 trains (we were late in starting, and the mike kept regurgitating portions of what

I presume was the last lecturer's spiel to have been heard here). The elderly ladies went upstream as boldly as if they had been salmon in the mating season."

From Cincinnati, two days later: "What to do between trains in a strange city where you have no room. [He was writing from the mezzanine of the Netherland Plaza, with the vacuum cleaner buzzing, and had had only orange juice and coffee for breakfast.] In a foolish moment of economy I said to myself said I, 'Brown, three hours in Cincinnati, three hours to kill, three mouths to feed at home, three dollars for a day-rate room at this hostelry. Which of these threes (discounting Faith, Hope, and Charity) is the greatest? Which can be most easily dispensed with?' After a moment's deep thinking, with the nearest cuspidor as my crystal ball, I said to Brown, 'the room,' with the three sweet 'T's' for which it stands—the Tub, the Toilet, and the Tranquillity."

From Chicago, February 7, 1941: "It's blowing cold by the shining big sea water. So far (knock on Grant Wood) no blizzards. But even in my hotel room, I feel like an uncaptured polar bear. . . . [The following sentence refers to a side trip for a lecture out of town, after which he is to return to Chicago.] To-morrow, I'll pull out . . . right after the lecture on the 4:50 train that will put me in here at 8:20. Then to bed for hours of sleep—then on to St. Louis so that I can get another hotel night's sleep before tackling the rest of the tour. I've just glanced through the Texas-Oklahoma-Kansas pages of the itinerary. Believe me they are formidable. Not only long jumps, but late trains, early risings, and day trips from nine to five before night lectures."

Three days earlier he had written a happier letter. It should be said that lecturers often meet one another on their road trips; Emily Kimbrough tells of having crossed John's trail, perhaps more than once. On another occasion John and Edward Weeks were booked in Canton, Ohio, for separate engagements on the same night; Weeks's train was late, and there was talk of combining the two audiences for John's lecture, but Weeks made it on time after all. The passages which follow, from a letter written in Chicago on February 4, 1941, tell of meeting not another lecturer, but an actress: Lillian Gish was in Chicago, playing in *Life with Father,* and John had telegraphed her for a lunch or dinner date. She replied inviting him to both. "Miss Gish is different," John wrote to Cassie. "She, like Cornell, talks of the theatre as if there were other people in it."

The letter was resumed in the evening. "Both luncheon and dinner with La Gish have been fun, the latter in particular. . . . Miss Gish's suite faces the lake. She has a sitting-room which bulges with flowers—roses with transcontinental stems, etc. Inasmuch as *Life with Father* will have been in Chicago a whole year next week. . . . Miss Gish is Queen of the May. The hotel is her court. Waiters, clerks, chambermaids, managers, and I presume even house detectives genuflect happily at the merest mention of her name.

"At lunch we talked of the war. Miss G. is an isolationist. She waxes violent . . . at what Mr. R. has done to involve us. Three times, she says, she has lived through history in the making. The World War, when hope was high. Italy (where she was making *Romola*) when Mussolini came into power. Germany after Hitler had putsched himself to the fore. She sees no reason why we should get mixed up in it again.

"All this, pro and con, with quotes of course from Dorothy Thompson, and much economic reasoning beyond us both, but carried on with a polite deference to each other's ignorance, lasted the hour. Meanwhile Miss G. was serving chicken à la king, coffee, and a salad. Then lecture time when I left.

"To my surprise (and I do think this was nice of her) she turned up at the lecture. . . . Miss G. didn't tell me she was coming, she claims, because she remembered I had told her that the sight of Dorothy [Gish] and her at the Colony had chilled my blood.

"During the lecture (fortunately not during the discussion of *Arsenic and Old Lace*) an old lady in the third row, a nice old lady of about seventy-six, fell over in a faint. The room was stifling; her heart just gave out. I jumped off the platform, helped push her in her chair [wheelchair?] to a dressing-room at the back of the platform; and followed instructions by stretching her out on the floor. Her poor old face was white as death. Truly I thought she had died. Then I went back to work and discovered, at the lecture's end, that she had recovered and was deeply upset to think of the commotion she had created.

"I've just had dinner [6:00 p.m.] (Miss G. was my guest to-night) in the little room off the grille they put at the disposal of La G. Good, good talk. Plays, people, George Jean Nathan, Jed Harris, America, the future, plays, John Anderson, plays, the theatre, the movies, you, the theatre, Preston, plays, Meredith, the theatre, you, and the theatre."

None of this kind of thing got into *Accustomed As I Am,* nor did John write of the many friends he made all over the country. He corresponded for many years with friends in Des Moines, in Tulsa, in San Diego, in a town near Portland, Oregon. Nothing about his Bread Loaf summers, the three summer sessions in Missoula, his course at Yale in 1931–32, or his four summers at Harvard. No mention of his lecture at the White House, in May 1939—he spoke as a dramatic critic. There is a nice chapter, which must be either largely fictitious or a composite, about a women's club president who brought her husband to meet John's train; the husband is represented as being disgusted with the entire proceedings until he and John had a chance to nip off for a couple of drinks. More literally credible is a brief passage from a letter to Cassie: "[In Milwaukee] it was fun . . . husbands' night at the Women's Club. In Hokinson circles that is something like the Coronation crowned with Mardi Gras."

While John was still a drama critic on the *New York Evening Post* and later on the *World-Telegram,* he occasionally flew back from his lecture tours to New York for important openings. Sometimes he took a month's leave from the paper. Later, after he had given up daily reviewing, these arrangements were no longer necessary. His schedule for 1947–48 had him speaking in New York, Greenwich, Connecticut, and Sweet Briar College in Virginia during early October. From October 21 to 31 he had a busy time: lectures in Oxford, Ohio; Cleveland; Erie, Pennsylvania; Terre Haute; St. Louis; Indianapolis; Franklin, Indiana; Chicago; Iowa City; Des Moines; Ames, Iowa; and Jacksonville, Illinois. November took him to Chicago again, to Pittsburgh, Fall River, New York City, Brooklyn, Pelham, Bloomfield, and Worcester. In December he spoke only in New York, Stamford, and Boston. But between January 11 and 26 he returned to Chicago, Bloomington, Illinois, and Indianapolis, visiting also Charleston, West Virginia, Nashville, Fort Wayne, Rock Island, Ann Arbor, Detroit, and Mt. Lebanon, Pennsylvania. February, only New York, Bronxville, and Charlotte, North Carolina. During March he went to Kansas City; Springfield, Missouri; Lawrence, Kansas; Dallas, San Antonio, Houston, New Orleans, and Oklahoma City. And in April he wound up his season with lectures in Chicago, Missoula, Spokane, Seattle, San Francisco, Fresno, Santa Barbara, Los Angeles, and Salt Lake City.

Among John's papers there is an even longer itinerary running from January 28 to March 15 of an unrecorded year, covering pretty much the whole country. All the hotels, trains, and buses are specified, with times of departure and arrival. It is an impressive document indeed. It must have been a schedule like this that Cassie was looking at when she said to John, referring to the zigzag itinerary (the story comes from their old friend Alfred de Liagre, Jr.), "Mercy, why do you have to go through all that?" "What a question!" John replied. "With two boys in private school, and both having their teeth straightened!"

That season his lecture was transcribed and mimeographed, so that it is possible to give an idea of it with a few quotations. The first thing one notices is the beginning of a change of emphasis— even to some extent of subject—which was to grow more pronounced during the 1950s. Before World War II his subject had been the theatre—"Broadway in Review"—but now his interest was taking in a wider stage. The lecture of 1947–48 runs about 10,000 words—John was a very rapid speaker—and it begins with a discussion of events then current; moreover, following that introduction, more books are discussed than plays, and most of the books were on political or related subjects. A few excerpts:

"In my youth I was brought up in simpler times, as some of you were. I was brought up, for example, on the Morris Plan rather than the Marshall Plan, and the change between the two is some indication of what has overtaken us as a people. . . . It was Secretary Marshall who in a single sentence stated what is your dilemma, what is my dilemma at the present time. He says: *'Our foreign policy has entered the American home and taken its place at the family table.'* "

Nineteen forty-eight was a presidential election year, the year when Truman was to upset all predictions by defeating Thomas E. Dewey, in spite of the rival and diversionary candidacies of the Dixiecrat Strom Thurmond and former Vice President Henry A. Wallace. John spoke of Wallace as the only person at the time who could "talk about the contemporary world and ignore Russia. . . . Mr. Wallace has a way of talking about the contemporary world as if he were an utterly benevolent and fine professor of algebra who somehow for a whole year had given a course in algebra but miraculously forgotten to mention the letter X."

He spoke of the current best-seller lists, headed by *Peace of Mind* by Rabbi Joshua L. Liebman. He expressed a favorable opinion of the book, but continued: "Any book that seemed to peddle serenity to this present world, as if serenity could be purchased at Walgreen's, would be bound to win a wide and grateful public everywhere." His opinion of *Cannery Row* and *The Wayward Bus* by John Steinbeck was more critical. Of the latter he said: "I as a lecturer, in other words as a wind instrument, travel frequently around this country and often go to towns which can be reached in no other way except by bus. And ever since I have read Mr. Steinbeck's book I have gotten on bus after bus hopefully, and I can only report with great melancholy that the experience which seemed to be the common experience on Mr. Steinbeck's bus has never overtaken me . . . nor have I seen a Greyhound bus with a motor powerful enough to pull so lusty a crew."

He quoted from an article by Louis Bromfield, which had appeared in *The Saturday Review,* the sentence "Even after the cruel testing of two world wars, we intellectually as Americans are precisely where we were in this country at the time of McKinley." And John added, "We have fought maturity more successfully and more stubbornly in this country than we have ever fought the most alarming of our enemies."

The center of gravity of the lecture is the state of the world. John discusses *The Goebbels Diaries* and *The Ciano Diaries,* Rebecca West's *The Meaning of Treason,* Trevor-Roper's *The Last Days of Hitler.* Also John Hersey's *A Bell for Adano* and his *Hiroshima; The Gallery* by John Horne Burns and *Back Home* by Bill Mauldin; and James Michener's *Tales of the South Pacific,* not yet converted into a musical by Rodgers and Hammerstein.

Not until almost two-thirds of the way through the lecture does John get around to plays: *Mr. Roberts,* by Joshua Logan and Thomas Heggen, based on Mr. Heggen's novel; *A Streetcar Named Desire* by Tennessee Williams. Then he turns for a glance at motion pictures, and back to books—Toynbee, Gunther's *Inside U.S.A.,* Frances Perkins's *The Roosevelt I Knew,* and a few others—before devoting a few hundred words to the current musicals: *Finian's Rainbow, Brigadoon, Allegro,* and *Annie, Get Your Gun.* Then to the classics: Judith Anderson's performance in the Robinson Jeffers translation of *Medea,* and Katharine Cornell in *Antony and Cleopatra.*

In conclusion he said, "If I read four books, I find I can read only three modern books, and for the fourth book I must turn to some volume of indisputable merit . . . some classic possessed of those qualities which A. B. Walkley described as the qualities of self-renewal. If I didn't do that, I should die of spiritual and intellectual scurvy. And the great book I mean to mention this afternoon is a book which is so applicable, indeed so popular that even Elsa Maxwell has heard of it. And I am speaking of Thucydides' *The Peloponnesian War.* . . . Of the Athenians who died [following the Syracusan disaster under Alcibiades, whom John called "the Jimmy Walker of ancient Athens"], Thucydides said these glorious words, and he said them with that radiant brevity which was the Greek genius. He said, 'Having done what men could, they suffered what men must.' "

John concluded with a sentence which Thucydides may have inspired: "We are lost if we surrender our belief in man's will and in man's reason and his connection with the Godhead, and once we lose those beliefs it seems to me we are doomed, indeed."

John began his lecture career as a client of the James B. Pond agency. When the Pond agency was dissolved he switched in the 1934–35 season to Lee Keedick. In his files there is a copy of a contract between him and Keedick, dated June 2, 1950, for the forthcoming seasons through 1954–55. It provided for Keedick's commission; for John to pay a share of his advertising expenses, and all of his hotel and traveling expenses. Keedick, of course, was to arrange the bookings, buy the tickets for John's transportation, and make his hotel reservations. From all indications the relationship between John and Keedick was a happy one for many years.

In March 1947 John had occasion to write to the article editor of *Cosmopolitan* magazine, who had in preparation a piece about him; John's letter objected to the statement in the article that he received five hundred dollars a lecture and gave a hundred lectures a year. His letter said that the figure was more like sixty lectures a year; and his fee was lower in the vicinity of New York than when he was on tour. Moreover, he considered it poor taste to publish financial figures. The editor replied that these figures were exactly what his readers were interested in. Be that as it may, if John's gross fee was five hundred dollars (as it probably was then—later it went up to seven hundred and fifty dollars) the terms of the contract make it clear that this was before his agent's commission and his considerable expenses.

A few miscellaneous notes on his lecturing: In 1945 he wrote to some friends, "I am jumping around the country like a kangaroo afraid of being raped." Lectures are not commonly subjects for reviews in newspapers, but Keedick's files contain scattered reviews from various places and written at various times. As one reviewer from Houston, Texas, said: "Brown is the most notable development in the talking machine since Edison's time." Boston often reviewed him. The January 1963 Bulletin of the Women's Educational and Industrial Union of Boston announces John's fifteenth consecutive annual lecture before that organization. Meanwhile, John had been to Bread Loaf in 1950 and 1951— probably for only one lecture each visit.

On the occasion of his fiftieth lecture at Town Hall in New York, on March 29, 1950, the event was a very special celebration. Bennett Cerf, who was then writing the weekly department "Trade Winds" for *The Saturday Review,* devoted a column to the event in the issue of April 29.

Not only the usual throng of adoring females, but a liberal sprinkling of follow critics, authors, and producers elbowed their way into the jammed hall, and when they were called upon to say a few words their good-natured jibes reflected obvious affection—and sheer envy. . . . Dick Watts suggested that one way to cure mass hysteria would be for John's lovely wife, Cassie, to accompany him on all lecture tours, reminding other ladies by her mere presence that for anybody else, as far as John was concerned, there definitely would be no tomorrow, and not even much tonight.

Mr. Watts told the present author that John spoke as if he were speaking individually to every woman there—"and with a bit of a leer." Alfred de Liagre, Jr., said, "The probable explanation of John's popularity as a lecturer is that he made the women of America think of all the things they hadn't done with all the gentlemen they hadn't met." * And Louis Kronenberger, undoubtedly speaking of the same occasion, said that all the women there were craning their necks for a good look at Cassie, to see what the woman was like—or at least looked like—who had hooked the prize catch. These comments of John's kind friends, two of them colleagues from the Drama Critics Circle, contain as much innocent merriment as they do truth.

More thoughtful remarks on other occasions come from Edward Weeks, then editor of the *Atlantic* and John's fellow lecturer. Said Weeks:

> Fair, auburn-haired, with a Scopas profile, he was the best talker of us all; he had an outrageous wit and he emphasized his points with his chin, lifted when he was in earnest, lowered when in doubt or in mirthful acknowledgment that he had been scored on. [That was at Harvard.] . . . He taught and he lectured. One reason why his lectures, of which he delivers some eighty a year, are so supremely popular is that he acts throughout them, pouring out, with his hand at the back of his head . . . a blend of parody, witticism, and interpretation. He gives unsparingly of himself on stage and off, knowing that a lecturer is paid for both, and his perception of this country, which he lightly discloses in *Accustomed As I Am*, has been growing at the rate of 40,000 miles a year.†

On January 29, 1953, Lee Keedick wrote to John:

Dear John,

I cannot let this day pass without telling you, however feebly, how proud I am of you on many counts.

First, let me speak about what you have done for lecturing in America. You have lifted it by the boot straps from more or less obscurity, freak grazing and quick money grabbing by sentimentalists, to a position of dignity, respectability and influence. You have established the fact that no one can really succeed at lecturing without thorough and painstaking effort and research, comparable to that expended in writing a book. You have made slackers appear pathetic and ridiculous

* He endeared himself forever to the present author's mother-in-law by greeting her after each lecture in Boston—where she lived and was a member of the aforesaid Women's Educational and Industrial Union—with a cheerful greeting, "Well, how's Maude Adams?"—whom he always said she resembled.
† From Mr. Weeks's book, *In Friendly Candor* (Little, Brown, 1959).

—you have revitalized and made lecturing an institution that must be recognized as a force in molding public opinion, and rightfully taking its place with the newspapers and the best-sellers that endure. If every lecturer measured himself by the standard you have set, every hall would be packed and the morons eliminated from the lecture field.

Secondly, I am proud of your example of sacrifice for country, and your telling efforts to preserve America and make it a better and greater place for our children.

Thirdly, I am proud of what you have done for education in general, and literature and the drama in particular.

Fourthly, I am proud of the fact that you are not an onlooker in this most exciting and depressing period of human history, but as lively a participant as the most militant could wish.

Age will not pall upon you ever, John. If such symptoms arise, I am sure you will smash them by starting a revolution in some backward and undeveloped country.

As ever,<br>*The Boss*

The following year, John wrote to a correspondent who had asked him whether audiences had changed during his career as a lecturer. "Over the past twenty-five years," he said, "audiences in women's clubs have inevitably changed with changed times. I would guess there are far fewer Helen Hokinson girls and far more college graduates. As the world invaded every American home, with war both as a memory and a threat, and with the draft as a reality to most families, there is, I think, a greater interest in world affairs and the overtones of contemporary events."

In the autumn of 1952, *The New Yorker* (issues of October 18 and 25) published a two-part "Profile" of John by Herbert Warren Wind, who accompanied John on one of his midwestern tours and gave a detailed account. The second part of the essay was devoted entirely to lecturing, beginning with a full account of the activities of lecture bureaus in America, leading up to John's unique career. Mr. Wind quoted several opinions of John as a lecturer, and mentioned a debate which took place in 1949 at Constitution Hall, on the rights of minorities, in which John participated and for which he received a congratulatory telegram from Arnold Toynbee. Mr. Wind's narrative continues:

A typical swing through the Middle West at the height of last season found Brown arriving in Detroit early one damp Wednesday morning in January after a peaceful night's rest aboard the New York Central's New England Wolverine. . . . He was scheduled to address the members of the Detroit Town Hall at eleven that morning. Estimating from experience that it would take him fifteen minutes to reach the auditorium and another fifteen for the pre-lecture formalities, and making his usual allowance for unforeseen complications, he arranged by telephone with a friend, Mrs. Edna Root, to pick him up at the hotel at a quarter past ten. Mrs. Root brought her Pontiac to a stop in front of the Statler on the dot of ten-fifteen, and Brown complimented her on her punctuality. A vigorous middle-aged lady, Mrs. Root was for many years one of the guiding spirits of the "old" Detroit Town Hall, which, before its dissolution in 1950, met at the Cass Theatre. . . .

Mrs. Root parked the Pontiac near the entrance to the theatre, and Brown hurried through the Egyptian lobby. Mrs. Kathleen Snow Stringer, the director of the new Town Hall, was waiting backstage for him. She seemed to be nervous, possibly because this was the first time Brown had appeared under the auspices of her organization. She showed him onto the stage of the still empty theatre, where he examined the lectern—something he does before each lecture. The lectern was six inches lower than the chest-high level Brown finds most comfortable for resting his arms, and this was immediately rectified. Brown asked the stage manager about the amplifier system, and was assured that he would not have to worry about talking too loudly or not loudly enough, because an engineer in the wings would be "riding gain" on the volume. However, a battery of spotlights playing on the stage bothered Brown. He is not fussy about lighting, but he always checks it before a lecture, since apparently few stage managers realize that speaker may well be blinded by the glare. This was precisely the trouble now, but the stage manager said that unfortunately no other lighting arrangement was possible, and Brown resigned himself to a "blind lecture"—one in which he is unable to see beyond the footlights to read the faces of his audience and must depend solely on his ear to tell how his points are going over. . . . Mrs. Stringer . . . then led him to a dressing room backstage. . . . Brown drew his stack of lecture cards from his briefcase and, flipping through them, trimmed ten minutes of his lecture by removing seven cards. [He always spoke from notes on a series of cards, seldom if ever from a prepared manuscript. On this occasion he had been asked to speak not longer than an hour and ten minutes.] Two bright-eyed ladies in mink jackets, friends of his, entered the dressing room as he was slapping an elastic band around the diminished deck. "You've grown a little heavier, John," one of them remarked in the midst of an exchange of news. "In exactly five minutes, you'll see just how heavy," Brown replied. . . .

The first half hour of the lecture produced only a few small patches of the humor that audiences have come to associate with Brown, and the breakneck speed with which he presented the fairly hefty thoughts on life and literature expressed by Shaw, Hemingway, Shakespeare, Burke, and Faulkner (particularly in the novelist's speech on accepting the Nobel Prize) put a perceptible strain on his listeners as they tried to keep up with him. It was not until he turned to lighter thoughts on the lighter arts that the auditorium took on the convivial, easygoing mood that audiences expect from a morning with John Mason Brown. The parts of the lecture the Detroit audience especially enjoyed were Brown on the "Spanish-moss, swamp, and boll-weevil school of Southern literature"; Brown's tirade against comic books. . . . Brown on the younger generation's ability to read a book and listen to the radio simultaneously. . . . Brown's epigrammatic comparison of Shaw's "Caesar and Cleopatra" and Shakespeare's "Antony and Cleopatra" ("The first is the brilliant work of a vegetarian. The second could only have been written by an Englishman living when there was no shortage of beef"). . . . When Brown, in his wind-up, solemnly recapitulated the heart of Faulkner's speech and some of the related themes of his initial half hour, the audience was far more receptive than it had been the first time around.

There was prolonged applause at the conclusion of the lecture, but it was constrained in comparison to the high-pitched ovation Brown received when he entered the L'Aiglon Room, a restaurant in the building, where several hundred members of the Detroit Town Hall were assembled for their customary post-lecture "celebrity luncheon." [One gathers from Mr. Wind's account that John's lunch consisted principally, if not entirely, of two double bourbons and coffee.]

Most of the questions that Brown answered in a twenty-five-minute period after downing his coffee—reading each of them to the audience in the author's own words—sought his opinion of current books, operas, and plays. There were two questions somewhat off this beat, and to these he devoted more time. In dealing with the first, "Do you think Katie Cornell is losing her stuff?" Brown, biting off his words with a sudden frosty indignation, advised the gathering that he detected in the wording of the question an intentional disrespect for Miss Cornell, which he considered quite out of line. "Miss Katharine Cornell is a distinguished actress who is properly referred to, by persons discussing her as an actress, as Katharine Cornell, not Katie Cornell," he said. "If the person who submitted the question is presuming an intimate acquaintance with Miss Cornell, she is also in error. Miss Cornell's friends call her Kit, not Katie." (Brown did not think Miss Cornell was losing her stuff.)

When Brown came to the second off-beat question, "Do you think that women as a group suffer from a lack of intelligence?" his good spirits returned in force. . . . "I think of you as the Typhoid Marys of culture, and as such you perform a very valuable function for this country."

So off the travelers Brown and Wind went to their next stop, Muncie, Indiana. This necessitated taking a night train; they were able to sleep in berths, but were obliged to get off at 4:30 in the morning. John, in good spirits, said to Wind, "You asked for it." (After the publication of the "Profile," he wrote to a friend, "Now that the *New Yorker* pieces are over, I can put on my fig-leaf again.")

To conclude the chapters here is David McCord's introduction to John's talk at the St. Botolph Club in Boston on May 6, 1958—too late to be included in *Accustomed As I Am,* and published here for the first time, by Mr. McCord's kind permission. He was at that time president of the club, and he and John had long been close friends.

### BALLAD WITH A BROWNSTONE FAÇADE

I've heard some introductions: none sublime,
Most of them long. O little word so brief—
T-i-m-e; we say it, and we chime
"Of which procastination is the thief."
Procrastination? Nonsense! No! Great grief!
The thieves of time so common, town or gown,
Are all these chairmen—chief offenders. Chief,
How does one introduce John Mason Brown?

In colleges some have a go at rhyme,
And all would prove him Proust to their Moncrieff.
Can wit soufflé this speaker in his prime?
Does withered grapefruit appetize good beef?
Booth, Coquelin, Duse, Beerbohm Tree in leaf—
I'd gladly speak of *them* and their renown,
But offer you this week's *aperitif:*
How does one introduce John Mason Brown?

John Mason Brown! What teacher in our time
Has won from art your conscience in belief?
No man shall rise ahead of you and mime—
As well attempted by the dumb and deef.
Some greenroom ghost shall spring to my relief:
"Accept this scepter, since you have a crown,
And failed to gnarl about a fee or fief."
How does one introduce John Mason Brown?

Envoy

Prince, I have struck I think a vein or reef:
*Judge, critic, wit, great humanist!* "Sit down,"
They cry. I shall. I'm folding up my sheaf.
How *does* one introduce John Mason Brown?

# Chapter Eight

# The Second World War

John's next book following *Accustomed As I Am,* also published in 1942, was *Insides Out: Being the Saga of a Drama Critic Who Attended His Own Opening.* This is the account of a hernia operation, written in the same manner as *Accustomed;* lighthearted to the point of frivolity, it is the book of a man who refused to take himself seriously, inside or out. But the purpose of the operation was altogether serious: it was to enable him to meet the physical requirements for enlistment in the Navy. He entered, in October 1942, with the commission of Lieutenant, USNR.

The surgery was performed under a spinal anaesthetic, so that John was conscious the entire time and was able to see things which patients who undergo surgery unconsciously never know. It seems that John's candor made some of the nurses indignant when the book came out. When John wanted to get up a day or two after the operation, one of the nurses remarked that such a proceeding might lead to evisceration; now, thirty years later, a surgical patient gets the impression that his surgeon wants him to run a hundred-yard dash down a hospital corridor within twenty-four hours of being stitched up.

The operation was performed by Dr. Henry W. Cave. There were two American editions of the book, as well as a British edition. John gave copies of all three to Dr. Cave, with inscriptions as follows:

"The hero of this book and of all his countless patients, including John Mason Brown."

"For Marse Henry [Marse because Dr. Cave was a Kentuckian, though not from Louisville], my candidate for permanent Secretary of the Interior."

And finally: "For Marse Henry Cave, the obstetrician who delivered me of this book."

(Incidentally, Dr. Cave did not send bills to servicemen; John later gave Dr. and Mrs. Cave a large, handsome Lowestoft tureen.)

Soon after receiving his commission, John was having lunch with a friend in New York. Cassie had taken a job in the Steuben glass retail store on Fifth Avenue; this was mentioned, and John said, "Yes, that takes a lot of the shine off this gold braid."

An official release of the Bureau of Naval Personnel, dated September 11, 1944, gives a brief summary of John's career in the service. Following his appointment, "and after a month's duty in the Third Naval District, he was transferred to London, England, where he was Assistant to the Chief of Staff of the Commander, U.S. Naval Forces, Europe, serving in that assignment for four months. He returned to the United States in March 1943 for duty in the Office of Public Relations, Navy Department, Washington, D.C."

Not until April 1943 was John assigned to the staff of the Commander, Amphibious Force, Atlantic, Rear Admiral Alan G. Kirk. John had met Admiral Kirk briefly in London, earlier in the year. At that time the Admiral, upon hearing from John that he wanted to see what the war was like, had him assigned to a minesweeper working off the coast of Britain. This lasted only a brief time. After John was recalled to the United States and when preparations were made for the invasion of Sicily, he was assigned to to the flagship *Ancon*, called, for security reasons, the *Spelvin* in John's book *To All Hands: An Amphibious Adventure*, which appeared before the end of 1943. A foreword by Admiral Kirk ex-

plains its origin. After saying that the task force comprised many
ships, and that it was most desirable "to make the fullest use of a
really great asset which the Armed Services of the United States
have in abundance," the Admiral continues:

Our success in combat comes often from brilliant individual initiative.
But before a person can act independently without throwing out of gear
a carefully drawn plan he must have some idea of what it is all about.
. . . Our soldiers and sailors are the better for knowing the score. This
reliance upon the individual is nowhere greater than in amphibious
warfare. During our attacks we are poised precariously—one foot on
land and the other in the water.

In the case of the flagship . . . it was our good fortune to have at
hand Lieutenant John Mason Brown, a trained journalist who is especially gifted in the art of public address. He possesses a keen and ob-
servant eye with reflexes quick enough to translate astonishment into
inquiry. Thus his reactions were immediate—and the meaning of
things had to be established at once.

With the salient happenings of the day recorded, the manuscript was
approved by my Intelligence Officer and the flagship at broadcast time
each afternoon was studded with groups and knots of men, listening to
this yarn of our daily lives and the news of great events.

John was listed as Bridge Announcer, and two days out from
Hampton Roads Admiral Kirk explained what he wanted John
to do: make daily broadcasts to the crew describing what was
going on. The book consists of some thirty of these broadcasts,
preceded by an introductory note called "This Is a Democratic
War," in which John explains that the broadcasts were the
Admiral's idea. One brief passage from that chapter demands
quotation:

No one could be less courageous than I am and have less of the hero
or even the warrior in his make-up. I expected to be scared to death,
and probably will be next time. Instead, I felt a strange exhilaration—
the kind of foolish desire to laugh at danger which roller-coaster addicts
know when the car is poised at the top of the first and steepest drop.
Not that I was unaware of what might happen momentarily and did
not dread it. But I found this danger, when so much faith and hope
were involved, a heady stimulant. The pleasure I felt in being *there*
was greater than any nervousness I knew.

Usually each broadcast was prepared in advance to last about half an hour. "Needless to say, during the night of the invasion there was no manuscript to read from." That night John broadcast intermittently from 11:30 p.m. until eight in the morning, "reporting extemporaneously at irregular but frequent intervals." That chapter, called "Battle Station," the nineteenth in the book, consists of unwritten broadcasts "which I have approximated here as faithfully as possible from scrawls in my notebook. It was a night," he says by way of understatement, "which is hard to forget." It was the night of July 9–10, 1943.

The chapter is too long to be quoted in full; a few passages must suffice.

11:30 P.M., July 9
"H" hour, the hour of hours, is almost here . . . the attack is scheduled to begin at 2:45 A.M.

When we passed Malta—unconquerable Malta—toward the middle of the afternoon, and later came to Gozo, we knew our next island was Sicily. We are near Sicily now, still moving towards it in the darkness. . . .

Already we have had our hints of "D" day's approach. Throughout the afternoon the gray sky has been filled from time to time by coveys of Spitfires. Several convoys have come within sight on the lunging waters. Six aircraft, said to be hostile, were reported twelve miles away from us in the late twilight. . . .

Let the cynical laugh, but we have seen something of a miracle tonight. All afternoon our hearts have grown the heavier with the increasing heaviness of the sea. Things have looked bad for us—very bad—these past eight hours or so. . . .

By 2:30 P.M. the Mediterranean was being swept by a 30-knot wind. As the waves rose under sullen skies, they subjected the little PC boats now with us to a terrible beating. . . . The prospect of trying to send such landing craft into the beaches against such odds was disturbing, to put it mildly.

Many of us remembered the Spanish Armada's fate . . .

Then suddenly, a little while ago, the miracle of which I spoke occurred. No matter where you may be stationed, you must have felt it. The wind died down almost as abruptly as it had started. . . .

Midnight, July 9
Before daylight this morning a heavy bombing attack is scheduled to be made on all Sicilian airfields. . . .

Those paratroopers we heard heading inland will have been dropped with others during the night in the area of the Task Force to our west. The guns we hear at first will not necessarily mean that the Italians and the Germans have spotted us. . . .

12:45 A.M., July 10

That crunchy, bumpy noise you may have heard five minutes ago was our anchor on the way down. It's blacker than coal up here. Our ships are still slipping into position. They are gathering like conspirators. We can't see them, but we can feel them, the way in a dark room you know some one else has entered. . . .

Don't be alarmed by the submarine just off our port side. It's one of ours. I hear the sight of it cost a soldier his dinner. He had wandered out on deck to get some air and see the show in which he will soon take part. Tonight's second slab of ice cream and the see-sawing of the Mediterranean had not been getting along too well. The soldier was holding his head in his hands when, to his horror, one of his eyes rolled open to discover the periscope, the conning tower, and finally the whale's back of a submarine loom out of the tar-colored waves beside him. "Jesus Christ!" he is reported to have said, at the same time that he said good-by to the ice cream and raced below.

Everything else is under control.

At 2:40 a.m. John reports that H-hour has been delayed until 3:45, owing to the choppy seas. At 4:15: "The Fourth of July was never like this! . . . Our big guns appear to have got two of those prying [enemy] searchlights. They have been snuffed out for quite a while." At 4:45: "Those planes are enemy planes. . . . They are headed for our beaches, dropping flares over them." At 5:15: "Good news. Word has just been received that initial landings have been accomplished on all our beaches, and that, in general, slight opposition has been met with from the ground forces of the enemy." At 7:15 the ship weighed anchor to move closer to shore. And finally:

8 A.M., July 10

For the moment, all's quiet. We have just dropped anchor. And after shaking hands with the Admiral, General Middleton of the 45th Division has gone ashore. In the same boat with him went Clark Lee, the INS correspondent. Fires are still smoking off the beaches, and guns rumbling intermittently.

The chief news is that there seems to have been no serious opposition. A message from the shore says, "Considerable artillery and prisoners taken."

That's good news to sleep on. And the Chief of Staff urges that you do sleep, your duties permitting, and sleep as long as possible. You deserve that sleep and may need it tonight. It should be a happy sleep.

The late Russell Briney (husband of Melville O. Briney, who wrote *Fond Recollection,* quoted at the beginning of this book) wrote in the *Courier-Journal* of November 7, 1943:

The reader [gets] a new kind of sense of participating. . . .

The broadcasts, by the testimony of Admiral Kirk, were highly successful. His listeners surely have not heard many people who could be as gay and more than a trifle bawdy at times and still at other times as lucid and eloquent about the meaning of this war as Lieutenant Brown was in his remarks upon the German prisoners—"the world's problem children, these men, only they are man-sized." Or, for another example, his reflections upon the fall of Mussolini, headed in this book, "Balcony to Let." *

After Sicily, John evidently had a few months back in New York, where he had a reunion with his family—Preston was now seven and Meredith three—and saw his book through the process of publication; also he must have put in some time doing public relations work in Washington. Late in 1943 he was in England again, working in London as a public relations officer and waiting for D-Day. He gave a Christmas broadcast over the BBC, with a special message for Preston and Meredith—he asked them what they got for Christmas. Apparently what he did as a public relations officer was to see reporters—or fend them off; write news releases and speeches to be delivered by his superior officers. On February 12, 1944, he wrote to Cassie:

* In both the Sicilian and the Normandy invasions one of John's shipmates was Richard T. Cragg. On the *Ancon* Lieutenant Cragg was Current Operations Officer in charge of the Combat Intelligence Room, where all activities of both sides were tracked. (Later, on the *Augusta,* Cragg's rank was Lieutenant Commander.) John spent a good deal of time there in order to get information for his broadcasts. "John's job," writes Mr. Cragg, "included public relations with the members of the press and as you can well imagine, he filled this job with excellence because he knew many of the reporters assigned to our flagship."

"Still grounded, and impatient to get on. I ache . . . to get closer, and can hardly wait for the word that I can get going. . . . We've [John and his friends] had to agree, each one of us, that in wartime it is necessary to take an Oriental or Mexican attitude towards time." Another passage in the same letter is of special interest, in view of the later biography of Sherwood: "Do you know any of the inner details of the Sherwood–Elmer Davis row, or the causes for the three OWI resignations in London?" * It goes without saying that many passages from John's letters home, omitted here, are full of love and concern for Cassie and the boys.

He got closer, without delay, if only for a short period, presumably in February. On March 2 John wrote to Edith Hamilton † from a Fleet Post Office address: "Recently I have been having an exciting time of it, leading a truly amphibious life. For two weeks I was in Africa and Italy with the 5th Army and with the British as an observer. I wouldn't take anything for this insight, however brief, into the rigors of army existence. The sight of Naples, or rather what is left of it, is not a cheering one. I hadn't been there for twenty years, and remember it in terms of *Our Hearts Were Young and Gay*. The shock of readjustment was considerable. So was the growing used to being a member of a victorious force, a feeling which I found as uncomfortable as if I had turned up uninvited and roistering at a stranger's funeral. From Naples north to Cassino the signs of war are everywhere. We reached the monastery the day after the bombing when the ruins were under heavy fire. The second day in the Cassino area our shelling was even more severe. Even so there was something Parthenonlike about the monastery on the top of that magnifi-

---

* Elmer Davis was director of the Office of War Information, with headquarters in Washington. Sherwood was overseas director, based in London. Sherwood wanted to be independent of Davis, and Davis said no. The whole episode is admirably set forth in Roger Burlingame's biography of Davis, *Don't Let Them Scare You* (Lippincott, 1961).

† John's great friend Edith Hamilton, author of *The Greek Way* and other books widely read and widely admired.

cent mountain. It was on the second day that we managed to jeep across the Rapido under German fire into the American-held outskirts of Cassino." (Edith Hamilton's reply appears in Chapter Thirteen.)

It is odd that, although he evidently sent a carbon copy of this letter to Cassie, he does not mention it in his letter to her written the very next day: "What have I been doing in the off hours? Nothing which in retrospect stands out. A threat of flu which sent me bedwards for a day and which was downed in time. Dinner one night with Bob Sherwood, Lady Colefax, Geoffrey Kerr, and Robert Henriques which was good enough fun, interrupted by a mild raid. Lunch yesterday with Johnny Schiff at the apartment of that same Polish count who last year was saying so confidently that the European phase of the war would end ninety days after the last German was expelled from North Africa. His excuse? The failure of the Army to do what he would have advised, which is as good an out as any. . . .

"I ache to write. But what can be written? The messenger boy activities of the job, plus the office confinement and routine, leave you fairly depleted (not tired) by six p.m. Then there is Security, which never ceases to leer. And the question of what in uniform you *should* write. Moreover, there's the constant, subconscious distraction of the war itself, the sense of futility."

On April 1 he wrote Cassie asking her to persuade Major Donald Oenslager to "reconsider his present decision [to remain in the service where up to now he had been an expert in the field of camouflage]. . . . He's done enough—done an excellent, needed, distinguished job. In his new work [as Intelligence Officer], regardless of how much he likes it, he's apt to find himself stuck off in some dreary spot, doing what thousands of younger men could do. . . . The thought, for example, of Thornton W[ilder] sitting in North Africa, by-passed by events and squandering his irreplaceable talent, is to me lamentable. . . .

"I've been speaking lately as I wrote you I was going to. On Thursday I spoke before the Women's Voluntary Services. . . .

I was supposed to be explaining America to the English—a ticklish assignment—and I must admit I was nervous both from being out of practice and the wonder as to how what I had to say would strike a British audience. [He was reassured by a letter from Lady Reading, which he quoted.]

"God willing, I'll pull off Monday night's speech. It's to the Navy here—about eighty officers in a dinner club; the speech on 'Words Are Weapons Too' that I wrote you about."

This letter goes on to describe a dinner party given by Lady Colefax at the Dorchester. This may be the appropriate place to put in a note about Lady Colefax—Sibyl Colefax, but not Lady Sibyl Colefax, because her father was not a peer.* It appears that Lady Colefax followed up these occasions by sending chits to her guests for the "ordinary" they had enjoyed—that is, a complete meal with all courses included, at a fixed price. But Hamish Hamilton, head of the London publishing house bearing his name, says that she was, with Emerald Cunard, one of the two great hostesses of their time. "At Sibyl's," he writes, "one met every celebrity who either lived in London or visited it, Wells, Huxley, Bennett, Maugham, the lot. She was the most kind-hearted and generous person in the world. . . . Unfortunately she dashed off brief letters in an illegible handwriting so that the posthumous attempt to collect her correspondence led to nothing."

Lady Colefax died in 1950. The London *Times* obituary, printed on September 26 and written by Alan Pryce-Jones, was headed "A Great London Hostess." "With her disappears, perhaps, the last great London *salon,* which had nothing to fear from the great literary *salons* of the past. . . . At the age of seventy . . . she possessed the art of mixing generations and kinds of people." John himself kept a large file of newspaper clippings

---

* The author's English friends have been extraordinarily kind and patient in explaining this to him. John's consistent misspelling of her name ("Colfax") has been corrected throughout these letters, but not his references to her as "Lady Sibyl Colefax."

about her, and considered writing an article about her for *The Saturday Review*.

On the occasion of the dinner at the Dorchester, John mentions that there was no air raid that night. The guests included the Duchess of Westminster, Captain "Angie" Biddle Duke, Lady Mountbatten, "and 'Chips' Channon, a very amusing, lightweight M.P. with an acid tongue and a strong hatred for Lady Astor. ('I hate her,' he said, 'because she has made women ridiculous, America absurd, and the House of Commons a joke.' . . .)

"Lady Mountbatten . . . was fun about Lord Louis, about Irving Berlin, about Noël Coward, about the government's attitude toward women." (She said that if she lost a leg in the blitz the government would pay her only half the compensation they would pay a man.)

Barry Bingham, publisher of the Louisville papers and an old friend of John's, was also a naval officer and in London when John was there. He says that they used to go to the theatre together, and that no theatres in London were hit during the blitz. They saw Turgenev's *A Month in the Country,* also a production of *Peer Gynt* so far from perfection as to reduce them to laughter; at the end, when the elderly couple departs from the stage, John remarked, "Boy gets girl." Bingham and John took a trip together to Glasgow, in an automobile chauffeured by a gob who was somewhat devil-may-care in his driving. At one point, when death seemed to be lurking round the corner, John said, "Tell Cassie I loved her."

John told David McCord two anecdotes of this period. At one point—this may have been earlier—Admiral Kirk ordered John to take a course in electronics. Soon he wrote the Admiral saying that in his civilian milieu, the theatre, the worst sin was miscasting.* The second anecdote is definitely from London. Admiral

* John gives a slightly different version of this episode in one of the Serrell Hillman interviews. He said it was calculus, not electronics, and complained to the Admiral that in trying to make John learn calculus Admiral Kirk was giving aid and comfort to the enemy.

Kirk gave John some letters to mail. John innocently put them in the British post office. When the Admiral heard this, he blew his top. "But," John explained, "when I mail letters I naturally take them to the post office."

On April 6 he wrote Cassie: "Work, even when trivial, is SECRET. Hence all these letters are lopsided. . . .

"Well, now to publishable news that includes work. Here it is the end of the week and I've never dropped you a line to tell you how the Navy dinner went at which Sherwood and I spoke. Barry was the chairman, and a most charming one. . . .

"Bob Sherwood, at his own request, followed me, speaking about the pamphlet work behind enemy lines of the OWI. He was, as always, eloquent in a rustic furniture way; a kind of Lincolnian Cicero in birch-bark. . . .

"As for me, doing the snowplow job, I had the generalities. Even so I prized them. They had to do with the age-worn cleavage between the men of action and the wordmen; between deeds for their own sake and deeds as merely a means to an end. . . . How it went I do not pretend to know. I know only that it is over; and that no china was tossed."

The same letter describes another of Lady Colefax's parties, one at which Harold Nicolson was present. Nicolson said he suspected that Woodrow Wilson had suffered his first stroke in Paris. " 'At least,' said Nicolson, 'after his initial attack, I saw Clemenceau leave his room and come to Lloyd George, saying, "Good. Good. He is sick! He is sick!" ' Poor evidence, if you ask me, but a good story."

John's book about the Normandy invasion, *Many a Watchful Night,* is quite different in design from *To All Hands.* Necessarily so, because Admiral Kirk's flagship, the cruiser *Augusta,* was not at sea as long as the *Ancon* had been, and in any case everybody on board must have known it was headed for the French coast. The book begins with events and emotions of June 5, 1944, the eve of D-Day. Then it flashes back to the months John has been writing about in his letters. He discusses the impact of the Americans and the British on each other: "If the British knew and admitted that they needed us, any American who thought, not twice but just plain thought, admitted and knew that we needed them. Had they not stood alone, we might not have been able to stand at all. We were both the stronger when we stood side by side. . . .

"We came hungry to a land where food was scarce. And the British entertained us in their homes. We came thirsty to pubs and clubs where the liquor supply was low. And the British, though no less thirsty, did not appear to mind. The sole comment of an English girl, a Wren, when she watched a group of our Sahara-throated sailors gulp down in a single hour a village pub's liquor supply for an entire evening, was 'I say, you Americans don't seem to savor your pleasures, do you?' "

*Many a Watchful Night* (the title is from *Henry IV., Part 2,* but the spirit is the spirit of *Henry V,* with the young King about to invade France; and many of the epigraphs and quotations in the book are from that play) explains that there were two United States Naval Commands in London, Admiral Stark's, which was shared with the Army, and the Task Force under Admiral Kirk, who was Commander of the Naval Forces participating in the invasion. Admiral Stark's was the senior and more permanent organization. John gives an affectionate characterization of Admiral Kirk: "a fighter, gruff, imperious, dogged, and willful. . . . But he was much more than that. . . . He was no mere sea dog in the manger. . . . He got along famously with people who by type and profession would not get along with one another. He read omnivorously when he had the time, and liked to laugh, even at himself.

"No one enjoyed more than he did, for example, the answer given by a young cook from Philadelphia when the Admiral, exhausted by a long, hard inspection tour, was going through the galley of a South Coast base. 'How's the chow?' asked the Admiral perfunctorily. 'Excellent,' said the boy who prepared it, grinning. 'Are the men gaining weight?' 'Well, sir, I don't exactly know,' replied the cook, smiling more broadly. 'You see, sir, I don't have to weigh 'em; I just have to feed 'em.' "

John had been in London during the winter of 1942–43, preceding the invasion of Sicily, and he gives a picture of the contrast between the London of that gloomy, desperate time, even before the Allies' landing in Africa, and the London of 1944, with hope and excitement in the air. He particularly contrasts himself and his contemporaries (he calls himself middle-aged; he was only forty-three) with the young men, who "take to modern warfare with an aptitude middle-aged novices cannot hope to equal." He describes the air raids. "Going to bed knowing there is apt to be a raid at some unpredictable hour is not alarming. It is merely a bore." Not that the raids were boring when they came. "London continues on her way, ignoring the sky as best she could, but not forgetting the war. Her streets, her hotels and restaurants, her stations and her stores, her factories and her libraries, her schools and her churches and her theatres were all crowded. So were her air raid shelters."

One episode John thoroughly enjoyed, and he conveys his enjoyment to the reader in a chapter called "Back to Methuselah." This was a visit to Bernard Shaw at Ayot St. Lawrence, made in the company of Lady Astor and McGeorge Bundy—Lieutenant, later Captain, Bundy, USA, Admiral Kirk's military aide. Bundy says that he went along at Lady Astor's suggestion, so that a staff car could be used and she could save her petrol ration. Lady Astor was particularly interested in seeing that Shaw, now approaching eighty-eight (the age of Captain Shotover in *Heartbreak House*), was being made comfortable and generally taken care of. Shaw took them round the garden; admitted he was writing an article "because I'm being paid twenty-five pounds for it"; and to John's dismay, said he was about to write a new play. "By the time we had followed him back to the house, he had already lunged into sex, marriage, primogeniture, cattle, the English clergy, Norman architecture, and Victorian bad taste."

Shaw discussed the Navy—"for no apparent reason, except that

I was wearing blues." He said that men joined the Navy for enjoyment, became bored with the life but stayed for promotions and the eventual pension, then gradually went crazy. As an example he spoke of a man who took his ship five times across the Bay of Biscay without ever putting into port; "then they threw him in the brig." Those who become captains are "segregated on their bridges. If they are not mad before this, they go mad then. And the maddest of all become admirals. Tell your Admiral this." Apparently no mention was made of John's lunch with Shaw in 1932.

Before the invasion there are more letters to Cassie. On May 7 John wrote: "I presume the papers at home bristle, bulge, and are bogged down with rumor stories about the invasion. Certainly the papers here are cluttered with such stories. What Rommel has to say about the surprises in store for us. . . . What the Air Command predicts will be the increased bomb load dropped on the Continent this month, an invasion prayer by the Dean of St. Paul's—'Let God Arise!' . . . Yes, and Herr Dr. Walter Lippmann, holding forth most pedagogically on morale and what ought to have been done about it in America. . . .

"It all is a sure sign of the quickened tomtoms. It all *must* add up to a pyschological weapon hard for the German nerves to stand, because, under the strain of waiting, nerves are jittery even here. And every night, and every morning the roar of the RAF and USAAF planes can be heard—going in, coming out.

"Lord! Lord! Lord! But what a moment in history this is, and how fateful are the decisions which will be made. Milton once spoke of darkness visible. Just now, without listening, all of us above the chatter of our daily living can hear that sibilant inrush of the world holding its breath."

And the following day, May 8: "Last night you were both thought about and talked about *often*. Your old maestro, Alfred Lunt, wanted full news of you. As I do, God knows. . . ." The letter describes a party given by Charles Collingwood: among the guests were Mr. and Mrs. Edward R. Murrow, Lynn Fontanne, Robert E. Sherwood, William S. Paley of CBS, and Ernie Pyle. Alfred Lunt cooked mushrooms, noodles, asparagus tips, and string beans.*

"The talk? Good, very good. Fontanne full of theatre. Interesting on the subject of why Stark Young's play was not ripe for production. 'Beautiful scenes. But then whole pages filled with things Alfred and I could not understand. Neither could Noël. I gave it to him to read; he's so sympathetic to authors. But Noël refused to read it after the first three pages. He has a passionate hatred of the deliberately unclear.' . . .

"Ernie Pyle wanted to know if Lynn and I weren't the oldest of old friends. We admitted we had seen each other three times before, and explained the actor-critic feeling about fraternization. To Ernie, so full of GI sweetness and light, this doctrine seemed 'obnoxious.' 'Why,' drawled he, 'I don't understand it at all. I couldn't write about one of my pilots or soldiers without knowing him.'"

The letter goes on to explain that although Pyle was willing to risk his life on the ground (where he was later to lose it), he would not fly, as Murrow did. "The question arose, Paley asking it, if Ed Murrow wasn't foolish to keep going on missions. Wasn't he more valuable here in London, explaining, as he has admirably explained since the blitz, the war as Britain has endured it. 'I don't go for that stuff,' said he. 'I can't write unless I've experienced the thing myself, and I hate this theory of unexpendable people. There's no one that important.'"

That brings us to the verge of D-Day, and back to *Many a Watchful Night*. Not until Part III of the book, which consists of the final five chapters, do we come to the invasion. John tells the story rather than repeating his broadcasts, though he quotes generously from his broadcast—or broadcasts—to the crew of the *Augusta* on the eve of the invasion. He explains the stupendous size of the invading forces, describes the coast of Normandy, warns that the invaders are going to meet the stiffest

* The Lunts were in London playing in Sherwood's *There Shall Be No Night*.

kind of opposition. The description of the battle itself is so condensed that it cannot be summarized, only sampled. "We do not have to be told that H-hour is at hand. On all sides it announces itself with a booming and banging, a banging and booming. There never has been such a wholesale Knocking at the Gate. Battleships, cruisers, destroyers—they all let go. The entrance march is played by an orchestra composed entirely of kettledrums." There is a surprising absence of counter-fire. "The Navy guns, aided by spotters, have evidently done their clean, precise, devastating work. We gather from the general silence that they must have neutralized most of the shore batteries. They have gone where our planes could not go. They have reached in under the ten-foot blocks of cement which hood the enemy strong points and offer them the protection of submarine pens. Against these they have obviously scored Annie Oakley after Annie Oakley. . . .

"Although our Air Force has performed a major service brilliantly, disrupting enemy communications, bringing in paratroopers and gliders, and throwing the Germans off the scent . . . it has been able in many cases to scratch no more than the surface of these strong points. On one fearless low-altitude flight after another, however, our Air Force has swooped down on these beaches, photographing the snaggle-toothed underwater obstacles, the barriers, the mines, and the gun emplacements."

The *Augusta* lay off Normandy six days, shuttling between the two American beachheads, "enabling Admiral Kirk to check upon the needs and progress of the operation. [The shuttling] likewise carried General Bradley where he had occasion to go. . . .

"The nights . . . never surrendered to the day's illusion of calm." The account proceeds to tell in detail what happened on the night of June 7—taken as a sample of the other nights. It was the night of a full moon, making the ships conspicuous targets. "The whir of motors—including enemy motors—was the only match needed to set off the fireworks. . . . Then the gun-

ners on the near-by LSTs and transports had themselves a field
day. Let one gun go, and guns followed almost everywhere."
Later: "Except for sporadic explosions on the beaches, the night's
excitements now began to taper off." Every night was alike; for
John, "Each night vibrated with enough disturbances to justify
from four to fourteen brief reports and reassurances over the
public address system to the men below." But surprisingly, "Each
night the Germans sent up no more than thirty or forty planes
over the whole invasion area."

General Bradley invited the correspondents aboard the *Augusta*
to come ashore; this made it possible for John, owing to his
daily broadcasts to the ship's company, to go with them for
three all-day visits. There follows a description of the beaches—
"a freight yard in the sand, a freight yard without trains or
tracks." Once ashore, the General left them on their own. Hanson
Baldwin of *The New York Times* "kept track of the higher
strategy for us with the fine eye and knowledge of a professional."
They talked to many soldiers; saw cows grazing in meadows;
bridges which the Germans, in the speed of their retreat, had neglected to blow up, together with some that had been destroyed
and quickly repaired by the Army Engineers. "We saw stunned
peasants standing in little groups on sidewalks rough with rubble and glass." One elderly couple was trudging away from
their ruined farmhouse, carrying what they could salvage in a
baby carriage. "At General Collins's headquarters, incidentally,
we saw two GIs bring in a frightened Nazi in green-gray. He was
a uniformed sniper, left behind the retreating German lines to
operate alone. . . . Snipers were plentiful and costly." They
saw Nazi prisoners. "For the most part, these Nazis were thin,
scrubby, and sorry examples of the Super Race. They bore no
resemblance to the fine physical specimens we had brought back
from Sicily and Africa." They included men from countries
Germany had conquered; they included boys as young as sixteen.
John and his companions visited hospitals and admired the courage of the doctors and corpsmen, listened to wounded men laugh-

ing with relief at having survived—"until they remembered Jack or Jim who had not been so lucky."

"The smell of death was heavily upon this meadow. We, inhaling it, thought of Ernest Hemingway's description. . . . But even in war death cannot keep pace with life."

And from the final paragraph: "If only men could realize that the maintenance of a proud peace requires more vigilance than the prosecution of a just war. Yes, and equal courage. And greater character and characters. If only, among all the things this war has taught us, we have gained sufficient wisdom to make another war unnecessary and unthinkable. Because the last people on earth who want a war are the men in their right senses who must fight it."

John was to write, in February 1947, to a correspondent in Australia about *Many a Watchful Night:* "I didn't want it to be merely the record of a campaign. I wanted it to be the story of the emotions of war." The book was written soon after John's return to the United States (its copyright date is 1944).

During that summer he must have gone through a period of tormenting indecision: whether to stay in the service or not. By November the decision had been made; John wrote to a correspondent saying that Admiral Kirk "urged me himself to apply for inactive duty, saying I could be of more service just now out of uniform than in. Accordingly I have gone back to pen-pushing and public speaking."

After the Sicilian invasion, Admiral Kirk had sent John a letter of special commendation, and after the invasion of Normandy, Admiral Kirk sent a similar second letter:

The initiative, energy and aggressiveness you displayed in the performance of your duties during the planning and attack phases of the landing operations of the Western Naval Task Force in the assault on the coast of Normandy in June 1944 were such as to warrant my appreciation and sincere thanks for a job well done. I therefore take pleasure in commending you for your contribution to the success of the invasion of Europe.

These two letters are quoted in the release dated September 11, 1944, previously referred to. The release informs us further that "Lieutenant Brown has the American Area Campaign Medal and the European-African–Middle Eastern Campaign Medal."

In May 1945 John was awarded the Bronze Star. The citation follows:

In the name of the President of the United States, it gives me great pleasure to award this Bronze Star Medal to:

Lieutenant,
John Mason Brown,
United States Naval Reserve.

CITATION

For meritorious performance of duty as Force Public Relations Officer on the staff of the Naval Commander, Western Task Force, prior to and during the invasion of Normandy, France, in June 1944.

Lieutenant Brown ably coordinated and directed the dissemination of news and photographs of the Western Assault and was especially successful in effecting a harmonious liaison with the British Public Relations officials with whom he dealt. He was in large part responsible for the cooperation existing between the Public Relations officers of the Commander, U.S. Naval Forces in Europe and those of the Naval Commander, Western Task Force. Lieutenant Brown personally assigned the various correspondents to their places in the ships and craft so as to ensure a properly balanced coverage of the operation. By his continuous and skillful broadcasts on the course of the battle, he greatly contributed to the splendid morale of the officers and men of the U.S.S. *Augusta.* At all times Lieutenant Brown met his many problems with initiative, energy and unfailing tact.

The efficient performance of duty displayed by Lieutenant Brown was in keeping with the best traditions of the United States Naval Service.

HAROLD R. STARK,
Admiral, U.S. Navy,
Commander, U.S. Naval Forces in Europe.

210575

A few excerpts from letters written during 1945 round out the story. To Donald Oenslager on April 11 (in spite of the advice quoted earlier that Don should retire from the service and that

Cassie should try to persuade him): "Your V-mail * written en route [to the South Pacific], arrived yesterday afternoon. I can well imagine how much you had to give to the sea. Your generosities to Neptune were always unstinting.

"I know, too, the high contentment that is in your heart. There is no feeling in the world as warming as that inner sense of identification with a larger cause. The discomforts, even the loneliness and homesickness, are all made bearable because of it.

"As much as I hate to have you out of the country, as much as Cass and I miss you in this city and in our daily living, as seriously as your absence has subtracted from the theatre these wartime seasons, I would not for anything have had you denied the experience which is now yours.

"The privations, the denials—these are really the joys of the service; these, coupled with danger itself. Without them the whole gesture is futile; the whole desire frustrated.

"I had to smile, my valued landlubber, at your description of the crossings. Lord God! but don't I, as a low lieutenant, know the miseries of such voyages. The overcrowding, the dirt, the smell, and the wonderful comradeship. Thank you for awakening memories which I value immeasurably."

To McGeorge Bundy, May 22: "Recently, when out on a lecture tour, I picked up a copy of the *Atlantic* in Chicago. There —smacko—leading off the table of contents, was the name of a young man not unknown to me.

" 'What,' said I to myself, 'can this young man, who once pulled the covers off my bed, battered my head with the pillow, and threw me into the passageway of the *Ancon,* what can this young man have to say that will cause me to listen without protest?'

"The answer, Mac, is 'A lot.' I rejoiced in your letter to the learned prexies. I rejoiced in the wonderfully incisive quality of your thinking no less than in the sparkle of your phrasing.

* Oenslager says it must have been APO mail, not V-mail.

Again and again, on jaunts around the country, I have this winter been depressed by the number of university deans and presidents who have been against compulsory service.* From now on I'll never bother to argue with them. I'll merely send them your 'Open Letter' by the next mail."

Mr. Bundy explains that the scuffle on board the *Ancon* started as a pillow fight, became slightly acrimonious, then ended in amity. He does not recall what started it, but he mentions that the *Ancon* was a converted passenger vessel, and that he and John shared a stateroom on board. Meredith Brown suggests that the altercation may have arisen over the question of who should have the lower bunk. In any event, it seems clear that Bundy—about twenty years younger than John—won the decision.

To Mrs. Merriam in Missoula, August 3: "Being home with Cassie and the children—at least, having home as an operating base—has been sheer bliss. Like everyone else, when I was overseas I was homesick. And homesickness is one of the most draining of diseases. There is only one cure for it, as men everywhere know all too well, and that is getting home. I can't tell you how, when once home, I have resented having to leave the family for each lecture trip."

Finally, an excerpt from a letter to General Bradley, September 15. After congratulating the Veterans' Administration on having the General at its head, John writes: "The nearest I have come to you since Normandy was when a niece of mine was playing golf at the Hot Springs this summer. You may remember her; you may also remember the incident. . . . She was preparing to drive, utterly unaware that anyone was nearby. As her stroke was a weak one, she compensated for this by the vigor of her vocabulary. She tells me that a gentleman in uniform stepped forward, who was surrounded by other men in uniform. The gentleman in question said, 'I never realized that a girl would be able to out-

* Bundy's *Atlantic* article was an argument for universal military service—a position with which he no longer agrees.

swear me.' My niece almost died when she realized that the gentleman was you. She tells me that in her confusion all she could think of saying was, 'General Bradley, weren't you with my Uncle John in Normandy?' Somehow, even she realized that wasn't just the way to phrase it, so she kept quiet."

# Chapter Nine

# A New Center of Gravity

The first decision John made on returning to civilian life was that he would not resume daily newspaper reviewing. Roy Howard, head of the Scripps-Howard chain which included the New York *World-Telegram,* offered him his old job back; John wrote Howard on November 8, 1944, declining the offer. This letter was acknowledged, with regret, by Howard a few days later. *Variety* on December 13 reported that John had turned down the *World-Telegram*'s offer of $25,000 a year because of a difference with the paper's editorial policy. The only conceivable difference was a reluctance on John's part to review openings promptly— and certainly it was a reasonable policy on the paper's part to have openings reviewed promptly. John had had a dozen years of it; and now he had been through experiences which, even for one who had been incurably stage-struck at the age of eight, were more significant and more memorable.

Indeed, it was as much his emphatic desire to keep the war in the forefront of the American mind as it was his declining interest in the theatre that led him to accept Norman Cousins's offer (made at the suggestion of Amy Loveman, associate editor and Norman Cousins's right arm) of an assistant editorship on *The Saturday Review of Literature* (it was not until 1952 that the magazine called itself "The Saturday Review" *tout court*). On November 13 he wrote Mrs. Merriam:

"At present, although Roy Howard kindly asked me to return to the *World-Telegram* right way, I had no inclination to go back to a world of make-believe, when the real world is at war. . . .

"Praise be that the election is over. Praise be, too, that Mr. Roosevelt is in. In a weak-minded moment, when curtained in the booth and faced with all the stage-fright that predicament provokes, I found myself voting for Dewey, merely because I could not tolerate the thought of Truman. [As we shall see, John was to write an admiring piece in 1953, "The Trumans Leave the White House."] That night I went to Sister's [Mary Miller Lambert's: her second marriage was to J. D. W. Lambert of St. Louis] to a party which was almost exclusively Republican. At this party I spent most of my time on my knees, praying fervently for Roosevelt to get in and for God to forgive me. My one hope now is that the President will survive these four years. We need him desperately."

On the same day he wrote to Elinor Hughes, head of the drama department of the *Boston Herald:* "Thank you for understanding the difficulties of my recent decision [to return to civil life]. I assure you it has been much harder to make up my mind to go out than it was to decide to join up. My one desire is to be where I can do the most service. The war is heavily on my heart and in my mind, and will be long after the last shot has been fired.

"Just now I feel there is so much to be done in bringing the conflict home to those indifferent to it here. Also in bridging the inevitable gap between those who have been through it and those who have not. I want to fight for a better understanding of the returning serviceman . . . and for the civilized values of the world for which he has fought and of which he will again become a part.

"All this is a tiresome, pontifical way of explaining the motives leading up, first of all, to my application for inactive duty; and secondly, to my going to *The Saturday Review* rather than returning to the *World-Telegram*. I hope in this weekly page to be

able to deal with the plays, books, movies, and ideas which interest me, and thus to duck the fly-by-night horrors. It's going
to be hard enough as it is to settle once more in the land of
make-believe and vicarious living. However, with the *Saturday
Review* page, and a weekly radio program I am planning to do
for CBS, I should be able to have my say on the aesthetic matters
nearest to my heart. Meanwhile, I shall stump the country
speaking on 'what we really should have learned from the war.' "

His page, or department, in *The Saturday Review* was called
"Seeing Things"—and to make it abundantly clear what things
John was supposed to be seeing, the magazine reproduced draw-
ings of the tragic and the comic mask on either side of the title.
And John—who was to draw upon this department for several
books—did continue to review plays. He also lived up to his
word about writing on other subjects. In a long letter to Captain
Bundy, written February 9, 1945, he wrote: "I am working like
a dog. My hope is that it has some relationship—that, in spite of
the stray pieces for the SRL, etc., my efforts still have some bearing on the war. I would feel suicidally blue if I thought they
didn't. Although I yip and yodel, in ways of which you would
disapprove, to civilian audiences on the subject of the cleavages
which separate us here in America from those in the services overseas, my heart is most in the fortnightly talks I give at Army and
Navy hospitals. Lord! Mac, how those maimed youngsters do
wrench the heart, and set one wondering."

In *The Saturday Review* of January 5, 1946, John wrote an
article entitled "Lest We Forget" (reprinted in *Seeing Things*),
from which a few brief quotations may be taken. "Well, peace
has come at last. But certainly the peace into which we have
moved is not the peace any of us dreamed of during those long,
desperate, lonely war years. Certainly it has none of the ecstasy
about it which all of us, old enough to remember the last Armis-
tice, felt when World War I came to an end." He speaks of the
very limited number of serious books and plays about the war
lately ended, and dismisses as irrelevant the argument that the

period of gestation is always long for such works to appear. He deplores the state of mind of the public that "wants to forget the war itself." And, in spite of a few good books,

publishers assure our writers the war is taboo. So do booksellers. So do producers. . . .

Our lack of war exposure only adds to our difficulties in comprehending the problems of the peace. . . . If we would know what has been, what is, and what may be again, we cannot wait for poetry born of emotion recollected in tranquillity. Let's face it. Tranquillity is a luxury we are not apt to enjoy again in our lifetime.

In that same month John gave a lecture on "What We Should Have Learned from the War," a subject on which he had written in *The Saturday Review*. The *Courier-Journal* reported this lecture, beginning with a quotation from it. "We have been living under the illusion of peace. And now we have been given a second chance, a second chance which we do not deserve. . . .

"We incessantly and insanely repeat that we are the most powerful nation in the world, and if we are that puts us in the position of the largest boy on the block, and the largest boy is usually the most despised." He believed we had "imperiled the things we fought for" by bringing the troops home too soon, by relaxing rationing, by walking out on commitments because our leadership failed to explain the need for them. He considered our attitude to the Negro "a tragic example of hypocrisy," and he said that *Black Boy* by Richard Wright should be required reading.

Meanwhile, he had been expressing his observations and feelings in his correspondence. To the present writer, who was then with the OWI in Paris, he wrote on September 15, 1945. After some personal remarks—including the news that Donald Oenslager had returned from Guam and would not be going out again—he wrote: "Norman Cousins's impressive editorial on the atomic bomb in the SRL has been widely reprinted in daily newspapers throughout the country, and is now to be brought out in book form by Viking. . . . [John's ellipses] The Viking

Press asked me if I would edit a volume for their portable library. 'Whose?' I asked Marshall [Best]. 'Oscar Wilde,' said he.* Needless to say, I declined, assuring him that the thought of a portable Oscar Wilde was something that I could not confront my boys with. . . . I am awfully depressed by the news stories that come back here, telling us of how outrageously the GIs have been behaving in France, and Belgium, not to forget Germany. . . . *Omnibook*,† which is now sponsoring my 'Of Men and Books' program on WABC, gave a party for me and Gertrude Lawrence at the Rainbow Room last night. It was really a nice party. This, as you well know, is something to say of any 'literary tea.' . . .

"I am back at the SRL now. And have resumed my Saturday broadcast ["Of Men and Books"] whenever football permits. I gather that in this country the pigskin would win over Pushkin every time. In other words, like you, my dear Southerner, I resent all sports that compel us talkative fellows to be quiet."

On November 14, he wrote to Brooks Atkinson in Russia; Atkinson was taking time off from Broadway to act as a foreign correspondent for *The New York Times*. "I read you and read about you happily, proudly. The chill of a Russian winter may be upon you; but here we have been exposed to the dullest, grayest, drizzliest fall known to the memory of a nation that dotes on cough syrups, vitamin pills, and purgatives. I am one Southerner who likes the cold. Sometimes I wonder if Mother didn't have me in the icehouse. . . .

"The feeling of let-down is still upon me. Everywhere one senses the sickness of the world. Here an appalling number of the old selfishnesses have reappeared. People, fat, sleek, and untouched, seem incapable of realizing the agony to which most mortals have been exposed. They cry for girdles; they cry for

---

* Later edited by Richard Aldington. John was to edit a book for Viking's Portable Library, *The Portable Charles Lamb,* and write the introduction for another, *The Portable Woollcott.*
† A periodical then flourishing, devoted to book condensations.

gas; they cry for nylons; they rejoice in having shoes unrationed. But they still seem to ration their sympathies cruelly.

"Our old love, the theatre, seems just now as confused in its small way as is the larger world for which it attempts to speak. I doubt if ever there has been a season more stillborn than this one. Tonight *The State of the Union* opens—the Lindsay-Crouse play—and of it great things are expected. Last night I saw Bob Sherwood's *The Rugged Path*. It had been damned pretty generally by the boys. And was excoriated by Burton * in one of the most unpardonable and scurrilous reviews that I have read in all the years that I have been writing and reading about the theatre. But as an editorial [the play, not the review] it is well felt. Certainly it is not boring. Certainly Spencer Tracy gives in it a magnificent performance.

"The disquieting thing is, Brooksy—and this is something I have felt for a long time—that the 'boys' on the aisle who have only been 'here' judge what they see by standards utterly divorced from those who have been 'there.' I suppose the simple truth is that no one undislocated by life, unremoved from the seeming serenity of this country, can be expected to imagine what life outside consists of. . . .

"I am loving my job on *The Saturday Review*. I enjoy writing once a week, and having time, even though, as you once put it, someone steals my watch. Norman Cousins is really doing a fine job with the magazine."

As the foregoing letter indicates, John had by no means given up seeing plays and writing about them. Indeed, it was during this period that he was president of the Critics Circle. Less than half of the first book collected almost entirely from his *Saturday Review* pieces consists of reviews of plays, and of these a considerable number are reviews of revivals and classics. These include Katharine Cornell's revival of *The Barretts of Wimpole Street,* which she had performed overseas for the troops and

---

* Burton Rascoe, who had succeeded to the drama critic's post at the *World-Telegram.*

now brought to New York; and Gertrude Lawrence in *Pygmalion* (John called this review "Eliza off the Ice," and compared Miss Lawrence's Eliza Doolittle favorably with some Elizas of previous productions). Incidentally, after taking the *Saturday Review* job, John became more relaxed about having friendships with people of the stage; Katharine Cornell, the Lunts, and Miss Lawrence all became good friends of his. As for Miss Lawrence, John had known her husband, Richard Aldrich, both at college and at the American Laboratory Theatre. After her performance in *Lady in the Dark* he called Miss Lawrence "the happy pelvis."

Among other revivals of which John preserved his reviews in *Seeing Things* were Margaret Webster's production of *The Tempest* and the condensed version of *Hamlet,* which Maurice Evans (one of the few actors who had played it uncut) staged for the troops. There were new plays, several of them still vividly remembered: Mary Chase's *Harvey,* Tennessee Williams's *The Glass Menagerie,* the Rodgers-Hammerstein musical *Carousel,* based on Molnár's *Liliom.*

Besides his comments on plays, *Seeing Things* includes John's comments on some of his fellow critics, notably Alexander Woollcott and George Jean Nathan. The piece on Woollcott was written as the introduction to *The Portable Woollcott,** and is a posthumous personality sketch with some first-class anecdotes. The piece on Nathan, published in *The Saturday Review* in

---

* It is amusing to note a passage from a letter of Woollcott's to Alfred Lunt, dated May 26, 1942, written from Bomoseen, Vermont: "In a nightmare last night I found myself arriving at a handsome, elegant, old-fashioned summer hotel somewhere in the White Mountains. A war benefit was to be staged in the big dining-room as soon as the waitresses could clear away the tables. I discovered with progressive discomfort that, under the management of John Mason Brown, all of us would be expected not only to attend the performance but to partake in it—that, in fact, each of us was expected to do one of Ruth Draper's monologues. My own distress derived from the fact that I not only had less than an hour in which to learn mine but that no one could tell me which one it was. They could only say it was the one with which I always made Alfred Lunt laugh so. At this point I woke screaming and was discovered to be in an appalling state of nervous indigestion." From *The Letters of Alexander Woollcott,* edited by Beatrice Kaufman and Joseph Hennessey (Viking, 1944), pp. 232–34.

November 1945, is largely an expression of astonishment—
while giving Nathan his due as an eminent, brilliant, and indefatigable theatre critic—that he had remained entirely un-
changed in a world of upheaval, while at the same time admitting
that the astonishment would have been even greater if Nathan
*had* changed: "this would be a surprise indeed, comparable to
finding the Statue of Liberty sitting down or The Thinker standing up." At the end John wrote that he wished Nathan would
put aside his scissors and paste and write a real book. "Above all,
I wish that, though rightfully proud of his head, he would not
continue always to be so ashamed of his heart." And the final
paragraph:

> Mr. Nathan remains the hedonist he was in a period of security even
> in these times of danger. He is a critic whose ideas are almost all theatre-
> born. He has his aesthetic opinions which are many, varied, smiling,
> and excellent. But he has none of the social convictions which were the
> source of Shaw's strength [as a critic]. The pity is that, though he is our
> foremost critic of the theatre, he so seldom widens his interest to include
> life.

This is an appropriate place to mention that John was an
excellent mimic—it was one of his resources as a lecturer—and
he was particularly good at imitating Nathan—who did, to be
sure, make it comparatively easy owing to his habit of talking
through clenched front teeth.

Although the bulk of *Seeing Things* is a collection of reviews
of plays produced in the season 1944–45, the book begins with a
short section called "Parents and Children" and ends with a
long section, "The Soldiers' Music." Here he includes the essay
"Lest We Forget": "Tranquillity is a luxury we are not apt to
enjoy again in our lifetime." He expresses disappointment almost amounting to outrage at Noël Coward's book *Middle East
Diary:* "Mr. Coward wanders through the horrors of war in
these pages as tight-lipped and dapper as if to him the war were
a sequel to *Design for Living.*" He returns to the theatre without
abandoning the war for a piece about Paul Osborn's dramatiza-

tion of John Hersey's novel *A Bell for Adano* and for reviews of other war plays. There is a rueful chapter, called "Ringside Seats," about the difficulty of hearing, through a fog of static at a summer hotel, the broadcast of the proceedings on board the U.S.S. *Missouri* marking the end of the war; but the ruefulness was less for missing the speeches of President Truman and General MacArthur than for the placidity of his fellow guests. "Perhaps it was just as well there was static. Perhaps there was static everywhere, even for those who could hear. Certainly few of the people who did hear could hope to understand that the war was over or what peace would mean.

" 'I'll bet we can get real girdles this winter,' beamed one plumpish woman. The ceremony was over. Peace was here." That essay was published in *The Saturday Review* of September 15, 1945.

In 1946 Norman Cousins had the editorial perspicacity to send John abroad. John wrote to his Uncle Preston on June 1 mentioning the forthcoming trip, planned for several reasons: "*The Saturday Review* is sending me over. . . . First of all, I am to go as their correspondent. Second, as their editor [associate editor?]. Thirdly, to do some broadcasting in England for BBC. And fourthly, to collect material for next winter's writing and lecturing here." On June 10 he wrote to Mrs. Merriam: "In many ways I hate going. But what is left of my conscience compels me to do this. I feel so violently about our present indifference to the outside world that I am hoping to pick up enough firsthand information from which to talk, write, and broadcast next winter, and perhaps be able to do a teeny-weeny midget bit of good." He left on June 13.

In London he stayed first at the Savoy, later with Hamish Hamilton, publisher in England of almost all of John's books. It was no doubt during this visit—Hamilton tells the story—that John was invited to a large and elaborate party given by Michael Redgrave (he was not yet Sir Michael) and his wife at their house in Hammersmith. The guest list was extensive, and preparations extraordinary. Unfortunately on the evening of the party an impenetrable fog settled over London. John was one of the dozen or so guests who managed to get to the Redgraves'. When he took his departure, he remarked, "That was one *fête* that was not *accomplie*." It may have been on the same London visit—obviously it was before the death of King George VI—that John found himself in a group including Dame May Whitty and presumably at least one other American besides himself, for it must have been an American who fed John the perfect line: "What does it take to make a Dame?" John at once answered, "In America any man can make a dame, but in England it takes the King."

During this visit the London Drama Critics gave a luncheon in John's honor. One of the critics, James Agate, tells of this festivity in *Ego 9*—the ninth volume of Agate's diary-autobiography. "The party took place in the Mikado Room [of the Savoy Hotel]. Somebody saying that Winston Churchill was lunching in the next room, J.M.B. said, 'Ah, the Sorcerer Room, I feel sure.' " Agate's contribution to the occasion was to relate an anecdote of an encounter with John on a previous occasion, at the time of the lend-lease bargaining between Britain and the United States.

*J.A.* Tell me, Brown. Why do you Americans, delightful individually, taken collectively add up to a nation of twerps?

*J.M.B.* All right, Agate. Why, with you Britishers, is the converse the the case?

John's later correspondence contains two comments on this passage. In his letter to his friend Alan Dent, another London drama critic, he wrote on September 1, 1948: "I have enjoyed reading around in *Ego 9*. . . . I was, of course, amused to discover that he had included that charming luncheon the London critics gave for me at the Savoy. But, coming as I do from the Hemingway-Caldwell country, I was sorry that he had reduced the derisive noun we both used to 'twerp.' It was stronger when it began with 's' instead of 't,' and possessed four letters rather than five." And as long afterward as 1964, John commented further in a letter to Serrell Hillman of *Time:* "The Agate retort was got off at the Ivy. . . . I will never forget Jimmy Agate sitting there when I came in, with two volumes of his *Ego* series on the table and one in his hands. It was one of the oddest forms of navel-contemplation that I have ever seen."

On July 5 John visited Admiral and Mrs. Kirk in Brussels, the Admiral then being our Ambassador to Belgium. No copy of a bread-and-butter letter turns up in his correspondence; presumably he sent his thanks in his illegible hand. And there seems to be no later comment on this part of his trip in other letters, although he had written to friends, before his trip, that he expected to be with the Kirks for a week. Actually he stayed in Brussels only a day or two. Although he had not mentioned it in the letters to his Uncle Preston or to Mrs. Merriam, quoted above, the real reason—at least the principal reason—why *The Saturday Review* sent John abroad in 1946 was to visit the war crimes trials at Nuremberg. According to Norman Cousins, *The Saturday Review* had no reason to keep this a secret. John's reason must have been his uncertainty whether he was going to get there. Communications in Europe were still chaotic; Nuremberg itself was in considerable part reduced to rubble. One did not simply go to an airline or to a travel agent and buy a ticket. John managed, in Brussels, to pick up a plane ride to Nuremberg—whether or not with Ambassador Kirk's assistance is not known. The Ambassador did probably give him an introduction to Francis Biddle, former Attorney General of the United States and now the United States member of the International Military Tribunal. John got back from Nuremberg to London on his own.

John wrote two articles on the Nuremberg trials, published in *The Saturday Review* in August 1946, and reprinted in his second *Saturday Review* book, *Seeing More Things* (McGraw-Hill, 1948). When John arrived for what was necessarily a quick visit, "the trial had dragged on for nine months beyond the three that some had thought it would take. . . . No doubt the proceedings were becalmed. To me, however, they were anything but dull." The double essay, called "Century of Progress," begins with a description of the appearance of the defendants. "In the courtroom they were shadows of themselves. They bore little relation to what they had been." But on a lower floor of the courthouse was a projection room where an American sergeant ran a film called *The Triumph of the Will*. "In America I had seen the Dachau and Buchenwald pictures, and wished that they could be made compulsory for everyone, especially for those who, in the natural pessimism of these days of the letdown, wonder what the war proved anyway." The films shown in Nuremberg were uncut, and showed all the horrors, which John's article lists in detail.* It also describes the leading Nazis, shown in the film in the heyday of their triumph—"but in the courtroom they were different. They were fractions of what they had been. . . . A sorrier group of men than those who had found their Valhalla in the Nuremberg dock could scarcely be imagined. . . . Adversity had whittled away their persons no less than their powers."

The piece goes on to show us the defendants individually; Keitel, Jodl, and Goering still in uniform. The description of Goering is particularly effective, for Goering apparently was enjoying himself as the center of attention: "No matter how great the stakes, the stage was his, and Goering was ham enough to revel in the realization."

John goes on to describe the judges—the two Russians in uniform; the British judges no less British for having left their wigs at home; Francis Biddle of the Main Line and Judge Parker of North Carolina. And especially Mr. Justice Robert H. Jackson of the United States Supreme Court, the prosecutor for the United States. "Justice Jackson may not excel at either the banter or the mongoose tactics of a prosecutor. He is a jurist, not a dis-

---

* It is worth reading, even—or especially—after nearly thirty years; and fortunately it can be read, since it is included among the contents of *Dramatis Personae*.

trict attorney. He is a man who has fought for a principle—a great principle—and defended it magnificently."

And surely the following is as timely as ever.

Justice Jackson and his associates have battled to see that the law, instead of remaining static, grows to meet world needs. He has sought by legal means to have international aggression take its place among recognized crimes. He has emphasized the absurdity of subjecting petty malefactors to punishment while the great ones go scot-free. . . . He has felt the shame that we all should have felt because of what has been barbarous in a supposedly civilized age.*

Back in London, John apparently resumed efforts begun shortly after his arrival in June to make preparations for the dinner to be held in New York on Shaw's ninetieth birthday anniversary, July 26. He had seen Shaw briefly in June, and among his papers there is a copy of a cable to Jack Cominsky, publisher of *The Saturday Review,* undated and with no indication whether it was ever sent. "Saw him [Shaw] yesterday three minutes. Most unsatisfactory. Older, slightly confused, forgetful. Would discuss nothing. Strongly advise using best pieces Dodd Mead [volume?].† Do you want acid piece on horrors of interview?" Whether the cable was sent or not, it seems to establish that John did see Shaw, and on some date after June 20, when he wrote to Cominsky that he had seen Shaw's secretary, who told him that Shaw would see no one until August. But the secretary "assured me that though this is a firm, it was not a final, answer. He says the Old Boy won't let anyone discuss his birthday with him. . . . He urged me to write the Elderly So-and-So, which I have done at length. . . . Now everything depends on what the Aged Bugger answers. If he says 'No,' I'll still

---

* Justice Jackson returned the compliment: there are a couple of letters from him among John's papers praising John's account of the trial.

† *G. B. S. 90* was published by Dodd, Mead in 1946. It contains twenty-seven contributions, varying in length, nearly all by British and Irish authors, plus sixteen pages of photographs. None of those who spoke at the dinner is among the contributors. The book was published in England either before its American publication, or simultaneously.

keep trying. But I promise you that a Devil's Disciple will turn overnight into a Devil's Advocate."

Further evidence of John's calls on Shaw is supplied by a letter he wrote to Shaw's permanent secretary, Miss Blanche Patch, in May 1948: "I also remember the first time I met you, back in 1932, when I had dropped by to ask Mr. Shaw some questions about William Archer, A. B. Walkley, etc. Then, two summers ago, you were kind enough to see me and we had a long talk about Mr. Shaw and Mr. Loewenstein [Shaw's refugee secretary, the one previously referred to in this context]." This letter raises a question, in that it does not at all square with the account given by Dorothy Sands of John's Russian lunch at Shaw's house in 1932. Did he make another visit to Shaw that went unrecorded?

The word "also" in the first quoted line of the preceding paragraph refers to a slight contretemps, by now a thing of the past. In a piece published July 22, 1944, in *The Saturday Review*— which was to be the chapter in *Many a Watchful Night* about the visit to Ayot St. Lawrence—John had quoted a remark of Shaw's about Miss Patch which sounded slighting, if not derogatory. Miss Patch wrote to McGraw-Hill in September 1944 threatening suit if the passage appeared in the book. It was deleted. Miss Patch wrote again to McGraw-Hill in December to say that she had been hurt rather than angry; that Shaw's remark, when spoken, could be taken as jest, but sounded quite otherwise in print. In her reply, dated May 18, 1949, to the letter of John's just quoted, Miss Patch mentioned "that amusing outburst" of hers, and said she would never have gone so far as to sue for libel.

John flew back to New York, arriving in time for the Shaw dinner, though not without difficulty. He wrote Hamish Hamilton: "I had a hell of a time getting back. The grounded Constellation at first made it highly problematical whether I would be able to get a plane at all. The C54 I was lucky enough to be squeezed on had engine trouble as soon as we landed in Ireland.

We spent three desperate days there, being kept 'on call,' as they say in the greater houses. But home I did get at three o'clock in the pouring rain on Tuesday morning, having left London on a Friday."

The Shaw dinner (which was *not* a vegetarian dinner) took place as scheduled. It was a *Saturday Review* affair: John was the master of ceremonies; Harrison Smith, president of the Saturday Review Company, was chairman. There were about four hundred present. The speakers included John and Henry Seidel Canby from *The Saturday Review;* Howard Lewis, president of Dodd, Mead, Shaw's American publishers; Deems Taylor, music critic and composer of *The King's Henchman* and *Peter Ibbetson;* Leonard Bacon, poet and a frequent contributor to *The Saturday Review;* Lawrence Langner of the Theatre Guild; and the playwright Maxwell Anderson. Maurice Evans and Cornelia Otis Skinner read from the plays; and the dinner ended with a quiz program, a special production of "Information, Please," one of the most popular programs of the time, with Clifton Fadiman as moderator, Franklin P. Adams and John Kieran as permanent panelists, joined by different guest panelists from week to week. At the Shaw dinner Fadiman and Adams were joined by Louis Kronenberger, Margaret Webster, and Howard Dietz. The dinner was followed by a showing of the motion picture of *Caesar and Cleopatra,* with Vivien Leigh and Claude Rains.

In the course of his remarks at the dinner, John noted Shaw's inconsistencies, and gave the opinion that Shaw had been a buffoon to protect himself against malice and stupidity. "If he is vain he has a right to be." In the same letter to Hamish Hamilton, John wrote that, in spite of the difficulties he had encountered in London, "the Shaw dinner went off beautifully. It really was a distinguished affair, and not as painful as those things usually are. The old boy surprised us all by finally transmitting through the BBC a message which vaguely referred to us, but which we pretended was for us alone. I am glad for his sake that he did." The "message" included the sentence, "It's pleasant to be among friends." Shaw quoted someone as saying that he had no enemies, and none of his friends liked him.

So much for the Shaw dinner, except for a brief sequel in 1952. It came in John's reply to a letter from Lady Astor asking him to be chairman of an American counterpart to a national committee which had been formed in England to pursue various activities to honor the memory of Shaw, who had died at ninety-four in 1950. John replied:

"Your letter, most considerately typed, is a model of exposition. GBS himself could not have stated the whole project more clearly or more frighteningly. That I love Shaw, that I love his works, and that I am heartily in sympathy with the purposes of such a fund-raising campaign, you and your committee must have suspected by your thinking of me as a possible chairman of the American committee. But there are reasons, valid and formidable ones, why I think it fairest to you and best for myself not to accept. I am a critic by profession, and critics, as Shaw knew, are the last people to work with organizations. They have to be free agents. Fund-raising is not their affair. Once they have become propagandists, they have sold their birthright (if, indeed, they have any right to be born). . . .

"It's hard for me as a Kentuckian to say no to my Rebel friend from Virginia. But I know that you will understand my reasons."

John had concluded *Seeing Things* with the text of his commencement address at the University of Montana, delivered in 1942. He concluded *Seeing More Things* similarly, with excerpts from his commencement address at Clark University in 1947. He spoke here, as he had written before, of the war and the perpetual crisis that succeeded it. There is much else in *Seeing More Things* beyond the scope of dramatic criticism: the double essay on the Nuremberg trials, for example. Even one of the drama reviews—of *The Winslow Boy* by Terence Rattigan, a play about an English boy who was the victim of a miscarriage of justice— goes on to narrate the story of another miscarriage of justice, this one in a small Iowa town, Pacific Junction; the victim here was a Negro, bullied by the mayor of the town as a "vagrant," defended by six young war veterans, one of whom fought the legal battle to the end—against the advice of his friends and neighbors—and won it. The Negro, to whom no restitution was made, had moved elsewhere.

A few other subjects may be mentioned: a Sunday afternoon with Preston and Meredith at the Metropolitan Museum; a bus trip altogether unlike the one that was John Steinbeck's subject in *The Wayward Bus* (a trip John called "a sex safari"); a visit to Flushing Meadow in 1947, where the United Nations had its first home. There are essays on other books—not necessarily current—and reviews of motion pictures. Still the bulk of the book is drama criticism, even if the center of gravity is the state of the world. Sartre's *No Exit;* Katharine Cornell's revival, noted earlier, of *Antony and Cleopatra;* other revivals, including *Lady Windermere's Fan* and *King Lear*—these were some of the events of the theatrical season.

John received honorary degrees from some of the institutions where he spoke. He received such a degree from Williams College in 1941, and was later awarded several others. His degree from the University of Louisville in 1948 may be mentioned here, especially since *Seeing More Things* contains a chapter on revisiting Louisville, "The Going-Home Train," published in *The Saturday Review* in November 1946.

It is interesting to note that the commencement address at Clark University in June 1947 took place shortly before a serious —but fortunately short-lived—crisis. At the beginning of July, by way of a birthday celebration, John had an operation for a stomach ulcer. Cancer had been suspected, and he had been told so. To the relief of one and all, no malignancy was discovered. A few months later John wrote to his friends Mr. and Mrs. Warren Chetham-Strode: "Early in July they rushed me to the hospital to remove an ulcer which they feared was cancerous. What they took out was . . . a growth which was probably my only benign feature." And to another correspondent: "I thought I was going to miss the two-thirds of my tummy that they took away from me. But I suppose a dramatic critic is trained to be allergic to tripe."

Two years earlier he had written to the lawyer who drew up his will, Mr. Asher Lans of Coudert Brothers: "Many thanks for the will. You have turned it into such a work of literature that I can hardly bear the thought of dying. . . . If I wear a black tie today, it is in my own honor and because of the persuasiveness of your prose." After several paragraphs of family information, John added a postscript: "Since this is my second will, shall I refer to it as my New Testament, rather than my Old?"

# Chapter Ten

# Seven Men—and More

If the Nuremberg trials provided the center of gravity of *Seeing More Things*, as well as signaling a turning-point in John's career, the center of gravity of his next book, *Still Seeing Things*, is his essay on Robert E. Sherwood, prophetically entitled "On a Larger Stage." This was published in *The Saturday Review* of November 13, 1948, surely several years before John had an inkling that he was to become Sherwood's biographer. At the head of the essay as reprinted in *Still Seeing Things*, John wrote this epigraph: "Playwright-into-biographer, or the exciting growth of Robert E. Sherwood, a dramatist who has become as at home with the intricacies of world history as he has long been with the mysteries of stage and screen." The occasion of the essay was the publication of Sherwood's book *Roosevelt and Hopkins: An Intimate History*, which John reviews, but in the course of the review he provides a personality sketch of Sherwood and a backward look at the important plays of his career. And he also provides, whether consciously or not, a forward look at his own career.

He recalls the party in London just before D-Day, at which he and Sherwood were present, also Edward R. Murrow, Ernie Pyle, and Alfred Lunt and Lynn Fontanne. And the book *Roosevelt and Hopkins* makes John realize how much had been on Sherwood's mind that night, knowledge of past and coming events which he could not talk about; instead, Sherwood performed his

famous parlor trick—a rendition of a song first made famous by
Al Jolson, "When the Red, Red Robin Comes Bob, Bob Bobbin
Along." Sherwood did the number

grim-faced as death. A hat was slanted on his head, a cane was in his
hand. . . . I have seen Mr. Sherwood do his number once since then
—undertaker-faced and just for fun. But that night it was more than
for fun that he did it. It was in agony. He was not merely dead-
panning his way through an absurd routine. Like his own hoofer in
"Idiot's Delight" (a part Mr. Lunt had played), he was dancing in a
world where bombs were falling and mass annihilation would soon
begin.

John considered *Roosevelt and Hopkins* to be comparable in
importance to Winston Churchill's *The Gathering Storm.*

Here is the whole bulging cast of recent history—of the nation in the
first days of the New Deal and the W.P.A. years when Harry Hopkins
was more spendthrift with other people's millions than any Brewster has
ever been with his own. Here too, and in far greater detail, are the
nation and the world when this same Harry Hopkins, lion-brave, desperately ill, and by then selfless in his ambitions, had risen to the test
of tremendous times and soared to dimensions which even his enemies
have had to admit were heroic. Here are the records of two ill men
who were determined to make a sick world well.

There is no evidence that this was the exact occasion—or that
any other time marked the exact occasion—when John decided
to turn biographer. It remained for Norman Cousins, once more,
to give him his opportunity, and this did not occur until 1952—
which, coincidentally, was the year when John's short but not insubstantial biography of Daniel Boone was published in Random
House's Landmark Series (originally planned as biographies or
episodes of history written for teen-age readers). John's book
makes no pretense to original research, but it does well the job
it set out to do. Meanwhile, there were other activities. In September 1946 John had gone to Hyde Park to see Mrs. Roosevelt;
he wanted to write a story about Fala, the Scottie who had occupied the White House with the Roosevelts. Evidently he never

wrote it; it does not appear in any of his books, or in the files of *The Saturday Review* through June 1947. He was elevated to the presidency of the American P.E.N. Club and kept the job one year. In 1947 he declined an offer to edit *Town and Country:* "Writing is where my heart is." In 1948 Washington and Lee University conferred upon him an honorary Phi Beta Kappa membership. He was elected to the National Institute of Arts and Letters in 1950. In that year he gave a lecture to the Kentucky Educational Association warning of attempted censorship by minority groups. He spoke of attacks that had been made on *The Merchant of Venice* and *Oliver Twist,* considered anti-Semitic, and *Little Black Sambo,* considered an insult to Negro children—although Little Black Sambo is an East Indian, he is the hero of the story, and there are no tigers at large in Africa. "There is no tolerance by intolerance. You can't pretend what was wasn't and you can't pretend what is isn't." In October 1950 he and Cassie were invited by Mr. and Mrs. Nelson Rockefeller to a dinner for the Chairman of the Delegates to the Fifth Session of the General Assembly of the United Nations. They accepted, and John sat next to Gloria Swanson and danced with her.

None of this had by any means put a stop to John's theatre-going. Although *Still Seeing Things* includes a short essay on Helen Hokinson, written on the occasion of her tragic death in an airplane accident, and a much longer one on Charles and Mary Lamb, which had been written as the introduction to *The Portable Charles Lamb* * in the Viking Press series; although it contains numerous book reviews, and among other miscellany a reminiscence of one of his teachers at the Morristown School and a piece about the grandeur and misery of a summer bachelor in New York while Cassie and the boys were in Connecticut—in spite of all this, and of the Sherwood article, the bulk of the book is concerned with, if no longer quite devoted to, the theatre, in-cluding motion pictures. Among other plays reviewed are Arthur Miller's *Death of a Salesman; The Wisteria Tree,* Joshua Logan's

* Reprinted in *Dramatis Personae.*

version of *The Cherry Orchard* transplanted, without conspicuous success, to Louisiana; *The Cocktail Party* by T. S. Eliot; *The Madwoman of Chaillot* by Jean Giraudoux; Maxwell Anderson's *Anne of the Thousand Days; I Know My Love* by S. N. Behrman (adapted from the French); and the highly successful revival of *Caesar and Cleopatra* with Cedric Hardwicke and Lilli Palmer.

But the review that sticks most conspicuously in the memory is the review of Katharine Hepburn in *As You Like It*. It was not one of John's favorites among Shakespeare's plays; he evidently agreed with the remark Shaw puts into Shakespeare's mouth in *The Dark Lady of the Sonnets*, "It is not as *I* like it."

Mr. Shaw . . . pretended the popularity of Rosalind is due to three main causes: (1) she speaks blank verse only for a few minutes, (2) she wears a skirt only for a few minutes, and (3) she makes love to the man instead of waiting for the man to make love to her. Subject to dispute as such reasoning may be, there are two indisputably good reasons why Miss Hepburn's Rosalind deserves its popularity. Both of these are at their lower extremities encased in her slippers. For, regardless of how much prose she may utter, Miss Hepburn's legs are always poetry, and poetry that is easy to scan.

As a fan of Miss Hepburn since "The Warrior's Husband," "Morning Glory," and "Little Women," . . . I admire her gifts, I enjoy her looks. She has grace, breeding, and a sort of matter-of-fact elegance which is not without its own special glamour. Even so, as Rosalind she does seem to me to be something of a Connecticut Yankee at Duke Frederick's Court. Although she has her excellent moments and tries valiantly to give the play its song, I cannot help feeling that she mistakes the Forest of Arden for the Bryn Mawr campus.

But he concludes: "Heresy though it may be to say so, for me the abiding trouble with Rosalind lies with Shakespeare."

Brooks Atkinson had written a similar minority report for *The New York Times,* and on March 17, 1950, he wrote John a letter. "After reading your clairvoyant article in *The Saturday Review* let me welcome you to the doghouse. It has been pretty lonely for me there for a couple of months, although there is a sizeable gang of people who do not like Hepburn in *As You Like It.* My impudence in not liking her has really roused the country and my mail is full of anger, hatred and scorn. I hope you can take some of it off my back now, although I expect you will not be hated quite so ferociously. Your instinctive sympathy and good manners are less provoking than my waspish personality. You and I were both on the wrong side of *The Cocktail Party* * and *As You Like It.* I shall survive by hanging on to your coat tails." And a P.S.: "You said one thing I didn't dare mention—Bryn Mawr."

John replied on March 31: "Forgive me for not having acknowledged that delectable note of yours. There is no one with whom I would rather be in or out of the doghouse than you. May I confess, however, that to my surprise since I joined you as a DP from Arden I have received no letters of attack but several letters from people who obviously hope to enroll in our ranks.

"You would have had my thanks long ago had it not been for lectures, lectures, lectures; trains, trains, trains; and words that had to be written for the SRL. I am off fairly soon on a trek into the land of wisteria trees. . . . I have missed seeing you, and need and look forward to a good, long, old-time talk with you."

There remained one more book, largely but by no means entirely composed of drama criticism, to come from John's column, "Seeing Things." This was *As They Appear,* published in 1952, the same year as his *Daniel Boone.* This contains several book reviews, three pieces on Shaw, several reviews of Shakespearean revivals, a few miscellaneous pieces (one, which was widely admired, on comic books, called "Marijuana of the Nursery"). Also reviews of new plays by Clifford Odets, Maxwell Anderson, and Tennessee Williams, among others. It was also the season of *Guys and Dolls,* based on Damon Runyon's stories, and a revival of John O'Hara's *Pal Joey*—these two constituting as elegant a pair of native lowdown American musicals as ever existed. John

---

* John had written of *The Cocktail Party:* "In my opinion the drama is a medium which seems to resist [Mr. Eliot's] advances. . . . Mr. Eliot in *The Cocktail Party* has not yet found a plot, a poetic idiom, or a dramatic method which realizes his hopes or our dreams."

found the Runyon characters sentimental under their toughness, but "no such inner core of tenderness is present in *Pal Joey*." He found it inimitable, and also unprecedented, except by *The Beggar's Opera*.

In November 1950 John wrote Hamish Hamilton that he would like to write an article about Lady Colefax. Amy Loveman told John that Louis Bromfield had pre-empted the idea, to which John replied that Bromfield had been sitting on it for weeks and still no article. "I had been planning an essay on the underestimated talents of a hostess, the good that she can do, etc., etc., and wanted, of course, to use Sibyl as my illustration." Meanwhile Shaw had died and John was asked to do the lead article for *The Saturday Review* on him. This article, called "Professional Man of Genius," ran in the magazine November 18, and was reprinted both in *As They Appear* and in *Dramatis Personae*. Apparently this disposed of the Colefax idea.

During the first half of 1951 John was in correspondence with Norman Cousins with a view to revising his responsibilities. He proposed writing ten articles a year on subjects of his own choice, and he proposed breaking with the theatre. To this end he suggested keeping the title "Seeing Things," but dropping the masks in the logotype; also that he become a contributing editor instead of an associate editor. He suggested further that any release of this news should be held until a new theatre critic was assigned. Henry Hewes, who had joined the *Saturday Review* staff as John's assistant, gradually took over the drama department.

On June 29 John summed up his point of view in a long letter to Cousins.

"I am afraid this won't be the final letter you expect and that I am very anxious to write. I am still, as Sean O'Casey's Juno would say, 'in a state of chassis.' I want to aim at the ten special pieces we have been discussing; in other words, to write about stuff that is not Broadwayese or even theatrical and to have some freedom of choice. I also wish with all my heart to get away from the thralldom of a weekly piece and be able to ponder and read, weigh and reappraise, for two weeks or more, stuff that may take two weeks in the writing. Naturally, I am as reluctant as Mr. Thurber's [actually Kenneth Grahame's] dragon to give up the theatre, since it has been my major field of concentration for more than twenty-five years.

"Frankly, I am still feeling my way around towards a solution. What I have in mind (and this is why I have urged you to let me retain the title 'Seeing Things') is that from the readers' point of view there would be no drastic, outward break. I would continue the department on the basis of serializing a major article; add theatre notes which would adequately cover important shows; and, if need be, in the case of something outstanding contribute the kind of article that for these past six years I have been contributing to my department.

"Let me give you an illustration. The musical version of *Seventeen* which I saw two nights ago would in a working period merit two paragraphs in *Briefly Noted*. It would not at any time or under any circumstances justify a full column. I should think from the readers' point of view it would be more interesting to have the column about something which presumably mattered and yet, in the *Time* sense, to be kept *au courant* with what is worthy of coverage in a national magazine.

"I am confident that this problem, which as we discuss it seems so intricate, can be solved simply in actual practice. Remember that for my lectures I shall have to see all the significant productions anyway. Then, in spite of the magnolia and jasmine in my bloodstream, mine is a ruggedly New England conscience when it comes to work. Calvin Coolidge, in a happily forgotten volume, once urged the nation to 'Have Faith in Massachusetts.' I ask you and my cherished confrères on the SRL to have some faith in me.

"I can't persuade myself that this problem is as difficult as the cease-fire in Korea or the tanker problem in Iran. So, for God's sake, let's regain some sense of sanity, which means an active sense of humor."

In a postscript John mentions that he is about to take

Meredith, now approaching eleven, on a trip to Montana, corresponding to a trip west he had made with Preston several years before. He suggests that he and Cousins talk the whole thing over on the telephone before he leaves. And he says that he sees no reason why Jack Cominsky, publisher of the magazine, should fear any loss of advertising revenue from these various proposals.

It is difficult for anyone who has known John, Cousins, and Cominsky to believe that the matter of advertising is what underlay the faint touch of acrimony in that last quoted sentence; rather it should be ascribed to an impatient nature.

In any event, Cousins gave John his great opportunity in 1952. (For the record, it may be noted that John had turned down an idea suggested by Cass Canfield of Harper & Brothers, apparently one of several that Canfield had proposed; this one was "How to Keep the Mind Free of Dry Rot." John declined, saying "I feel happiest when people are my subject rather than abstract ideas.") People were indeed to be his subject—and, incidentally, Harpers his publisher, for the book that was to be the product of Cousins's assignment. Let John tell of it, in his prefatory note to *Through These Men.*

I am . . . grateful to Norman Cousins for giving me the opportunity to have a look into our own politics. Being grateful to him has been a habit of mine since I joined his staff on *The Saturday Review* more than eleven years ago. [*Through These Men* was not published until 1956.] In a rash moment he asked me to cover the Republican and Democratic conventions in 1952. Once started with writing about figures on the national scene, I found it hard to stop, and this book is the result of my addiction.

The book begins with the reports of the two conventions that John wrote for the magazine. The year 1952 was when the very conservative Senator Robert A. Taft of Ohio seemed in advance to have the Republican nomination in his grasp, but the opposition, including Lodge, Brownell, and Dewey, united behind the unbeatable Eisenhower—a matter of delight to the opponents of Taft in both parties, but of some chagrin to Democrats when they found that their highly distinguished candidate, Governor Adlai E. Stevenson of Illinois, who might have defeated Taft, had no chance against the overwhelmingly popular Ike. Following the conventions, John traveled with the two candidates during parts of their campaigns. His account is entirely fair to both; Stevenson is shown as the more effective campaigner, but each man had difficulties with his supporters. One might guess that John's preference was for Stevenson, but he almost ostentatiously preserves his neutrality—which, in a news report, is as it should be. His second chapter concludes: "Through it all, however, it became increasingly clear how fortunate we were to have such men to choose between."

John had first met Stevenson in Washington soon after D-Day. Subsequently, when John lectured in Springfield, Illinois, Governor Stevenson gave a party for him. On October 9, 1952, a month before the election, John wrote Stevenson (whom he called by his first name): "Thanks for your enchanting letter with its unforgettable reference to the Democratic convention as 'the one I happened to attend.' That statement deserves the Nobel Prize for modesty, understatement, and charm.

"My sincerest thanks also to you and to William Flanagan for allowing me to travel with your party through Connecticut, Massachusetts, and Virginia. That trip for me was more than a journey. It was a conversion, as I muttered to you when I had the pleasure of seeing you for a moment after your AFL speech. In next week's issue of *The Saturday Review,* which they are sending to you airmail, I have tried to state my admiration for you. [This article was presumably incorporated, in substance, into the chapter of *Through These Men* called "Stevenson Speaking"; but this chapter includes numerous references to publications and events of years later than 1952.]

"But this is what is really on my mind. Do you remember those words spoken by Oliver Cromwell just before the Battle of Dunbar which Judge Learned Hand is fond of quoting? They run, 'I beseech ye in the bowels of Christ, think that ye may be mistaken.'

"I am thinking just now how mistaken I may be in having the temerity to make a suggestion to you. I am also well aware that my suggestion may turn out to be wrong from the point of view of the hard-boiled politicians. But I feel what I am about to say so strongly that I cannot resist running the risk.

"The papers inform me, and some of your own hard-slugging attacks on Eisenhower appear to back them up, that your advisers are urging you to lay it on thick as far as the General is concerned. I am one of your countless devotees who wish you would ignore that advice. Along with your other warm admirers, I wish that you would let Mr. Truman do that kind of in-fighting for you. By this I do not mean pull your punches. I mean only that I hope you won't be tempted to use brass knuckles verbally. Can't you lambaste the General's confused policies and apparently lost gift for leadership without attacking him personally? And, in the long run, wouldn't it be politically wiser?

"Please, please, at least during the last two weeks of the campaign, start speaking again in the high tones of your welcoming address, your acceptance speech, your fine talk in Los Angeles, your definition of Asiatic policy, and the admirable address you delivered at Richmond. I honestly think that it is what the country wants and needs and looks to you for. I certainly don't want you to abandon your humor, wit, or high literacy. My humble plea is merely to have you also release that full eloquence which you command and that altitude of feeling, thought, and phrasing which makes you so uncommonly outstanding and indispensable an American leader.

"Here's to you and an overwhelming victory."

John was among those who spent the evening of election day with Stevenson, hoping against hope in the face of mounting disappointment. The following day he wrote to his defeated friend: "It is over. It did not end as some twenty million of us hoped it would. Yet we, the disappointed, were never prouder of you or more convinced of the calibre of our candidate than when you made that memorable statement of yours which is so fine and moving in its gallantry. Those were the words of a great man and in themselves representative of a victory of the highest kind. . . .

"Here's to you—and to '56 (and I don't think I need my head examined)."

The chapter on Stevenson in *Through These Men* is immediately preceded by two long chapters on Eisenhower. Published when Eisenhower's first term was coming to a close, it is a well-rounded account of the important personages, including the Vice President and members of the cabinet, with emphasis on the most important cabinet member, John Foster Dulles, Secretary of State. As to Nixon, he made a statement for which he was roundly upbraided by his friend Mary Bingham (Mrs. Barry Bingham) in her review of *Through These Men* published in the *Courier-Journal* for May 20, 1956. "What David Cohn has called 'the blight of objectivity,'" wrote Mrs. Bingham, "somewhat afflicts Mr. Brown's handling of his material. Only the most firmly cultivated objectivity surely could lead a man of his impeccable taste to say that, in the famous Checkers broadcast, Nixon's 'frankness came through as disarming, his honesty beyond question.'" (John had said, however, on the preceding page of his account of the broadcast in which Nixon attempted to justify his acceptance of a private fund to apply against his political expenses as a senator—the revelation of which nearly cost him his nomination—"within the first fifteen minutes of his allotted half-hour Nixon had told all, fighting with every weapon including tear gas.")

As to Eisenhower, one has the odd impression, on rereading now the two chapters devoted to him, that John put the President on the defensive and then proceeded to defend him, with that cultivated objectivity to which Mrs. Bingham was to call attention.

The Eisenhower chapters are in turn preceded by one entitled

"The Trumans Leave the White House." John had been to Washington early in January; on the sixth he saw Mr. Truman for fifteen minutes. He was in the White House again two weeks later, on Inauguration Day. He found Mr. Truman ready to turn over the cares of office, with no regrets either for anything he had done as President or for the end of his term. "He was spruce, kindly, and above fatigue. He held himself erect, moved briskly, and was in top-notch physical form. . . . As a politician long accustomed to the hard blows exchanged in elections, he had forgotten most of the wounds he had given and received during the campaign. As a Democrat, he was sorry to have had his party lose. As a President, he was anxious to have the policies for which he had battled continued here and abroad. As a man, however, he looked forward to the freedom Americans have but which is denied their Presidents."

John had written to Stevenson advising him to let Mr. Truman do his in-fighting for him; a little later on John was looking forward to 1956. As it turned out, Truman's support of Stevenson in 1956 was definitely weaker than it had been four years earlier; he had even favored Averell Harriman for the presidential nomination. John himself wrote to a correspondent in September 1956 that he felt encouraged, but not confident. "Adlai's campaign is far less to my individual liking than the 1952 one—pitched lower, more partisan, and more scolding. Nonetheless it is plainly a campaign that the country likes. . . . I'm certain that he has not changed one iota deep within himself in those qualities which are splendidly and uniquely his."

In November 1955 John had written another long letter to Stevenson: "You may remember that, like many others, I have the impudence to write you from time to time Dutch-uncle letters. Mine at least have the virtue of being very occasional.

"Of course, I am passionately interested in you, your candidacy, and your election. You know that. And I know what a tough spot H.S.T.'s stubborn waverings and Ike's illness have put you in. You have done a magnificent job with the Godkin lectures. And only last night I realized how admirable you are as a travel writer when I found you in competition with John Gunther and Ruark in *Look*. But now I am thinking of November 19 and the announcement of your candidacy. I read with interest your Duluth speech. It was fine for Duluth, but I do hope the announcement will be pitched differently.

"I had a long talk two hours ago with Norman Cousins, who tells me he is going out to see you. He and I both feel so passionately the same way about this speech to come that I trust you will forgive me for daring to offer my advice. The spokesman of the party that is out always suffers the disadvantage of becoming a scold. His is the easy dart-throwing job of the nondoer that makes dramatic critics so universally unpopular. You can throw darts with the most superb felicity. But please, I beg of you, in the speech don't do that. It is too easy. Furthermore, I personally believe at the moment it is very bad politics.

"Ike's illness has changed the whole picture. If he were well, you could stoop to whistle-stopping. But since he is ill and, as I believe and hope, there is every possibility that you will be the next President, I beg of you not to do that. Since Ike's illness has taken him out of politics and made him unassailable, I think it would be tremendously wise of you to make your speech *above* politics, after announcing that you are running.

"Regardless of parties or personal preferences, let's face the facts. Following the heart attack, there was an immense decline in confidence in this country, as the stock market reflected. What the country is looking for is some person who in Ike's manner can restore that lost confidence. I believe you can do it if you will speak as a statesman in the terms of an inaugural address, rather than as a campaigner hitting the tank towns.

"Furthermore, I think—after you have paid the full and proper tribute that I know you feel to Eisenhower as a man—it would be a surprising but immensely popular venture. You could disentangle him from his administration and yet emphasize the outstanding points in his leadership, promising to continue those you think best and giving full credit where credit is due.

"You are much bigger than any of the bosses. Listen to yourself, not them, because you are now the biggest guy in the country.

"Forgive me, and all good luck."

Needless to say, Eisenhower recovered sufficiently to run for a second term, to prove himself once again unbeatable, and to last out his full eight years in the White House and several more thereafter.

On November 9 John wrote Stevenson: "I am just one of the millions who remain faithful to you and grateful to you, too. Once again yours was an extraordinary service to what is best in the democratic processes in this country. I congratulate you on your eloquence and courage, your conscience and industry. Don't ever think that what has been has been in vain. All of us are better for what you are and what you have done."

There are four more chapters in *Through These Men:* they are of substantial length, and in fact occupy the second half of the book. The subjects are Henry Cabot Lodge, Felix Frankfurter, Walter Lippmann, and J. Robert Oppenheimer. "Like anyone else," wrote John in his prefatory note, "I could have chosen others to serve as mirrors of our present. . . . Even if my choices had been different, I would have approached them in the same way. I would have tried to root their present in their past, suggest the backgrounds against which they have moved, and trace the symptomatic changes in their thinking which our changing history has brought about. Above all, I would have written about them as individuals no less than forces, and as forces because of what they are as individuals." He proceeds to repudiate the "great man" theory of history, and to state, quite accurately, that many more persons are involved than those whose names head the chapters.* Yet his remarks, just quoted, are those of a biographer, not of a historian.

* That is why the present author has borrowed Max Beerbohm's title for the title of this chapter, adding "and More."

Of his old friend Henry Cabot Lodge, John writes with personal warmth and detailed knowledge of Lodge's career in public service. In the Senate at the age of thirty-four, he tried to keep this country out of the European war, "accepted the inevitable" by voting for Lend-Lease, and "by May 1942 he had flown to Libya with one of the first American units to arrive in North Africa. There as a major in the first American tank detachment he saw action under General Auchinleck with the British Eighth Army." Recalled to Washington in July, he was told by Secretary of War Henry A. Stimson that he would be of more value as a senator than as a soldier. Lodge chafed at this decision, but ran and was reelected in 1942. After a tour in 1943 with four other senators to investigate the conduct of the war, he resigned from the Senate and rejoined the Army. In 1952 he supported Eisenhower for the nomination, and after the election was appointed Ambassador to the United Nations, with cabinet status. He was still in that post when *Through These Men* was published; the campaign for the Vice Presidency in 1960, the mission to Saigon, and the ambassadorship to the Vatican were still to come. But if the public account was limited by time, this is more than made up for by the personal portrait.

The essay on Felix Frankfurter is more informative and descriptive than anecdotal, though there are a few good stories, and there does emerge a three-dimensional portrait of the man. Frankfurter, it appears, did not like to talk about himself, and referred those who wanted to write about him to his friends. He had many friends, as well as his share of enemies, among them the late Westbrook Pegler. These enemies lend drama to the account of the hearings following Roosevelt's nomination of Frankfurter to the Supreme Court and preceding his confirmation by the Senate. The opposition to Frankfurter arose from several matters: among them were his defense of Sacco and Vanzetti and his active role in the New Deal, where he is shown as playing the part of a highly successful catalytic agent for the President.

The next chapter is entitled "A Preface to Lippmann," Walter Lippmann having written, among numerous other books, *A Preface to Politics* and *A Preface to Morals*. Again he was writing about a friend, though not one of so long standing as Lodge. John accurately calls Lippmann a "philosopher-journalist," and follows his career through his years on *The New Republic,* the *New York World,* and, after the demise of that important liberal newspaper, his syndicated column, "Today and Tomorrow." At Harvard he attracted favorable attention by writing "a blistering review" of *The Privileged Classes* by Barrett Wendell, who assuredly considered himself a privileged character. Another faculty member who "seemed to feel his own superiority beyond question" was George Santayana, but Lippmann became his admirer and disciple. His principal interest, however, was to be politics, not philosophy, and John's chapter traces the course of Lippmann's thinking, including some changes of mind for which he was accused of inconsistency. He had many critics as well as many followers; criticism never got under his skin.

As in the chapter on Frankfurter, the Sacco-Vanzetti case occupies a prominent part in the chapter on Lippmann, who was editor of the *World* at the time of the execution of Sacco and Vanzetti in August 1927. Many people believed—many still do, for the conviction and subsequent execution made a *cause célèbre* of the case—that the trial had been grossly unfair, and that the report of Governor Alvin T. Fuller's advisory committee which reviewed the case and upheld the verdict left much to be desired. The committee was headed by President A. Lawrence Lowell of Harvard. At that time a popular columnist was Heywood Broun, who had been at Harvard with Lippmann, and who wrote in the *New York World* a series of vigorous, highly charged attacks on the Lowell committee.

Broun approached the Sacco-Vanzetti case frankly as an emotionalist, Lippmann no less frankly as a logician. . . . Lippmann was as disturbed by Broun's violence as Broun was amazed at Lippmann's calm. Lippmann felt that such unrestrained invective was more an individual indulgence than a public service, since it was bound to anger Governor Fuller and stiffen his resolve not to stay the execution. As Lippmann saw it, it was all very well for Broun, who did not face the electric chair, to insist out of the most sincere high-mindedness that nothing less than a pardon or a new trial was satisfactory to him. To Lippmann, however, the saving of the lives of Sacco and Vanzetti was more important than the airing of anyone's views.

American journalism, so often charged with irresponsibility, was never more responsible than in the full-page editorial by him which appeared in the *World* on August 19, 1927. It remains a model of cool reasoning and detailed exposition. Facts, not fury, were Lippmann's concern, and he marshaled them with masterly logic as he reviewed the case, stressed the doubts it had raised, and pleaded for a stay of execution and a new trial. On the day following the execution Lippmann carried moderation to a point which outraged Broun. He wrote an editorial in which he praised such valiant defenders of Sacco and Vanzetti as Felix Frankfurter at the same time that he paid his respects to the members of the Lowell committee for having bravely done a disagreeable duty. Broun held that such "sportsmanship," while desirable at a Harvard-Yale game, was shocking when, as it seemed to him, two innocent men had been murdered.

Enough has been quoted from *Through These Men* to give an idea of its flavor and style, and perhaps enough has been said to give an idea of its organization. There is no question that John's venture into fresh woods and pastures new, as represented by *Through These Men,* was a successful one. If there is one element which a reader who had followed John's other writings might miss here, it is his wit. John's wit was spontaneous, as everybody knows who knew him. In an essay of 1949, "Pleasant Agony," he said that writing did not come easily to him.

When I think of the one-legged kittens that land on my pages; when I remember the false starts, illegible scribblings, unfinished sentences, discarded drafts, changed constructions, and altered words which mark my beginnings, my continuings, and my endings, I blush with shame and, like the voyagers in Dante's realm, abandon all hope.

Maybe so, but none of this agony went into those passages, however brief, that were unquestionably spontaneous, witty eruptions of the geyser. Also his letters—most of them, at all events—

are the fruits of that same spontaneity; surely he could not have been so prolific a correspondent if agony had been involved. And none of his letters are perfunctory.

Whatever qualities of John's earlier writing may be absent from *Through These Men,* they are more than made up for by the force and character of the final chapter, "In the Matter of J. Robert Oppenheimer." Mrs. Bingham, who had commented adversely on John's objectivity regarding Mr. Nixon, calls this résumé of the Oppenheimer case "sensitive, fully explored and deeply sympathetic . . . an important addition to the file on that tormented subject." The chapter on Oppenheimer is about as long as the two chapters on Eisenhower put together. The story is a complicated one; although it is now twenty years old, most people must be familiar at least with its outlines. Many loyal and thoughtful Americans considered the proceedings outrageous and, on the part of some of Oppenheimer's opponents, vindictive. Beginning with a letter to J. Edgar Hoover written by William Liscum Borden, formerly executive director of the Joint (Congressional) Committee on Atomic Energy, the matter —that is to say, Borden's accusations—went to Eisenhower, and to other high officials including especially Admiral Lewis L. Strauss, chairman of the Atomic Energy Commission. With Oppenheimer's refusal to resign as a consultant to the commission, the Personel Security Board, a committee of three headed by Gordon Gray, took over and conducted an investigation that lasted from April 12 to May 6, 1954, and resulted in a two-to-one decision to recommend lifting Oppenheimer's security clearance. John comments on Gray's "strange tolerance," during the hearings, "of the ruthless tactics of the Board's counsel, Roger Robb, who again and again behaved as if he were a district attorney out for blood." The AEC backed up the board's recommendation by a vote of four to one. The dissenter on the board was Dr. Ward V. Evans; on the commission, Dr. Henry DeWolf Smyth. Before his appointment to the Atomic Energy Commission, Smyth had been chairman of the Physics Department at Princeton. He was the author of *Atomic Energy for Military Purposes,* popularly known as "The Smyth Report," released by the United States government in August 1945 and published in book form by the Princeton University Press in September.

Senator Joseph R. McCarthy had not yet been punctured by Joseph N. Welch during the Army-McCarthy hearings; that was not to happen until June. McCarthy had been taking every opportunity to horn into every situation that might create trouble for Eisenhower and publicity for himself; John thinks it possible that the shadow of McCarthy may have added influence to Borden's letter. John believes that the procedures followed at least had the good result of saving Oppenheimer "from McCarthy, the Klieg lights, the cameras, the microphones, and the cruel and tawdry circusdom of a Congressional hearing as conducted by him." McCarthy was still chairman of the Senate permanent investigations subcommittee; he did not finally lose his influence until the Senate voted to censure him in December 1954. The November elections had returned a Democratic majority to Congress, so that the Republican committee chairmen were going to be replaced anyhow. But in McCarthy's absence from the proceedings, perhaps Robb was enough.

John's chapter follows the case in detail; there is no space to summarize it here, and a summary would in any event lose the dramatic impact of his presentation. John had not only studied the voluminous records, but had gone to see Oppenheimer and interviewed him at length. On May 7, 1956, Oppenheimer wrote to John: "I am glad that you wanted to put me into the book. I am, of course, not one to judge the product, except . . . confirming that it is, as far as my knowledge goes, remarkably free of error. I have read, and liked enormously, what you have written of others. . . . It is clear to me that to the last chapter [the one on Dr. Oppenheimer] you have brought even more study, more struggle, and more thought. I only hope that what I think of the chapters I can judge, others will think of the chapter I cannot."

In John's files there is a note dated May 10, 1956, from Senator Clinton P. Anderson of New Mexico, who was at that time chairman of the Joint Congressional Committee on Atomic Energy. Senator Anderson wrote, "I had hoped that if you came down here we might discuss the chapter on Dr. Oppenheimer." And added in the margin, with a pen: "You have the right dope on that!—C.P.A."

*Through These Men* had a good press—John was by no means a prophet without honor in his own country—but by far the best review was that in the *Times Literary Supplement* of September 21, 1956: a long review—as Edith Hamilton was to write John, more of a tribute than a review—with emphasis on what the book had to tell Europeans, the English in particular, about our political character—and characters. It concludes: "Mr. Brown's mind and methods offer Europeans a delightful, informative guide to contemporary American democracy. They should mark it well. It may reflect much of their future."

## Chapter Eleven

# Harvard Again

In 1949 John was elected to membership on the Board of Overseers of Harvard College, for the customary term of six years. He had never lost connection with his alma mater; as we have seen, he had given courses at the Harvard Summer School for four years beginning in 1937, and in the spring of 1940 he delivered the Winthrop Ames Memorial Lectures at the university. The subjects: English Comic Writers: Wilde, Maugham, and Coward; Modern Tragedy: Eugene O'Neill and Maxwell Anderson; The American Theatre Comes of Age: Barry, Kaufman, and others; and The Drama of Social Significance: Odets, Saroyan, etc. (John seldom printed anything of lecture length; just how this material was worked into his books may be surmised from the essay "American Tragedy" [1949] published in *Still Seeing Things* and reprinted in *Dramatis Personae,* where it is followed by an essay called "The Tragic Blueprint," from the year of the lectures. "American Tragedy" is specifically concerned with O'Neill and Anderson.)

In 1947 a classmate, Robert F. Bradford, was elected Governor of Massachusetts; some members of the class were inspired to solicit contributions for the presentation of a chair by the class. John remarked to a classmate that he would be glad to contribute if it were to be an electric chair. Unable to resist a joke which he did not intend seriously, he was equally unable to resist abandoning it altogether, so when the time came he sent a generous contribution, with a covering letter: "Herewith my humble contribution to the unelectrified chair that we of '23 are presenting to the Governor. Will you please give Bob my warmest congratulations?"

In 1948 John was the principal speaker at the twenty-fifth reunion of his class. The talk has unfortunately not been preserved, but is remembered as a running comment on the autobiographies prepared by all the members of the class, except a few reluctant recalcitrants, and published in a stout and handsome volume shortly before the reunion, which took place in June, at commencement. Better records were kept of John's address to the fortieth class reunion. He spoke of the class as being "older in a younger America," and of Harvard, "where we have room for everything and space for nothing." As to the class, "in Shakespeare's chronology, he would be in the fifth age, the age of the justice, with good capon lined, full of wise saws and modern instances. But we are at once younger and older than that." Again he read from the class report some of the autobiographies, and commented on them, but the fortieth reunion volume was considerably briefer than the twenty-fifth. Also, as a consequence of time and tide, there were considerably fewer biographies. John's theme was the process of aging, and he accused Cicero in *De Senectute* of false optimism, comparing him with William Lyon Phelps, who had written of aging in a book called *Happiness*.

Harvard is the only major university to have a bicameral system of government. It is interesting to note that the university, in its printed description of the duties of the Board of Overseers, speaks of the Board as "one of the two central governing boards of Harvard University," but the Board itself is called the Board of Overseers of Harvard College—as the other board, commonly known as the Corporation, is officially the President and Fellows of Harvard College. The Corporation conducts the ordinary, day-to-day business, along with the faculty; the view of the Overseers is supposed to be "a longer, more contemplative one, reviewing carefully the actions of the Corporation and the Faculties to insure that the University remains true to its obligation to maintain high standards as a place of learning, serving the University with their counsel and taking action or offering advice as may be useful or appropriate."

The Overseers are nominated by a standing committee of the Associated Harvard Alumni, and each year five members are elected to the Board, which has thirty members. The term of office is six years. The Board of Overseers cannot initiate any action, and has no power over finances, which are entirely in the hands of the Corporation, but its approval is required for all faculty and administrative appointments to run more than one year and for the award of regular and honorary degrees, "and important matters of business are submitted by the Corporation that the Overseers 'may consent thereto if they see fit.' "

"Each member of the Board is expected to serve on one or more of the Visiting Committees established both to evaluate the effectiveness of the schools and institutions within the University and to provide them with encouragement and advice. Each Overseer chairs at least one Visiting Committee." The chairman of each Visiting Committee is supposed to be an Overseer; the other members need not even be alumni, but usually are. Every department of the university is Visited annually, "except for those Committees to Visit the Departments of the Faculty of Arts and Sciences, which meet biennially."

Apparently John's first Visiting Committee assignment was to the Committee to Visit the Arnold Arboretum; he remained on this committee only one year. For so urban a person as John, this experience may have proved educational. In 1950 he was appointed as a member of the Committee to Visit the Graduate School of Business Administration, and he remained on this committee until 1955. The assignment seems incongruous, and seemed so to John, who wrote to Dean Donald David of the Business School that this appointment would be "catastrophic to the financial security of the Republic." Evidently John was appointed to this committee by way of providing contrast to the other members—the phrase "court jester" has been heard in this connection.

His other committee assignments were more appropriate: Romance Languages and Literature, 1949–55 (chairman, 1950–53); Slavic Languages and Literature, 1950–52; University Library, 1950–55; English, 1949–58, and again, after his term as Overseer had expired, 1961–67—he was chairman of this committee in 1953–55, and vice-chairman in 1964–67. He served on the Committee to Visit Harvard College, 1954–63, and on Coordinating Committees for the Biological Sciences, 1949–50, and the Humanities, 1949–55. It can readily be seen that these activities were time-consuming, in addition to the meetings—at least eight a year—of the Board of Overseers itself. It can also be seen that they considerably enlarged John's range of friends and acquaintances.

As a member of the Committee to Visit the English Department, John often took the opportunity to visit classes, such as those of Professor Harry Levin and Professor Archibald MacLeish—both good friends of John's; MacLeish became a very close friend. On one occasion John dropped in on a class of MacLeish's in a course designed to elucidate the nature of poetry and what it can express that prose cannot. On this occasion MacLeish was discussing Ezra Pound. (The memory was still vivid of the Bollingen Award to Pound and the controversy caused by Robert Hillyer's attack on Pound and on the Award in *The Saturday Review*.) At the end of the class John went to MacLeish and said that he had always loathed and despised Pound, but that MacLeish had made him see Pound in terms of the poem he had been discussing, "Hugh Selwyn Mauberley."

The proceedings of the Board of Overseers are not made public; like those of the Corporation, they are known by their results, and by what references are made to them in the President's Annual Report. One story has leaked concerning John's influence as an Overseer. During one of the years of his tenure,

two distinguished men were under consideration for professor-
ships in the History Department. The objection was raised that
both men were at work on similar projects, which were biographies of Franklin D. Roosevelt; some of the Overseers apparently
felt that one was enough and that a choice should be made.
John remarked, in rebuttal, that he knew of an instance where
four different biographers chose the same subject. After a pause
for effect, he said, "Their names were Matthew, Mark, Luke, and
John." Both Mr. Frank Freidel and Mr. Arthur Schlesinger, Jr.,
were appointed.

Among the associations which John's service as Overseer
brought him was a renewal of his friendship with McGeorge
Bundy, who in 1953 became Dean of the Faculty of Arts and
Sciences, having previously been associate professor of government. Also he came to know President James B. Conant well.
Back in the 1930s, when John began teaching in the Harvard Summer School, he reported to a friend that Mr. Conant, on hearing
John's name proposed, remarked that he would be very glad to
have John Nicholas Brown. Now John Nicholas Brown of
Rhode Island was and still is a gentleman of considerable sub-
stance and distinction, a philanthropist and yachtsman. John
Mason Brown was achieving his own distinction, but not yet
any considerable substance. He did ultimately acquire a rowboat
at his summer place in Connecticut. (On an occasion years later,
John received a telephone call from some one who was trying to
reach the other Brown; the secretary who placed the call asked,
"Is this Mr. John Nicholas Brown?" "No," replied John, "he is
John *N.* Brown; I am John *M.* Brown; that is your initial mistake.")

Mr. Conant retired as President of Harvard in 1953, and was
succeeded by Nathan M. Pusey, with whom John's relations were
to be altogether cordial and cooperative throughout John's various activities at Harvard, during and following his term as an
Overseer. Harvard alumni will not be the only ones to recall the
courage and independence with which the new president fought

off the attacks of Senator Joseph R. McCarthy on certain members of the Harvard faculty at the outset of Mr. Pusey's administration. This was the period when McCarthy was at the height of his pernicious influence. Among his other assignments, John was chairman of the Committee on Honorary Degrees for the Board of Overseers during the academic years 1953–54. In 1954 Henry Cabot Lodge was to receive an honorary degree. On May 21, John wrote to Dean Bundy: "I know nothing about the writing of Harvard's citations. But I have read the first very rough draft of Cabot Lodge's Commencement Day speech. Although it needs a lot of working over, I think it has its points to make which are good in themselves and good for Harvard, too. His theme, not as yet clarified or developed as it should be, is the search for truth in education, the freedom for which Harvard has always stood, and the answer almost daily at the U.N. is just the opposite of truth. [This was during the first Eisenhower Administration, and Mr. Lodge was the U.S. Ambassador to the United Nations.] At one point, as I recall, he says it is incredible that so great an institution as Harvard, with its many and superb contributions to truth, should ever in the public mind be associated with what is pink or red.

"God knows (and I do, too, from my lecture tours) that a frightening number of people up and down the country do feel that Harvard is Communist-infested. It is a myth that needs emphatic killing, especially in these days of Furry [Professor (of physics) Wendell Furry, the faculty member most conspicuously under attack by McCarthy] when McCarthy has trained his guns on the University.

"I was wondering if an oblique point could not be scored in the phrasing of Cabot's citation without having Nate [Mr. Pusey] enter into any unnecessary and unwanted controversy. I have in mind some such phrase as 'stalwart champion of the United Nations as a world forum and a means to peace, and in that forum a quick-minded and eloquent defender of the truth that free men cherish.'

"If you think I am 'way off the beam, toss this into your waste-paper basket. If, however, you think there is anything, even the smallest seed, in the suggestion, you might bring it up with Nate. I don't think some such citation would do any harm."

The citation, which follows, is by no means out of line with John's suggestion.

HENRY CABOT LODGE
Doctor of Laws

Son of Harvard, servant of the Commonwealth,
an eloquent defender in the United Nations
of the truth that free men cherish.

John's principal interest at Harvard was the reestablishment of the drama as an important activity of the university. He had been profoundly disappointed when Harvard allowed George Pierce Baker to take himself and his 47 Workshop to Yale. In 1931 John made an abortive attempt to find support for the establishment of a George Pierce Baker Memorial Scholarship at Harvard; but 1931 was a poor year for fund-raising. In President Conant's Report to the Board of Overseers for the year 1950–51, he wrote, "Harvard is the only great university without such a theatre." And in his annual report for the same academic year: "The faculty is anxious to encourage those many undergraduate organizations that regularly produce plays; their efforts are now greatly hampered by the total lack of acceptable facilities." He called for a "scheme of fellowships connected with the dramatic arts" and "the construction of a theatre building to serve as a focal center." Whether or not John had a hand in these reports cannot be definitely said; he probably did. John had also drawn up a list of suggested names for a committee to further the project, not long before he received a letter from Professor Archibald MacLeish with the suggestion for reviving the campaign for a theatre.

In the first year of his presidency, 1953, Mr. Pusey said he was "all for" the theatre project. In a letter from John to Dean Bundy of October 20, 1953, he continues, after an expression of enthusiasm for Mr. Pusey's installation, as follows: "I do believe that he is really interested in the theatre project, and I hope as soon as he understands that it is already in the works he will give me a green light to go on with the fund-raising campaign. . . . My concern is not with a department. My interest is in getting an adequate theatre built." The phrase "fund-raising campaign" is a reference to the original plan to raise $1,000,000; there were numerous pledges but there was a time limit, and it was reached before the required sum was pledged. Some of the contributors renewed their pledges, others directed that their contributions be diverted to other causes. The matter was to become moot (not to say academic).

In a report dated October 8, 1956, President Pusey announced "A Program for Harvard College." The report was addressed to alumni and friends of Harvard. It stressed the need for higher faculty salaries, more Houses (like Eliot House, Dunster House, and the others in which undergraduates had lived since the inauguration of the House Plan during the Lowell administration); apartment houses for students and younger faculty members, to enable them to establish closer relations; new facilities for the Chemistry and Astronomy departments; a new health center. Various other needs were mentioned, including the need for a theatre. It was to be a three-year program to raise $82,000,000.

Once more out of chronological order, it is convenient to note here that on March 28, 1958, there was an hour-long radio program in support of the Program for Harvard College, in which at least twenty distinguished persons participated, including Senator John F. Kennedy, Robert Frost, McGeorge Bundy, Leonard Bernstein, Barbara Ward, Howard Lindsay, James B. Conant, and John Mason Brown. The program was broadcast over the nation-wide network of the Columbia Broadcasting System; Harvard University paid for the time. In addition, the program was carried by the Armed Forces Radio Services, the Voice of America, and several broadcasting companies in Europe, South America, and Asia—in order to reach as many Harvard alumni and other friends of Harvard as possible. Later the program was rebroadcast as a public service over the network of the National Broadcasting Company. In addition to the contributions by the sundry celebrities, there were "sound sequences of recorded statements" by undergraduates. The Editorial Committee comprised Professor Archibald MacLeish; Eric Larrabee, '43, then associate editor of *Harper's* magazine; and William Bentinck-Smith, '37, assistant to President Pusey. The executive producer was Laurence O. Pratt, '26, director of public relations of A Program for Harvard College. "Commercials" were contributed by President Pusey and by Alexander M. White, '25, general chairman of the program. It was reported that $35,000,000 was already on hand in cash or pledges. "Harvard handles the 60-minute stanza like a Palace pro * with confidence and pride," reported *Variety*.

Frank Pemberton wrote an article in the Autumn 1960 issue of *Harvard Today,* in which he said that "more than two years before the beginning of the Program for Harvard College, John Mason Brown, '23, together with Professors Archibald MacLeish and Harry T. Levin, began holding informal discussions about providing a new theatre for Harvard and its sister institution, Radcliffe. [Of Harvard's relation to Radcliffe, President Conant had once observed, "Harvard is not coeducational in theory, only in practice."] It was from these discussions that there developed the first concrete proposals later incorporated into the Program for Harvard, for this remarkable theatre."

Previously the Harvard Dramatic Club, the Harvard Theatre Group, and the Radcliffe Idler Club had to use Sanders Theatre in Memorial Hall, the New Lecture Hall, and the dining rooms of the various Houses for their productions.

What made the fund-raising campaign moot was the gift in 1957 of $1,100,000 by John L. Loeb, '24, an investment banker,

---

* Reference to the Palace Theatre on Broadway, where the best of the old vaudeville acts had been played.

for a modern theatre center for Harvard and Radcliffe. *The New York Times* of June 2, 1957, announced this gift, and the *Times* story credited Bundy, MacLeish, and Brown with having worked toward the theatre. John promptly disclaimed credit for himself; he wrote to David McCord on June 17: "I am delighted about the Loeb gift for the Harvard theatre. Believe me, I deserve no credit for it. Mac [Dean Bundy] and Nate are the ones who brought it all about. I only dreamed for many years of what they have made possible."

John prepared a two-page report for the Committee to Visit Harvard College, mentioning that Mr. Loeb's gift had been received. The idea was *not* to have Harvard's theatre become a professional training school like the Yale Drama School. The *Harvard Crimson,* the undergraduate daily paper, reported on March 9, 1959, that work was to begin at once on the Loeb Drama Center, to be completed in fifteen to eighteen months, as announced by President Pusey. The main auditorium was to seat 515, with a smaller experimental theatre to seat 100. The design was by a firm of Cambridge architects, Hugh A. Stubbins & Associates. The director from the outset has been Professor Robert H. Chapman, formerly of the English Department; before that he had taught speech and drama elsewhere. He had also collaborated with Louis Coxe in the dramatization of Melville's *Billy Budd.*

On August 6, 1960, shortly before the opening of the center, John wrote to David McCord from Stonington: "I had read the release about Chapman and wish him and the theatre well. He took me, and Preston and Meredith, through it some months back, and even as an embryo it looked a very exciting place. If I am invited to the opening, let's go together for the sake of old times and G.P. But I very much doubt, with Harvard's genius for amnesia, if I am remembered, and it really doesn't matter anyway. They have the theatre. That does matter." John was indeed invited.

"I send you a piece I did on John Marquand [recently deceased] for the Book-of-the-Month Club *News,* which I thought might, in part at least, be of interest to readers of the *Bulletin.* [The Harvard Alumni *Bulletin,* of which McCord was for many years the editor.] I do think the $10,000 prize in his name is a fine and exciting tribute.*

"Think of me at Breadloaf. I loved my summers there; just think when A. Woollcott, Red Lewis, and La Thompson [Dorothy Thompson, who was Mrs. Sinclair Lewis] were neighbors, and the dear Otis Skinners (and even Cal the Cool) nearby, and Benny DeVoto was hot on the spot. Ah, me! [DeVoto had died in 1955, but the impression he left on Breadloaf was indelible—as it was everywhere he had been.]

"The book goes [John's biography of Robert E. Sherwood]. Cassie and I, at the lecture season's end, splurged and took a dream trip to Sicily and Italy (for fun) and England (for fun and work) and now in this beloved little town I am happily working all day, each day.

"I reread your piece on Churchill at Harvard last week. What a honey it is! Repeated congratulations."

Not long before the Loeb gift was announced, John saw an undergraduate production by the Dramatic Club of *Hamlet,* uncut. He was sufficiently impressed to telegraph both President Pusey and Dean Bundy, on his return to New York, urging them to see the play: "It is as fine a plea for the theatre project as I know of." And on January 8, 1957, he wrote to the director, Stephen A. Aaron, a long letter of praise, reading in part as follows: "You undertook a Herculean job, and carried it out in a big, bold, and imaginative way. I have seen only one other production of the uncut *Hamlet*—Maurice Evans's. I realized in its presence, as I did in the presence of yours, how infinitely much we lose by being offered the usual truncated scripts.

* This prize was offered by the Book-of-the-Month Club for the best first novel by an American or Canadian author published during the eighteen months following Marquand's death. This made the time limit December 31, 1961. The novel chosen was *The Morning and the Evening* by Joan Williams.

"I think to a remarkable degree you brought out the full richness of the text, giving its meanings and relationships the proper priority, and abstaining from easy or showy tricks of staging." *

The Loeb Drama Center opened in October 1960, with a production of *Troilus and Cressida* presented by the Dramatic Club. There was a preview on October 14, followed by eight evening performances October 15–22, and a matinee on the twenty-second. On October 27 John wrote to President and Mrs. Pusey: "Cassie and I have been very much in orbit since that unforgettable evening when you opened the Loeb Theatre. I had to run up to Durham that same night to help open a new Arts Center at the University of New Hampshire. The day after that we flew to Belgium for a week and are just back.

"The University of New Hampshire has a lovely building but it does not compare in grace, beauty, dignity, and pliability with the Loeb. I cannot pretend that *Troilus and Cressida* is one of my favorite plays. I do know, however, that the Harvard Theatre is my favorite theatre in this country. I am so proud of it for Harvard and so proud of you for all that you have done to champion it and make it possible. From the beginning of your presidency you have been its staunch and imaginative friend. You shouldn't have mentioned me the other night, but, believe me, I was touched by your doing so. . . ."

On the same date he wrote a similar letter to Dean Bundy, saying, "It is a beautiful theatre. . . . And it is you and Nate who, above all others, have made it possible."

In 1958 John, no longer an Overseer, had felt obliged by the pressure of other obligations to turn down an opportunity to become president of the Harvard Alumni Association. He was,

* Mr. Aaron, now artistic director of the Washington Theater Club, in Washington, D.C., supplies the further information that the production was given in Sanders Theatre at Harvard. The orchestra seats were removed to produce a contemporary version of the Globe Theatre. The producer "chose to simulate daylight in order to give the audience a sense of what it must have been like to watch the original production at the Globe in 1601." So the ghost of Hamlet's father walked the day instead of the night. The participants, with the exception of one graduate student, were all undergraduates.

however, still a member of the Committee to Visit Harvard College, and in connection with a forthcoming meeting of that committee he wrote on November 3, 1960, to David W. Bailey, secretary of the Board of Overseers, a letter largely devoted to the new theatre: "Wasn't it thrilling the other night when, in the glorious excellence of the Loeb Drama Center, Harvard at last achieved a theatre! When I saw you, I thought back to the long campaign, to H. T. Parker and the *Transcript*. And when I walked back to the Commander [Hotel] and passed Brattle Hall, I again thought long and hard of you and even more insistently than at *Troilus and Cressida* or at Nate's for dinner. The smiling ghost of G.P. appeared to me. I wish he had lived to see that night."

In March 1961 Louise W. Bray, whose *Mis' Mercy* had been produced by the 47 Workshop in John's day, sent John a copy of a recent issue of the *Radcliffe Quarterly* which contained an article of hers on the opening of the Loeb Drama Center. John acknowledged it on April 3: "I couldn't believe my ears when, at the opening of the Loeb Theatre, no mention was made of G.P. Hence I am doubly delighted to have you and Agnes Morgan, Eleanor Hinkley, Dorothy [Sands], and Doris [Halman] write so feelingly and well about Mr. Baker. [All these women were connected with the theatre.]

"The older I grow, the more depressed I become at what older people forget and younger people have no way of knowing. I agree with you that the argument Baker should not have been mentioned because he went to Yale makes no sense at all, and ignoring his long and important services at Harvard and Radcliffe is the utmost in ingratitude. You and I know the reasons for his leaving and realize that, if Harvard had let him have his way, he would have stayed there. He never walked out on Harvard; Harvard walked out on him."

Chapter Twelve

# Family and Friends

John wrote about his family spasmodically and by no means co-piously. His longest treatment of the Brown family is in his book *Morning Faces;* this was published in 1949, but the writing had started, and separate chapters had begun to appear in *The Saturday Review,* as early as 1945, when Preston was nine and Meredith five. The war, from which John had returned a year before, was just over, and naturally John had on his mind all the feelings of a man rejoining his family, all the realizations of his good fortune in being able to do so. He expresses these in a short chapter describing the annual exercises of the final day of the school year —the private school which Preston and Meredith attended. "There are many, many moments when, in spite of ourselves . . . all of us find our eyes filled, our throats hurting. No tragedy is more moving in its misfortunes than youth is in its lack of them. . . . The helplessness of parenthood is its chief anguish." One of John's friends remembers that he worried about the boys when they were at camp, and jumped when the telephone rang.

John very wisely put this chapter second instead of first. It does not set the tone of the book, all the rest of which is humorous. A birthday party at the rodeo, where John spent most of the afternoon taking his sons' guests to the men's room. "I soon reached the conclusion that Aristotle must have had a rodeo rather than a tragedy in mind, when he spoke of the purgation of the emotions through pity and fear." And there was the boy who inquired, " 'What's a steer?' while every adult head in the row in front of me turned around to await the answer." There is the chapter, previously mentioned, on dancing school; the chapter on taking the boys fishing in their rowboat in Long Island Sound off Stonington, Connecticut, where the Browns usually spent their summers—the rowboat was the *Cassie B.;* the chapter about taking Preston to see Maurice Evans's production of the "G. I. *Hamlet*"—the cut version done for the troops—and Preston's genuine enjoyment of it, at the age of nine (but unlike his father as a boy in Louisville, Preston did not become stage-struck); the chapter, previously mentioned, about taking the boys to the Metropolitan Museum on a Sunday afternoon, with the inevitable separation and frantic search for the missing boy, who of course considered that his father and brother were lost, not he. The book ends with Preston's departure for his first year at boarding school (Groton); but perhaps most memorable of all is "Westward Ho!," the account of a trip that John and Preston made to Colorado when Preston was eleven, a trip that, alas, can no longer be made in the same way: the Twentieth Century Limited is no more. It still existed, however, in 1951, when John took Meredith on a similar trip to the West, but to Montana instead of Colorado. They went to Glacier Park, where they rode and fished. First, though, there was the same kind of royal, red-carpet experience on board the Century that John had described in *Morning Faces*. He loved trains (a good thing, too, considering how much time he had to spend on them during his lecture trips). Then several days in Chicago, where Meredith could not be detached by persuasion or force from the Field Museum. Meredith was a natural-born natural historian; at the age of eight or thereabouts he had developed an interest in volcanoes and became quite knowledgeable about them. In Chicago John finally rebelled, saying that he could not bear the sight of another stuffed eagle. So they took the Vista-Dome, on the Great Northern, to Glacier.

Evidently the trip went well—it's a pity John never got round to writing an account of it; although they acquired a guide with ambition to write for publication, and who attached himself to John much as the author of the unpublished manuscript "Forty Years an Ohio Doctor" attached himself to Sheridan Whiteside in *The Man Who Came to Dinner*. The riding was enjoyable (though there was another occasion when John, on a visit to Mary Miller in Arizona, undertook a ride of thirty miles or more in a single day, resulting in a loss of skin from a vital area, and a condition requiring the services of a physician). In 1953 Meredith went with his father to Utah, where John was to lecture.

There had been other trips which John never got round to recording; one is worth a flashback. In 1935, before Bread Loaf, John and Cassie took a Scandinavian trip, both by land and by sea, as Xenophon put it. They were accompanied by Cassie's brother, Dr. Richard Meredith, and their friend J. Hampton Barnes of Philadelphia. Cassie mainly remembers her duties as porter and courier at every change of trains. "Kate"—they must have been in a Shakespearean mood to call her that—"Kate, you go ahead, cross the tracks to the other train and get a compartment. And don't forget to take the coats on the racks."

In June 1953 he wrote to his Aunt Susan (widow of Uncle Preston) to thank her for some gifts, and adds: "This morning Aunt Mary, Cassie and I went to the Buckley School for Meredith's Commencement. We were really awfully proud of him. He had the highest average in the school—94—and therefore got the school's gold medal for scholarship and had the privilege of carrying the American flag in General MacArthur's presence (his son graduated). . . .

"During the past week from Groton we had equally cheering news from Preston. He wrote that he had just been made assistant baseball manager and editor-in-chief of *The Grotonian*. I think this shows a happy and healthy diversity of interests."

Three of the chapters from *Morning Faces* were to be repeated, two in *Seeing Things* and one in *Seeing More Things* ("Thrift, thrift, Horatio!"); except for the letter quoted above, there is little or nothing about the boys in their teens, at Groton and Harvard (where both made distinguished records), and in their early twenties at the Harvard Law School. One might assume that John, having for so many years depended on lecturing to maintain his standard of living, a career which took him away from his family so much of the time, wanted his boys to enjoy the benefits and pleasures of a less peripatetic life, and so influenced them; but the decision to go to law school was entirely their own.

As we have seen, John kept up a correspondence with friends all over the country whom he saw regularly on his lecture trips. To one such family, the Bruners of Des Moines, John wrote in October 1961 expressing his pride in both his sons. Preston had just passed his bar examinations; Meredith had graduated *summa cum laude* from Harvard College, and had won a traveling fellowship of $3000, enough to take him around the world.

With some of his other friends John corresponded regularly and intimately. He was on a first-name basis with everyone from Dean Acheson to Gene Tunney. His papers contain a considerable number of letters of condolence. According to David McCord, John said that when his friends died he had to believe in God—but God must be a Spaniard because he took such long siestas.

John was at the mercy of his own sense of humor, and could be quite outrageous when inspired. The inspiration of humor—the chance to say something amusing, and his wit was invariably amusing—was an irresistible force, and John by no means an immovable body. But he could disarm those few who might have occasionally taken umbrage by rejoinders like this: "My face is redder than the sea through which Moses made the first amphibious crossing."

One listener remembers a lecture of John's, given soon after he took leave of the Navy, in which—if the listener's memory is accurate—John said that Preston and Meredith came into the bathroom with him every morning hoping to see him cut himself shaving. Also, that in order to get them to read good books, he forbade them to read *Treasure Island* and *Huckleberry Finn*.

Meredith says there is nothing in this; they did stay with him while he was shaving, but for purposes of conversation, not *schadenfreude;* and that John himself read *Treasure Island* aloud to them. Nevertheless, it is quite possible that John gave the lecture as described; his friends would not put it past him. In any event he wrote a piece for *The Saturday Review* (May 10, 1947) in which he says that he lost the boys' attention after one chapter of *Treasure Island.*

Many of the anecdotes contributed by John's friends to this book must be given piecemeal; one does not lead to another except by virtue of having concerned John. To his friend Alfred de Liagre, Jr., who had been made a Chevalier of the Legion of Honor, he wrote in 1950: "I learn from this morning's paper that the French Government has at last caught up with you. For years, of course, I have known that you were part of a Cheval. But now I am overjoyed to learn that you are a full-fledged Chevalier." To Norman Cousins he once remarked: "I don't mind your looking so young, but you look positively prenatal." To another friend, he said of Cousins, who signed his editorials in *The Saturday Review* with his initials, that "N.C." should be taken to signify New Christ.

That friend, previously mentioned, was John K. Hutchens, then book reviewer on the New York *Herald-Tribune,* later to become, as a judge of the Book-of-the-Month Club, a colleague of John's. Hutchens remembers being taken to lunch by John at the Century Club. After finishing their cocktails, and being about to ascend to the dining room one flight above, John took Hutchens to the door of the reading room, and said, in the stage whisper of a professional lecturer, "That is the prostate room." Hutchens reports a certain rustling of papers among the members who overheard the remark. (John had a right to make the remark, as one who had had, or was going to have, a prostate operation himself.)

Alfred de Liagre, Jr., tells several stories in addition to the one about John's remark, previously quoted, when Cassie commented on his lecture schedule. Once when John and Cassie were at dinner at the de Liagres', the host had John's new book and asked him to autograph it. John complied, with the following: "Inscribed with admiration and in friendship," and signed it Alfred de Liagre, Jr.

John had an unfortunate habit of telephoning his friends and pretending to be somebody else. He did this once to a publishing friend, pretending to be Walter Winchell looking for items for his column. He had on occasion done the same to de Liagre. So, when de Liagre received a call from some one purporting to be Mayor John V. Lindsay, he assumed it was John, and kidded around until he discovered that it really was Lindsay, who wanted to enlist him in the service of the city. On another occasion, John's friend Francis Henry Taylor, then director of the Metropolitan Museum of Art, received a call after he had gone to bed, perhaps about eleven thirty, from some one who announced that Cardinal Spellman was calling. Annoyed and exasperated, Taylor went to the telephone prepared to give John a piece of his mind in no uncertain terms, but was deterred by an influence from on high—or at least from the vicinity of Saint Patrick's Cathedral—most fortunately, because it was indeed His Eminence calling.

John's friendship with de Liagre may be better illustrated by a serious anecdote. Archibald MacLeish's play *J.B.* was produced by de Liagre just on the eve of New York's most paralyzing newspaper strike; the absence of reviews could have ruined the play. John, being no longer a professional drama critic, was able to agree to de Liagre's request that he go and see the play, and if he liked it, give a few lines to Edward R. Murrow for possible quotation on his television program. John did think well of the play (which subsequently received the Pulitzer Prize), Murrow quoted him, and there were long lines at the box office the next day.

Mrs. Adrian Lambert has supplied several stories. An old friend of Cassie's from her native Harrisburg was the party of the first part in a prolonged courtship; he used to come to New York every Christmas and get Cassie to go with him to Saks to pick out a present for the party of the second part. After several such occasions, John remarked, "What this courtship needs is less Saks and more sex."

It happened that Mrs. Lambert's and Cassie's birthdays were exactly a month apart, and they had a habit of celebrating together, not necessarily with any one else present. One year, however, on Mrs. Lambert's birthday, there was a large dinner party. It had been agreed to say nothing about the birthday, but John let it out at dinner and suggested that each person present give Mrs. Lambert something he or she was wearing, whereupon one of the guests took off her diamond-and-emerald earrings and necklace and promptly dropped them in her lap.

Cassie has always been able to hold her own with John; her wit contributed to her enjoyment of his. There was the time when Mary Miller happened to read a newspaper story about a woman who shot her husband on Christmas Eve, only to find later that he had put a mink coat for her under the Christmas tree. "My," observed Mary Miller, "if it were I, I never would be able to wear that coat." "Where *would* she wear it?" asked Cassie. "To the death house?"

Cassie was and is a believing, church-going Episcopalian; John was believing but not church-going. (Nevertheless, in one of the Hillman interviews he surprised Hillman by saying he thought the influence of the church has *not* decreased.) On one occasion when their minister called, late in the afternoon, he found Cassie in a housecoat, John in old flannels; they had a cosy visit over a cocktail. On another occasion, the minister called at the same time of day, but the Browns were dressing to go out: Cassie in curlers, John struggling with his tie. "Jesus Christ!" said John, "tell him we're not here." The minister was duly so misinformed.

When Cornelia Otis Skinner's son (that is to say, Mrs. Alden Blodget's son) was married, at an interfaith ceremony without benefit of either Wagner or Mendelssohn, Miss Skinner was in a quandary, remarking that she was an actress, accustomed to cues. John was sitting near enough to observe, when he saw coming down the aisle a distinguished soprano and her husband, an equally distinguished Marine Corps general, in full regalia, "Cornelia can stop worrying about the music: here comes John Philip Sousa."

To Mrs. Vincent Astor he once wrote, regretting that he was unable to lunch on a certain day, "a schizophrenic is a split infinitive of a person."

Cass Canfield, of Harper & Row, John's last publisher, wrote in his interesting book of publishing reminiscences, *Up and Down and Around,* this paragraph: "I was very fond of the late John Mason Brown, a person of special wit; author, dramatic critic, lecturer. His conversation sparkled and I remember one of his observations when he attended a party given by a famous collector of modern art. Confronted by a massive sculpture by Arp, with a large hole in its middle, Brown exclaimed, 'Ah, a womb with a view!' "

The collector was the financier and government official William A. M. Burden (Ambassador to Belgium from 1959 to 1961), who showed the Arp sculpture to the present author and gave another version of John's comment. (Both versions are undoubtedly accurate; no reason why John should not have made different comments on different occasions.) The sculpture itself may be described by some one who is not qualified to describe or discuss modern art, as looking like a large (forty inches high) representation of the Greek letter theta, twisted and with an extra half loop at the top, done in cast stone. In this version John exclaimed, "Ah, Madame Ovary!" *

The Browns and the Burdens saw a great deal of each other, and Mr. and Mrs. Burden have kindly supplied some verses John

---

* The author has an uneasy feeling that the phrase "a womb with a view" may have been used earlier, by somebody else; after all E. M. Forster's book came out in 1922. But "Madame Ovary" was undoubtedly his; he had used it earlier, in conversation with a friend, to describe the visceral quality of the prose of the newspaper columnist Dorothy Thompson. He did not mean that it was Flaubertian.

wrote to them as bread-and-butter letters. Here is one dated April 3, 1943, when John was probably doing public relations work for the Navy in Washington, not long before taking off for Sicily on the *Ancon*.

> In Britain now, I have no doubts
> The King is eating Brussels sprouts.
> The Queen has sipped her royal tea
> And has not thought—at least of me.
> The Yanks tonight will dine on Spam
> And theatregoers have their ham.
> In cotton hose or plain bare legs
> The girls will chew on powdered eggs;
> Men hungry in their lonely hearts
> Must search Piccadilly for their tarts.
> Blackest bleakness will cover all
> The city lying near St. Paul,
> The night will bring its nightly fears
> The searchlights raise their mighty spears.
> *Then* England will arise once more
> To eat Brussels sprouts as of yore
> But luckier I, with Peg and Bill
> Can feel a more Lucullan thrill
> Can share their home, and not their lease
> And in war know the joys of peace.

If John's verses are less professional than Ogden Nash's or his friend David McCord's, by the same token they help to maintain his amateur standing as a humorist. Nor was he the only amateur humorist in the household. Cassie has been cited. Not so, as yet, Susan Frawley, the Browns' maid for nineteen years. She is said to have frightened visitors because she never smiled. It so happened that early in 1950 A. Whitney Griswold was dining with the Browns when the news came that he had been chosen as

President of Yale. Mr. Griswold had been at a matinée with John's Aunt Mary Waite; New Haven was trying frantically to locate him, and finally reached him at the Browns' after dinner. The following morning Susan, demonstrating an unusual insight into the vicissitudes that beset a university president, remarked, "Sure, and he'll never have as good a time as he had last night." On another occasion, when presumably John and Cassie were dining alone, John complained that the plates were not warm enough. Susan put him in what she considered his place: "Sure, and you're always the critic, aren't you?"

John's family and friends all too often observed that John was a wit, all right, but that they just couldn't remember anything specific he had said. Serrell Hillman, in an article about John called "One Man Chautauqua," which appeared in the April 1960 issue of *Esquire,* has supplied the following quotations—all within the context of an excellent over-all portrait.

A friend asked Brown . . . to make some predictions on the quality of the forthcoming Broadway season. Brown exploded: "Trying to judge a season before it opens is like wiping off the lipstick before you've kissed the girl."

[At one of the "Person to Person" interviews with Edward R. Murrow:] Before the program went on TV, with Murrow interviewing Brown and his wife, a technician walked up to Brown and said: "Mr. Brown, I'll have to recharge your batteries." Said Brown: "Young man, not even God can do that."

[Of John Gunther, among other comments:] "He talks at the drop of a pause, but he's the best listener of any nonstop talker I know."

[When he joined the *New York Evening Post,* John said that his salary] "was like a postage stamp without glue—you could look at it, but it wouldn't take you any place."

In a recent lecture, Brown mentioned Grace Metalious' racy novel *Peyton Place* ("I would never be mean enough to challenge her experience") and Vladimir Nabokov's *Lolita* ("I felt as if I were reading that section of Kinsey I didn't want to read, as illustrated by Charles Addams"). Of the young hero of the play "The World of Suzie Wong" who finds himself in a Hong Kong brothel, Brown said, to the vast titillation of his audience: "Even in *The Little Colonel Series,* I've never seen such sustained innocence. He obviously thought he was in the Y.M.C.A."

Mr. Hillman ended his article with a serious quotation, from John's graduation address at Groton. Here is part of the quotation:

> "Remember," he told the students, "you have been spared the unintentional cruelty of that kind of Progressive education which misleads the young into believing that they will always be free to do what they want to do, at the moment and in the way they want to do it. The reality of life is quite different. Most people spend most of their days doing what they do not want to do in order to earn the right, at times, to do what they may desire. . . . To say the world at present stinks is to underestimate its fragrance. To say that it must stink forever is a lie. . . . I trust that you and your contemporaries will earn the right to be known as 'the unbeatable generation.' "

John's friends are justified in remembering him as primarily a man who sparkled; but they remember him also as radiating the warmth of an affection as spontaneous as his humor; and this is the quality that emerges principally from his correspondence. We have seen some of his correspondence with Brooks Atkinson—this exchange lasted a good forty years. With other friends who lived in New York, correspondence is usually limited to bread-and-butter letters, like those to the Burdens—though these are the only ones John wrote in verse—when the Browns had been to stay with their friends in the latters' country places; and letters of condolence on the appropriate occasions. Thus we are deprived of what would certainly have been a most interesting and informative correspondence, if Donald Oenslager had not been a neighbor. The Browns did a great deal of dining out and a corresponding amount of entertaining; one of their friends calls it "worldly living at its best." Before the Second World War, John enjoyed parlor games at dinner parties; there was one game called "Who Am I?" that John was especially fond of; it is a question-and-answer game, and he often introduced it after dinner at Amy Loveman's. Amy consistently refused to get the hang of this game by no means through inability to understand—she suffered no such inability in any respect; she just didn't like it, but was invariably polite about it. After the war it seems that "Who Am I?" went into the discard and was replaced by conversations, and in conversation John was witty, spontaneous, often opinionated, often brilliant. Unfortunately there is no correspondence between John and Amy Loveman.

There are many letters that deserve quotation. (John's extensive correspondence with Henry Cabot Lodge and with Edith Hamilton will be saved for a separate chapter.) John exchanged letters with, for instance, John K. Hutchens, from his first summer in Missoula. Hutchens was on vacation that summer from Hamilton College, where he had just completed his sophomore year, and was writing for the paper, discovering, as he put it later, that he was not Richard Harding Davis. That summer he reviewed a production by John of three one-act plays, including Kenneth Raisbeck's *Torches*. John was to write Hutchens in 1956: "I count it among my privileges that I have followed your career, junior, ever since those faraway days in Missoula in 1923, when you reviewed most maturely my juvenile efforts." Meanwhile he had written Hutchens on numerous occasions, sometimes to thank him for a favorable review, sometimes to congratulate him on a new step in his career. In September 1938 Hutchens had joined the staff of the Boston *Transcript;* Hutchens says of this letter, "He must have known how nervous I was about going to Boston, and to sit at the desk of H.T.P., no less." John had written: "Please congratulate the *Transcript* for me! . . . I know you'll do a fine job. . . . What really pleases me is that I know H.T.P. would be happy—and proud. In other words, here's a fan letter from a renewed *Transcript* reader. What a grand page the paper boasted when the *Transcript* was the Parker house. What a grand page it will have now that it is in the hands of Hutch."

In 1948 Hutchens joined the book department of the New York *Herald-Tribune,* working with Lewis Gannett, and John wrote to congratulate him. A year later he thanked Hutchens for his review of *Morning Faces,* and in 1951 he congratulated him when Hutchens was awarded an honorary degree by his alma mater, Hamilton College. Finally, the letter of September 28, 1956, already quoted in part, went on to say: "Your excellent movie reviews on the *Post* (on which paper I will never forget you helped me get a job); your brilliant theatre reviews for the *Transcript* when you followed, and topped, H.T.P.; your sparkling work on the *Times* [*The New York Times Book Review,* of which Hutchens was for a time editor]; and your brightening of the *Herald-Tribune*'s book page these many years—all of these I relished as experiences and treasure as recollections."

He had a similar running but spasmodic correspondence with David McCord, spasmodic because during John's years as Harvard Overseer he saw McCord on many of his frequent trips to Cambridge. The letter of August 1960 about the Drama Center has been quoted. In March 1953 he wrote McCord: "Ours is, indeed, a friendship that goes back many years. I would take nothing for it and treasure it mightily. I too regret, and regret with my whole heart, that those miles of New Haven tracks have been so belligerent in keeping us apart. Cassie and I both look back with the pleasantest kind of nostalgia to our Cambridge summers when you were as accessible as a neighbor.

"I realize what an uprooting and subtraction Jim Conant's leaving means for you. Even I, who never got to know him as well as I should like to have but who always liked and venerated him, feel the loss keenly."

In 1953 John wrote to congratulate McCord on his receiving the Signet Society's medal; in 1955, to express appreciation of McCord's essay *Out of Smalle* [sic] *Beginnings* (the reprint of his commencement address at New England College, Henniker, New Hampshire, in 1954). "Congratulations on the whole of it, and special congratulations on the pages dealing with Greece. I don't think anywhere, even in Edith Hamilton, have I read a nobler or more beautiful evocation of what it is that all of us owe to that 'smallest nation which has had the largest cultural influence on the western world.'" On March 12, 1956, following the Signet citation quoted earlier, he wrote: "I am still treading on clouds from the other night and your citation. That's a beautiful piece of writing you did—written, to be sure, from the prejudices of a long friendship, but written as only a poet could feel, perceive, and write." The morning after John's talk at the St. Botolph Club in May 1958, McCord wrote John to say what a success it had been, and John wrote to thank McCord for the occasion and for the ballad introduction. On January 7, 1959, McCord having asked John what he thought of MacLeish's play *J.B.*, John replied:

> "Thank the Lord
> For Dave McCord.
> *J.B.* for me
> is fine to see.
> But I give Dave
> A bigger rave.

"(At this point, a person from Porlock interrupted me. So, incidentally, did two other unwanted and sinister characters known as Pneumonia and Pleurisy. But now I am recovered.)

"Happy New Year!"

Finally, in March 1962, John wrote: "From Brooks and other sources I learn that you are to retire. Stated as a fact, this seems to me as incredible as any of the feats of modern science or Glenn's world spannings or yesterday's two-way transcontinental hop. What comforts me is that, though you may retire as the little boy used to in the Fisk advertisement, you will never retire from life. The [Harvard Alumni] *Bulletin* and Harvard will lose your warming, charming, mesmerizing and polarizing presence in Wadsworth House. But you are the kind of person who will always be in orbit. This will give you more time for friends, and that is good for them; more time for writing, and that is good for everyone; and more time for sleeping, which will be good for you. You have done a wonderful job which, thank God, Harvard finally recognized. [In 1956 McCord had received an honorary degree—the first L.H.D. Harvard had ever awarded.] Every Harvard man recognized it long ago." McCord replied in kind, spoke of his plans for writing and travel, mentioned the years "since you and I (perhaps along with Thomas Wolfe) saw the Restoration unfold in Harvard Hall."

## Chapter Thirteen

# A Chapter of Letters

There are two sets of letters which, because of their intrinsic interest, their continuity, and the light they throw on John's character and personality, deserve a chapter to themselves. These consist of his correspondence with two of his most admired friends—friends with whom he maintained a close relationship for forty years or more. His correspondence with Edith Hamilton continued until her death in 1963; that with Henry Cabot Lodge until John's own last illness. Not all the letters survive, and if they did they would occupy a separate volume.

Excerpts from almost twenty years of correspondence with Henry Cabot Lodge not only illuminate their long friendship, but also throw light on the subject matter of *Through These Men* and some of the events that led to John's interest in public affairs. From John to Lodge, May 21, 1946: "Sire: You are a bum. You are a rush of bums. Not a syllable from you to tell me that you had decided to run for the Senate. I read it in our newspapers, with excitement, with pleasure. I was particularly pleased by the *Herald-Tribune*'s Lochinvar editorial. . . . But, in spite of your silence—I thought Coolidge was a man, not a disease, but he has proven contagious—I wish you well. I don't know whether all the old sailors in the waterfront houses of Brooklyn are for you, but this Old Salt is." Lodge replied on May 24: ". . . I am sorry that in the rush of events here in Massachusetts, my eyes didn't rise above the horizon and see you in New York. You know that anything that I do would never be complete without your participation. . . ."

From John to Lodge March 15, 1947: "Only recently I have been off in the South and Southwest on a lecture jaunt. You can imagine the pride and joy with which I picked up a copy of *Time* and read how the pros were pricking up their ears over two presidential prospects who were enjoying a sudden upsurge of popularity. I was no less delighted to read your fine Lincoln Day speech in Louisville. . . . I talked to my mother in Louisville over the long distance. She told me that my stepfather, Jim Stone, had seen and heard you there. He had left the meeting an ardent supporter of yours. . . ." Lodge replied on March 19: "I am glad you get good reports of my political activities. There seem to be waves or cycles in politics. For a while everything seems to click and then for a while nothing clicks. And the longer you stay in politics the less you know why or how those things happen.

"It was, indeed, a wonderful meeting and visit in Louisville and seeing your stepfather was a true pleasure."

At the conclusion of the Republican Convention of 1948, where Lodge served as chairman of the Platform Committee, John telegraphed him on June 25: "YOU DONE NOBLE AND THOUGH I AM NOT DEWEY EYED I AM A MEMBER OF YOUR LODGE PROUDLY AFFECTIONATELY JOHN MASON BROWN." From Lodge's reply, dated July 8: Thanks for your telegram. The job of Chairman of the Platform Committee was the most laborious and backbreaking task which I have ever had to perform in time of peace and, while it is not exactly as I would have wanted it, I think it is a good platform. It is the shortest we have ever had, the English is not too atrocious, and it does make rather a large number of very definite un-weaselish statements. In fact, as Arthur Krock says, instead of going back forty-eight years to Mark Hanna it goes forty-eight years ahead to where the Republican Party should be. As my life dedication is towards making the Republican Party a more modern and forward-looking instrument of public service, this naturally is pleasing.

"At the Convention I supported Senator Vandenberg, but I am very happy about Governor Dewey and shall support him with a great deal of loyalty and enthusiasm."

Just before the presidential election of 1952—on October 21—John wrote: "This comes to you from an inn in Granville, Ohio, where I am to speak to [Denison] University tonight. It should, it would, have come to you long ago, if only the turbulence of the past weeks (mild compared to what you have been undergoing) had not made letter writing an impossibility. But now I have a 'breather' for the moment, and cannot let another minute slip by without saying something which, as a devoted friend of yours, I feel I would be disloyal if I did not say.

"God knows, I want you re-elected to the Senate for the country's sake. God knows, never, never, never would or could I do anything that might in any way hurt you or be false to you. Certainly my having decided to vote for Stevenson, and speaking for him in a small way can hurt no one unless it is Stevenson. But I felt I owed it to you and our treasured friendship to tell you of my decision.

"I was jubilantly pro-Ike in Chicago, and can never forget the masterly manner in which you won him the nomination. But then came the Democratic convention, and Adlai spoke, and I responded (as who didn't?) to what he said. I have long been a shopper in politics, and these past months I have been shopping. If only this had not been an election year for you, if only you could have stayed with the General and continued to guide him as you did in Chicago, I would no doubt still be for him. But the victory you won for him, I think he has thrown away.

"I won't bore you with all the reasons which forced me after anguishing hours and weeks to reach my decision. I will merely say that after spending those four days on each of the candidates' trains, I had no other choice.

"Cassie remains pro-Ike and is beyond persuasion. So is Preston. So is Meredith. So the vote in the Brown family continues to be Republican. I am the renegade.

"This doesn't mean that I wouldn't give my eye teeth to be up in Massachusetts, licking stamps, ringing doorbells, etc., for you. You know that.

"I do trust you aren't exhausted from campaigning. I thought Truman lamentable in his Boston talk, and have heard from Francesca and John [Lodge's brother and sister-in-law] how low are the religious prejudices being used against you. You are constantly in my mind. With all my heart I hope you score the huge victory you deserve, and I feel confident you will."

The next exchange comes from another election year, but was prompted not by politics but by the publication of *Through These Men*. Lodge wrote John on May 11, 1956: "I have now read the book and want you to know how much I admire what you have done.

"I am not speaking of what you wrote about me—which is far more flattering than I deserve. That is naturally very pleasing, first because it is obviously helpful to a man in public life to have such things said about him by a man of your standing and secondly—which is far more important—I am deeply touched that after all these years you should have it in your heart to write as you have about me.

"But the book is noteworthy for many other reasons. It is interesting; it is instructive; it shows the hard polish of real knowledge and penetrating research. You have a tone of balance and a lack of chip-on-the-shoulder bitterness which are unusual and inspiring.

"You have a right to be very proud, and as your friend, I share that pride with you."

John replied on May 14: "Bless you for that fine letter. It means a great deal to me to have you approve of the book. I struggled hard to write it without the kind of easy indulgences in prejudice which so sicken me in most political commentaries. To have you say that it has balance and lacks the usual bitterness pleases me greatly. Profound thanks. I value your judgment as I do our friendship."

On July 30, 1960, directly after Lodge's nomination as the Republican candidate for Vice-President, John wrote to him and Mrs. Lodge: "You can imagine—No, that's downright silly—*You know* how Cassie, Preston and I feel about what has happened for the country by happening to the two of you. And Meredith, Germany or Italy or wherever he is at the moment, feels the same way, of that I am confident. I only wish he had been here to follow it all as we did in the newspapers and on TV, and to share the pleasure of your call from Chicago. Bless you for that. It will never be forgotten, nor for that matter will the pride and joy and tense emotions with which we watched you at the U.N. (you were superb, Cabot), then in Chicago, then as you approached the auditorium, then as the delegates roared their votes for you, then when the two of you (the handsomest couple in America) appeared on the platform, then when the demonstration began (and what a fine one), then when Cabot spoke admirably with great force and eloquence. . . ."

And after the election, on November 17, John wrote: "Cassie and I went to the polls and for the first time in years our visits there justified themselves, inasmuch as in the past we have usually canceled each other out. This time I pulled down the black lever by your name with a true lifting of the heart. For me, an old Stevensonian Democrat, to vote the Republican ticket was not an easy decision. It took hours of weighing and wavering. I found myself with little enthusiasm for Nixon, with slightly more for Kennedy, and with none at all for Lyndon Johnson. But my feeling about you was very strong indeed. It was strong—and this is an important point—in spite of my having been your close friend. I say 'in spite of' because to see a person that one has known in terms of the Presidential image is doubly hard. I saw you that way and see you that way, and may I quickly add that it was as President that I was thinking of you.

"Your hold upon the American imagination is much greater, I think, than almost anyone realized in advance of your nomination. TV and your excellent performances on it were responsible for this, and the fact that since 1952 you have spoken up bravely in defense of America, against Communism and without abandoning the statesman's role for politics.

"What you have decided to do I am, of course, eager to hear. I hope you will consider doing some lecturing on international subjects. . . ."

Finally, part of a letter from John, dated December 4, 1963, to Ambassador and Mrs. Lodge, then in Saigon. "Cabot, Cassie and I thought, was brilliantly wise to fly straight from Washington to the motel at Idlewild and dig in there, before facing the rigors of that long broken trip to Saigon. We were cheated, of course, by not seeing him. . . . But he was infinitely considerate to call, exhausted as he must have been by the tragedy through which the world had been, only he was included in it personally. I was interested (Cassie's a *Trib* reader, I read both) to see Reston coming out once again today for Lodge and Scranton as Republican possibilities, and saying that some were urging Lodge to come home and run, even as he had urged Eisenhower to do the same.

"I was shocked this morning to learn from a casual telephone call that some people are blaming Cabot for having Diem and Nhu assassinated. Old Polonius Brown said this is not true and thinks it ought to be answered swiftly and indisputably. I remember you, Cabot, lamenting the paid pickets at the Soviet Embassy and saying how mad a thing it would have been if anyone had taken a pot shot at Tito or Khrushchev during the overpopulated U.N. session. I don't know where such a story about you started, but I think it ought to be quashed. And if ever I encounter it again, I shall certainly do my best to kill it, as I did when I first heard it. . . .

"For all of us everywhere these have been absolutely bludgeoning weeks. Cassie first heard the news of the President's assassination at Philharmonic Hall where, after the first number of Beethoven, a man appeared on the stage and announced that he had news of the utmost gravity to report, told of the assassination, and said of course the concert was ended. I heard it after having had lunch at the Century with Alfred Lunt, interviewing him for the Sherwood book. We walked up Fifth Avenue, gay and laughing. An unknown person came up to us and said, 'I am sorry. I think it is true he has died,' etc. We then went into a store with many other people and clustered around a radio. After that we soon parted and, in a daze, I walked all the way home up Park Avenue, occasionally running into friends who were crying and many strangers with tears in their eyes who gave me piecemeal information. The next days of solid news coverage I will never forget, nor has anyone yet recovered from them. Work was impossible. Never before in history has a major tragedy become an intimate part of the living of so many families. How the funeral was organized in so short a time and how so many people flew from all over the world, including you, Cabot—these are things I will never understand. Since then, dizzied, unrecovered, we have watched what has been happening and taken heart in LBJ's excellent, dignified, and energetic beginning. At least we have taught others that immediate continuity is possible here. That is something. I feel the relief for that is genuine, in the midst of continuing despair, perplexity, and incredulity."

The letter continues with several paragraphs of personal news about friends and about the theatre—"pretty dismal this year" —and ends with a paragraph about the Brown family: "Preston continues happy at Davis, Polk, and delights in the life that he and his young lawyer friends have at their West Side home. Meredith, in his second year at the Law School, is on an advisory committee, and has shown me quite a good spy novel that he wrote last summer in Montana, about an attempted assassination of Nehru. . . . [John's ellipses] Cassie and I are both fine. I still labor daily and sometimes even fruitfully at the Sherwood and go out windbreaking over the country. But we don't like having the Lodges so far overseas. Please come home. . . ."

John's correspondence with Edith Hamilton has been mentioned. It spanned more than thirty years. Along with Elling Aannestad (editor of the book publishing house of W. W. Norton & Co.) and several other friends, he was one of those who influenced Edith *—the word "influenced" means something between encouraged and badgered—to write her first book, *The Greek Way,* when she was over sixty, and thus to share the grace of her learning and the splendor of her wisdom with an audience that has existed, replacing itself with younger members, for more than forty years and has never failed in appreciation. *The Greek Way* was published by Norton in 1930.

Read consecutively, the letters that passed between them amount to a recapitulation of John's career and part of Edith's —with comments by each on the career of the other—from 1930 until Edith's death in 1963, in her ninety-sixth year.

The first letter in the folder, from John to Edith and Doris Reid, was written from Missoula and dated July 1930 (probably a mistake for 1929): "I haven't written for two reasons. One has really been work, and the other was a mild peeve I felt when I rushed home from Baltimore Saturday night on the midnight in the hope (and on the promise) of seeing you all for a last full day. The story was a sad one, because when I got home, you two had gone [Donald Oenslager and other friends were in the country]. Not only was your old correspondent forced to face a sweltering Sunday *all* alone, but he was—and this is the saddest part of the whole sad tale to me—forced to leave for the summer without seeing you all again. And Doris, the beloved skunk, promised me she would be in New York on Sunday." He spoke of the progress he was making on his book *Upstage*—several chapters done and the expectation to complete the job by August 15. The letter is a long one, ending with expressions of deep affection.

In December 1931 Edith wrote to thank John for a book he had sent her—*Upstage?* By now she was working on her second

* This story is admirably told in the memoir of Edith Hamilton by Doris Fielding Reid, her long-time friend and close associate. They lived together in New York and Washington, and during summers in Maine. Miss Reid eventually became Miss Hamilton's literary executrix. John's letter commenting on her book will be quoted later.

book, *The Roman Way;* John had asked her to read a chapter of the manuscript to him. "As for Cicero," she wrote, "the lady type-writer has not finished with it, but when she does I will read you as much as you can bear. It is very, very dull."

Some time during the mid-thirties—Edith often left her letters undated—she addressed both John and Cassie; evidently she had been ill. "It is very good for a sick person to have their heart warmed the way you did to me. I looked happily at your flowers and ate greedily of your soup (I have an extreme liking for what used to be called *beef-tea*) and read John's indecencies with com-plete amusement, and his words of affection with something that went very deep. You are two of the dearest people in the world—and so important to me as I could hardly tell you."

John often mentioned Edith Hamilton in his reviews, not all of them reprinted; she seldom if ever failed to send him a note of appreciation; she always credited him with having been responsi-ble for her literary recognition. In 1941, apparently, John's friend and colleague John Anderson, drama critic of the New York *Journal-American,* had written about her; she wrote John: "Did you advertise me to John Anderson too? Whenever any one says something nice about my books I ask, 'Do you know John Mason Brown?' "

On February 2, 1943, when John was either in England or in Washington—it is difficult to follow his exact goings and comings in the months before he sailed on the *Ancon* to Sicily—Edith sent him a long letter for which he must have been grateful.

"Darling Johnny,

"On Sunday Norris Houghton gave a farewell cocktail party in your flat—and I was homesick. I wanted my Johnny. I wanted him to draw me apart into his study and say, 'I've something to show you.' I wanted to see him moving among the crowd and always dominating it, and everyone so happy if he stopped to speak to them. Everything more fun, the atmosphere a bit excit-ing, when he happened along. His place, where he belonged, ut-terly changed when he wasn't there. I didn't like that party. The only bit I liked was Catherine, so lovely in a deep red dress, so deep-eyed and sweet—and, well, pensive. She always is that now. We smiled at each other and she knew what I was feeling. I think she has perfect courage. And the children. They came in, Preston very erect and very grave. Somehow he looked proud. He did very little smiling. He said soberly to me, 'I'm coming to see you soon' —and repeated it when I said goodbye to him. But really he was quiet, not one bit happily excited as I have seen him at your parties. As for Meredith, he is simply the most engaging youngster. He trotted around, his face all over smiles, holding a fat little hand out to everybody, often forgetting he had shaken hands and doing it all over again, not noisy, beautifully mannered and just delightful. But it was Preston's aloof, grave little face, and his reserved dignity (quite accurate this, I assure you) which stayed in my mind. Well, dear, dear boy, they are a part of America worth fighting for. We are all just overflowing with admiration for Catherine. She said to me when I was asking about her work, 'Well, really it doesn't much matter to me what I do while John is gone.' Oh, if only this awful thing would end. But anyway that does seem a lot nearer than it did. . . ."

Edith wrote frequently to John while he was in the Navy; few of his letters to her during this period have survived. She wrote to him in January 1944 from Washington, where she and Doris Reid were then living, that Aunt Mary Waite and her husband had come to dinner and they had called up Cassie in New York. "She made us laugh by telling us how Meredith admired Preston as a superior being because his teeth fell out while Meredith's were immovable. She said you were at sea somewhere, she thought. Her voice quivered, but just for a moment. I admire and love her in all ways, but, I believe, most for her courage. What are the other virtues worth without it?" She mentioned that the *National Geographic* was using four thousand words from her book *The Great Age of Greek Literature* (This was a title which Norton, her publisher, thought of giving to an enlarged edition of *The Greek Way*. Fortunately the idea aborted; and nothing came of the *National Geographic* project). John replied on March 2 from a Fleet Post Office address—this is one of the few times during this period when a letter can be matched with an answer (It was different when John returned to civilian life): "As always a letter from you arrived as plasma. Thank you for your news of Cassie; for your vignette of the Waites; for your charming picture of your new house and for Doris's news and yours. I promise you, even though I feel no need to visit the dentist, I shall from now on devour each copy of the *National Geographic* until I encounter that article they have reprinted from *The Great Age of Greek Literature*. My respect for their sagacity has risen no end. What are they using for illustrations? You and Doris in Greek costumes?" The letter continues with the passage quoted in Chapter Eight (see page 140).

Edith replied on April 17: "I try my best to put myself in your place—see with your eyes—hear with your ears—and feel—what? I do not know how to begin to imagine it. In one sense we are living in the real world and you in one that is unreal—but in a more pressing sense, you are facing reality and we are sheltered and hidden from it. Dear John, when—oh, when—we meet, you must try to deepen and widen our grasp of things." Later in the same letter Edith speaks of the political gossip buzzing in Washington—"quite often diverting, and I assure you, not sparing anyone in high places." She said she was "exercising the greatest self-control" not to pass it on, "but the censor would never pass the letter. . . . 'Gobbledegook' is bureaucratic language. Here is a well-known passage from the Book of Genesis translated into it: The Office of Omnipotence authorizes the use of this statement: as of the present instant, and hereafter, and until revoked or amended by further order, illumination is declared requisite and mandatory.' I think that very nice."

Late in June 1944, when John had returned to the United States, Edith wrote: "The happiness it was to know that you, my dearest John, were here and not blasting Cherbourg was so great I almost wept. To think of you there with Catherine and the boys is a joy." And on November 2, when John had returned to civilian life, she wrote: "I am deeply happy that you have decided as you have done. To me it is the clearly right decision. I am sure it was hard for you to make it, and I honour you for it. I myself know no one—in my own circle—who gave up anything approaching as much as you and Catherine did when you joined the Navy. You two did your share in a way that was beyond praise. . ." She went on to discuss an article on the British which John had written for *The Saturday Review* and which was to be a chapter in *Many a Watchful Night*.

John replied on November 9: "I am, of course, delighted that you liked the English chapter. But what really pleased me was that you so completely understood the dilemmas I have recently faced. This decision of getting out has been the hardest I have ever reached. I only hope I was right. My head insists I was. It tells me I can be more useful speaking and writing here than I would be on a non-operational job in France, or stuck off drearily as a public relations officer (God forbid) on some atoll two thousand miles out of the action in the Pacific. One thing I would never consent to do, if I had any choice whatsoever. That is to remain in New York or Washington in uniform and at a desk job. Unless it is action, no Roxy usher consolations for me.

"I must admit I feel strangely naked without my uniform. I find myself wanting to go up to unknown sailors and explain that I too was once in on it. It's an exiled and disquieting feeling. However, that too will doubtless pass." Then he went on to explain his decision to abandon daily reviewing and join *The Saturday Review*.

On July 26, 1945, John wrote: "I can't resist following up our talk of the other evening with a letter, however inadequate. . . .

"I am having lunch today with your old-palsy-walsy, Warder Norton. Yes, with Storer [Lunt], too.* So you may be certain you

---

* William Warder Norton, founder and president of W. W. Norton & Co., died late in 1945. Storer Lunt succeeded him as president of the company and later became chairman of the board. John published with Norton up to and

also will be having lunch with us; at least conversationally. The book on religion [*Witness to the Truth*] sounds highly interesting. Will it include those fine lectures you delivered in New York, and which I blame Beelzebub for having to miss? . . .

"You asked me if I am doing a book. The answer, dearest Edith, is for once an emphatic 'No.' I feel as surprised at not doing one as Queen Anne must have been on those rare occasions when she failed to find herself pregnant."

Early in 1946 John wrote to Edith about a piece on Thomas Mann she had written for *The Saturday Review* in the late 1930s. It was a critical piece—she considered Mann pretentious. "Mann's Joseph books [wrote John] are my idea of sheer torture. In fact, my suspicion is that in many respects, and in spite of the skill of *The Magic Mountain,* Mann is the most overrated writer of our time. Perhaps that's just my own antipathy to the Teutonic mind." But of course Mann was one of the first, and one of the most distinguished and outspoken, of the German opponents of Hitler.

And so the correspondence continued, during the years while Edith was living in Washington, with comments on each other's writings, on family, friends, ideas, notions, travels, summers in Stonington (John) and in Maine (Edith). Incidentally, not all of John's comments were uncritical. In 1945 John wrote Edith that her paragraphs were too long; that she used "that" as a relative where "which" would be better or where no relative was needed; and that too many of her sentences began with a superfluous "and." Edith took this gracefully and gratefully (perhaps with a small grain of salt).

After John's operation for an ulcer early in July 1947, Edith

---

including *Accustomed As I Am* (1942) except for *Letters from Greenroom Ghosts,* which was published by Viking. Later he had several publishers—chiefly McGraw-Hill, until he went to Harpers with *Through These Men, The Worlds of Robert E. Sherwood,* and *The Ordeal of a Playwright.* Viking published *Dramatis Personae* and the two Portables, *Lamb* and *Woollcott.* All Edith's books were published by Norton with the exception of her *Mythology,* which was commissioned by Little, Brown.

wrote him on the eighth: "I feel that I know more what you are feeling this minute than other people who have not had it themselves. I had two operations as serious—almost—as there could be and I knew one of them was for cancer. And that was in 1916! So I am a living monument to what surgery can do. But I know too all the nastiness and weariness. . . ."

John replied on July 17, in a letter addressed to Edith and Doris Reid: "I am dictating this on the roof of the Roosevelt Hospital. I am able to walk. In fact, do quite a bit of it. I walk just about as much as an unsuccessful streetwalker. My diet is still on the diapery side, but even so I am up to purée of spinach, eggs, soups, chocolate milk shakes, etc., and in another week or two should be eating practically what everyone else eats. . . ."

John had been planning to write an article for *The Saturday Review* to be published as near as possible to her eightieth birthday anniversary; he had some clandestine correspondence with Doris Reid about it during May and June; but the operation put an end to that project. On August 5 Edith wrote: "Doris has just told me about your plan for my birthday. How like you, dearest John, and like no one else on earth. It is not to be, but except for the cause—my dear, dear boy—I can hardly feel a regret, the knowledge that it was planned is such a very great happiness— and wonder. There are no words at my command to say what I feel. The memory of it will help me through bad moments. I have not many that are fit to put with it. (Oh, *that!* Substitute a *which,* please.) . . . Rest in what you have done for me, dear John, and never give a thought to the paltry consideration of factual accomplishment. 'Whether the ideal commonwealth exists in fact or not is of little importance. Each man can have it in his soul.' Socrates, of course. You have put a lot into my soul."

John did write an article about Edith for *The Saturday Review,* published March 2, 1948. It was occasioned by the publication of *Witness to the Truth,* and was largely a preview of that book. Edith wrote him in appreciation on March 21: "I think I feel a little dream-like, as if only in a dream could a thing happen to me like your article. Deep down what I think is this: the completest give-away is always the writer's. Whatever else he may set down, he always sets himself down. And in this article my dear John appears, clearly to be discerned by all who love him. . . . (Once, some twenty years ago when I was sick, you sat on my bed and read me *Othello,* and could not keep your voice from breaking when you came to his words after Desdemona's death. You were so young and so ardent and so touching.)"

When, in the mid-fifties, the *Times Literary Supplement* had published its laudatory review of *Through These Men,* Edith wrote John, calling it "more than a review, it is a tribute—and a glowing one. Dear John, do take it as some reward for all your effort and work. It is what Cicero said was the greatest reward, praise by one who knows." John replied with thanks a week later: "The review did please me but no more than your thinking of me and writing in such lovely terms."

The next letter of Edith's to be quoted is dated May 30, 1957, and in its final paragraph it contains an important piece of news. It should be explained that Margaret Hamilton and Dr. Alice Hamilton were Edith's sisters, both of whom were to survive her and to live to even more advanced ages. Margaret Hamilton was an educator; she died in 1969 at the age of ninety-eight. Dr. Alice Hamilton was a distinguished pioneering authority on industrial diseases; she lived to be a hundred and one and died in 1970. They lived in Hadlyme, Connecticut.

"Margaret wrote me yesterday from Hadlyme that she and Alice 'were listening [on television] to John Mason Brown on language' and he said emphatically that *most* could not be used with *unique.* 'I used the word in speaking of Edith Hamilton. She is the author of *The Greek Way* and has just brought out *The Echo of Greece.* I said she is not only a great person, she is unique. You cannot add a qualifying word to unique. It stands alone—as does she.' Darling John, you have done so much for me and you go right on doing more. How can I speak my gratitude for it all. I wonder what would have happened to me if you had not taken

me up. Beyond all question the success I have had is most of all
your creation. There is nothing to do about such a debt, only
accept it gratefully and humbly. When nice things happen I see
you at the back of them. They would not have come to me without you.

"Do you know that I am going as a guest of the Greek Govern-
ment to see the performance of *Prometheus* in July? Well, dear
John, that is your doing. It is going to be great fun. Of course
Doris goes with me and Storer Lunt, too." *

On August 29 (She had turned ninety on the twelfth) she wrote
from Sea Wall, Maine, to John: "I have had many thoughts of
you during the last two months. The journey to Greece was delightful and is bound to do a great deal for my books, and the
Book-of-the-Month Club [which offered *The Greek Way* and *The
Echo of Greece* as dividends] is something I never even dreamed
could happen to me. It has all come to me, dear John, primarily
through you. If only there were some way to show you my gratitude. Just today Storer Lunt sent me the *Christian Science Moni-
tor*'s account of what happened in Greece and the article began
with a quotation from you. I shall never give up trying to thank
you, and I shall never succeed in putting any part of what I feel
into words.

"We got back from Greece on my birthday, and for the moment anyway, I felt as I lay on the rocks watching the tide that
I would not give that up for the Parthenon. . . ."

John replied on September 5: "Thank you for those lovely,
though totally undeserved, words in your most welcome letter.
Needless to say, Cassie and I, the boys, the Oenslagers . . . and
all of your countless admirers followed with delight every detail
of your conquest of Greece. The *Time* story moved us pro-

* The whole story of this journey, in which Edith was made an honorary
citizen of Athens—to her tremendous pride—is told as well as anyone could
tell it in Doris Reid's memoir, previously mentioned. The Greek Government
in 1957 was of course the government that existed before the coup of the
"Colonels" and the imposition of a military dictatorship.

foundly; so did *The New York Times,* and so did that glorious picture of you in *Life.* . . .

"You ask for our news. We returned yesterday, all four of us, from Stonington and are dug in here now. Preston's seven weeks abroad earlier in the summer with three friends proved a wonderful success. Meredith has been working with me on the Sherwood biography and has been of immense assistance. We have had a placid, happy summer. I have had to come down each Sunday for "The Last Word," the television program I have been on since January, but I've had four or five days in the sun every week. As a family, we had a lovely four days at Vineyard Haven, where we found Aunt Susan in great form and Aunt Mary somewhat frail. Within the next two weeks Meredith returns to Groton for his last year and Preston to Harvard as a senior. It all goes too swiftly."

After Edith's death, at the end of May 1963, John wrote a memorable eulogy of her for *The Saturday Review* of June 22, "The Heritage of Edith Hamilton." Too late for *Dramatis Personae,* it has never been reprinted. Therefore it deserves to be quoted extensively.

When she died three weeks ago at ninety-five, Edith Hamilton was unquestionably aged but remained ageless. She was as old in the wisdom of which she was the embodiment as she was young in her relish of today's trivia and gossip. To those of us, and we were many, who came to know her well after she was sixty she was never Miss Hamilton. No matter how many decades younger we were and in spite of our reverence for her, she was Edith. Not freshly. Not presumptuously. Not coyly. She was Edith on our lips and to her face because she was Edith in our minds and hearts. She was Edith as if it were a place-name for friendship, Edith with no trespassing upon her dignity, Edith because she was as much at home in our worlds as she was in ancient Greece or Rome.

When she was born on August 12, 1867, the Civil War had been over for a little more than two years. . . . This . . . far distant world into which Edith was born . . . bore little or no resemblance to the world in which she died. But she was not given to looking back, at least not to the altering years through which she had lived. Although the past was her passionate concern, the past that absorbed her was not her own.

It was the Athens of Socrates, Plato, Thucydides, or Aeschylus, or the Rome of Plautus, Cicero, Horace, or Caesar, or the Jerusalem of Christ and St. Paul to which she turned when she looked back. They were so near to her and she in spirit to them that she was able to make them present to us.

Edith was brought up in Fort Wayne, Indiana, an unlikely stockade in those days, one might think, for classical literature. But the classics in the original were nearer to cultivated people then, and Edith's father was a cultivated man. Blessedly for us and her, he "knew nothing about softening the rigors of study." By her own telling we know that he started her reading Latin when she was seven. Greek, no doubt, came soon thereafter. Although she approached them first as lessons, in no time she was reading them for pleasure and as naturally as if they were English. She learned the hard way, mastering the inescapable disciplines of education. The drudgery on which knowledge is based never smudged for her the delights to which it leads. Instead, they proved the guarantee of those delights. . . .

Although I have read her books again and again, I can still hear her reading them. I can see her, slim as a girl, with a bird's grace and the dignity of a Mrs. Siddons, seated in the corner of a sofa with the light pouring on her snow-white hair, her dark eyes shining beneath her black eyebrows and her noble forehead, as she would adjust her sometimes noisy hearing aid and reach for her manuscript. She had a reading voice that was not quite like her speaking voice. It was thinner, a little strained, lacking in the sonorities of her daily speech. But what she read was music.

Although she wrote brilliantly about St. Paul, beautifully about Jesus, revealingly of the prophets of Israel, with deep knowledge of the outstanding Romans, and with particular charm about Horace, Greece was the love of Edith's life. . . .

In her essay on tragedy she pointed out that the tragic heroes and heroines belong to the only genuine aristocracy of this world—the aristocracy of truly passionate souls. . . . Edith was one of the passionate large-souled. Her life, however, was no tragedy. It was a triumph. It was crowned when, at eighty-nine, having been decorated by the King of Greece, she stood, noble and exultant, on the stage of the ancient theatre of Herodes Atticus at the foot of the Acropolis and heard the Athenian Mayor proclaim her a citizen of Athens. Striding to the microphone, she cried out in strong, clear tones, "I am an Athenian! I am an Athenian! This is the proudest day of my life."

An Athenian she always was, with the gift of making us all Athenians while reading her.

There is a postscript: a letter of John's to Mrs. August Belmont, dated July 24, 1967, about Doris Reid's book on Edith.

"Dearest Lady B.,

"So cheering to get your letter, and so good to learn that you feel the same enthusiasm I feel for Doris Reid's book on Edith. Her assignment was not easy. Edith, that beguiling, multiple creature, was the most human of goddesses. No one ever carried learning more colloquially or yet could be more noble in her wisdom. I too look back with shining happiness to those days in Maine when you and I met with Doris and Edith.

"In her book I think Doris has approached Edith in exactly the right way, doing a personal memoir rather than a formal biography. With you, I agree Edith comes through laughing, gay, sage, at play and at work. It pleases me mightily to learn from Doris how well her book has gone.

"All goes well here. We are expecting momentarily news that Sylvia, Meredith's wife, has had her baby. Naturally, we are mighty excited and will be relieved when the suspense is over."

It was—and is—a boy.

# Chapter Fourteen

# The Air — Off and On

John was broadcasting the radio program "Of Men and Books" over WABC (later WCBS) as early as December 1944 (He had made one appearance in November 1943 to discuss *To All Hands*), and he was to be on other programs during the next two decades. Now radio and television programs, like the actors in Prospero's masque, have a way of melting into air, into thin air; but not quite like that insubstantial pageant faded, they may leave a rack behind. (A rack, according to the late George Lyman Kittredge, is "a drifting cloud.") John kept the scripts of his broadcasts on "Of Men and Books." (This program was broadcast on Saturday afternoons, and was therefore dumped when the broadcasters wished to put on a football game instead, which led to the acidulous comment by John already quoted—see p. 160.)

Of one columnist (not Walter Winchell nor any one practicing the art today) he said: "He is able to create the illusion that he dipped his pen in a keyhole rather than an inkwell." Of an unnamed Englishwoman, mentioned in connection with Nancy Mitford's novel *The Pursuit of Love,* he said: "Suddenly this English female swept into view. She had those elbows out of which empire is made. She pushed her way down the line, saying to each American as she passed, 'If you will just let me go first, I shall be out of your way.' "

There is of course a great deal about Shaw. Four of John's

best essays on Shaw are preserved in *Dramatis Personae* under the general heading "Headmaster to the Universe." "Mr. Shaw's dislike of birthdays is of long standing. In fact, it has existed for many of those ninety years that he has been standing, bolt-upright, looking like Satan lost in a snowdrift; as thin as a soda-straw; and as erect as an exclamation point." This may well be part of what John said in his talk at the Shaw dinner. On the broadcast he followed these remarks with the description of Max Beerbohm's well-known cartoon of Shaw standing on his head, with the caption: "Mild surprise of one who, revisiting England after a long absence, finds that the dear fellow has not moved." John himself commented: "Yet the truth is that, while pretending to stand on his head, Mr. Shaw has held his head high and turned the Victorian world upside-down." And in another broadcast he speaks of Shaw's letters—"those amazing letters written by that old Casanova of the ink-stand."

Significant for John himself is a passage from his review of Gertrude Lawrence's autobiography, *A Star Danced:* "It is not surprising that a great number of men—men who emerge from Miss Lawrence's pages as invariably tall and young—fell in love with her. Nor is it unnatural that she fell in love with them. Until she and Lt. Commander Richard Aldrich, the last of the tall young men, were married, Miss Lawrence seems emotionally to have had Mr. Chamberlain's talent for missing the boat." Miss Lawrence had had an unsuccessful first marriage—otherwise this sounds like John before he began to court Cassie seriously in the autumn of 1932.*

He said that Dickens had an ambulance-chaser's absorption with death, and he told the audience about the teacher in Louisville with the perforated paddle. He gave an account of Gertrude Stein at the Dutch Treat Club † in New York: " 'I am going to

---

* See Mr. Aldrich's book *Gertrude Lawrence As Mrs. A.* for the story of the Aldriches' married life.

† The membership of this club is largely composed of writers, publishers, advertising men, literary agents, and others in the field of communications,

speak to you,' she said, 'on the Nowness of the Now.' On the Nowness of the Now she spoke for at least twenty minutes. She spoke wittily, sagely, and . . . while she was speaking, I could have sworn that I understood precisely what she meant."

Finally, from a broadcast on the art of parody, especially as practiced by Wolcott Gibbs of *The New Yorker:* "If I mention Beerbohm this afternoon, it is because my first subject is Wolcott Gibbs . . . by all odds the best parodist to have written since Beerbohm. The real truth is that, as a parodist, Mr. Gibbs is every bit as good as Mr. Beerbohm. If you doubt me, you have only to turn to the delightful pages of Mr. Gibbs's new book, *Season in the Sun and Other Pleasures."* He mentioned Gibbs's parodies of Sinclair Lewis's *Cass Timberlane,* Erich Maria Remarque's *Arch of Triumph,* of John P. Marquand, and of Noël Coward's autobiography, *Present Indicative;* Gibbs's piece was called *Future Conditional.* "He realizes it [parody] means that one man is not only writing *like* another man, but writing *against* him, too. Criticism in action: criticism which is creative no less than re-creative."

Wolcott Gibbs wrote John on December 8, 1946, shortly after that broadcast:

I am greatly in your debt. You are such a good critic, in the sense that you always seem aware of the author's intention, and, of course, one of my lasting admirations as a writer, too. I'm afraid I'm not really within a hundred miles of Beerbohm, who could keep these things in a lower key than I'd ever dare and who had a kind of genial cultivation far beyond my gifts, but it gives me something to dream about, anyway.

"Of Men and Books" was on the air—with intermittent periods of suspension, each of a few months' duration—from 1938 to 1948. John took on these solo literary discussions on December 9, 1944, and continued with the program until January 11, 1947. Another CBS program, "Tonight on Broadway," was broadcast

---

who have lunch in a hotel ballroom and invite celebrities to speak, sing, or play to them.

both on radio and on TV. John was not connected with the radio program, but he joined the television program on April 27, 1948, in the role of interviewer and narrator: it was a series concerned with the theatre, featuring interviews with stars and excerpts from Broadway plays. The program was broadcast weekly from April 6 to May 25, 1948; it was resumed on October 2, 1949, and ran till the end of the year. After joining the program John appeared every week but one until his final appearance on October 30, 1949.

On the CBS radio program "Invitation to Learning," which was devoted to literary discussions by prominent people, John made thirty-four appearances between October 15, 1944, and May 4, 1964. The subjects for discussion ranged from plays by Shakespeare to plays currently running on Broadway; from Addison and Steele to Orwell's *1984*. The program of June 26, 1960, has been preserved in print; it is a discussion by John, Philip Noel-Baker, and the moderator, George Crothers, of Shaw's *Arms and the Man*.

Apparently John's first television program was "Critic-at-Large," broadcast by the American Broadcasting Company from August 19, 1948, to April 20, 1949. In a letter dated September 9, 1948, to his Aunt Mary Waite, whom he addressed as "Mamie darling," he described what may have been a typical program. "The television program has turned out to be fun. Its scope is infinite; its subject-matter changes each week. It is called 'Critic-at-Large.' So far, the topics have ranged from dramatic criticism, the justification of columnists, and the spiraling cost of living, to . . . writers of World War I compared with those of World War II. Next week it's democracy and the draft; the week after that, *Hamlet*. On the cost-of-living program we had Senator O'Mahoney from Wyoming, Mr. George Shea, the editor of *Barron's Weekly* and, of all people, an authority on this subject —Al Seldis of Seldis Brothers Market right across the street.

"Last night was, I think, really a good show. It was good because the panel consisted of young Bill Mauldin, who is photogenic, alert and very bright; James A. Michener, the author, as you know, of *Tales of the South Pacific,* and a brilliant and charming man; and Orville Prescott, the *Times* book critic. When we discuss modern art, Francis Taylor will take the conservative Metropolitan point of view; Jim Soby will espouse modernism; and Walter Stuempfig, the painter, will speak for the young artist.

"Each week the American Broadcasting Company allows me to have the panel for dinner at the Sulgrave, where the ad lib discussion is quickly outlined. Al Seldis was the life of the party the night he came. You would love to have seen Senator O'Mahoney being most senatorial and full of Dale Carnegie charm. 'Why, Mr. Seldes,' said he, 'delighted to meet you. I've read you with pleasure for years.' 'Not me,' Al replied. 'Oh, yes indeed I have. You're too modest.' 'If you have, you must have been reading slips in my store,' was Al's rejoinder, as the Senator's face fell and I tried to explain."

John was on the NBC television show "Who Said That?" seventeen times between June 1951 and June 1954; the program had begun late in 1948 and continued into July 1954. John served as quiz-master, feeding quotations or partial quotations to the panel for identification or completion (it must have reminded him of his first encounter with Cassie and the American Laboratory Theatre). Previously he had been quiz-master on another NBC program, "Americana," from December 1947 to April 1948. He appeared several times on the NBC radio show "Conversation" in the mid-fifties; twice on another NBC radio show, "Biographies in Sound," both times in 1955: he discussed Shaw and Helen Hayes. Four times in the sixties he was a guest on NBC's "Today" show. It should also be mentioned that on May 10, 1949, he had appeared as a panelist on the program "Town Meeting of the Air" and had had his say about censorship; he used the substance of his remarks in his article later that year, "Wishful Banning." This was by no means the only time John used his broadcast material in his writing; another instance is his essay on comics, already mentioned, "Marijuana of the Nursery."

From 1957 until late in 1959 John was a panelist on the television program conducted by the lexicographer Bergen Evans, "The Last Word," broadcast on Sunday afternoons by CBS. The panel, which invited different guests at different times—they included Joseph N. Welch, John Gunther, H. Allen Smith, Mary McCarthy, Aldous Huxley, and P. G. Wodehouse—discussed the denotations, connotations, proper usage, and perhaps occasionally the etymology, of such words and phrases as widow's weeds; dumbbell; nerve, cheek, gall; *lose* your temper; tuxedo; Roman holiday; *crack* of dawn. On the difference between "jealous" and "envious," John took the occasion to quote *Othello*. Other subjects included the difference between *modern* art and *contemporary* art; *right* versus *privilege;* try *and* stop me. On one program John was the only one who took exception to *irregardless* (We saw in the preceding chapter how he felt about *most unique*). Once Ann Landers, the syndicated columnist who gives advice on personal problems, dilemmas, and quandaries, asked, "Can you say 'pregnant' on this program?" "You just did," observed John.

John would use the word *cop,* but not to the cop's face. "Not the first time," he remarked, "that I have disagreed with Mr. Hoover" (J. Edgar Hoover had written a letter saying that the word *cop* was degrading to law enforcement officers). And on another pair of words too often carelessly interchanged, he said, "I *confess* I have read *Lolita.* I *admit* I haven't read [whatever it might be]."

In February 1957 John was interviewed by telephone from Louisville; the interview was conducted by Bill Ladd, TV Editor of the *Courier-Journal.* John was surprised by the success of "The Last Word."

"No one had a great deal of hope for it when it started, except perhaps Bergen Evans. But it seems to have caught the audience and people are talking about it in the streets. . . .

"Evans called me and asked if I would be a member of a panel on his CBS show on Sunday afternoon. I was idle that day, so I said I would.

"After the show, he asked if I would be a permanent panelist, the only permanent member. I said yes, thinking the show would probably last a few weeks at best. Now it looks as if the word permanent was used advisedly."

[Mr. Ladd continues:] There is no preparation for the show, Brown says. . . . Brown thinks this is good. Not knowing what words they will discuss until they get on the air leads to relaxed comment.

Mr. Ladd recalls John's work as a summer reporter for the *Courier-Journal,* and quotes him:

"I'll never forget an undertaker who had a business in Louisville when I used to check them every night at deadline. [Neither John nor Mr. Ladd seems to have been aware of the appropriateness of this word.] This man in his ad used a picture of his casket with the words under the picture, 'Use my casket and you will never use another.'

"That was truly the last word!"

In July of the same year John gave a lecture at "a large American University," unspecified by Charles Mercer, the Associated Press writer whose report was published in the *Courier-Journal.*

He remarked at a dinner party that he would like to see a television program which was about to appear that night.

The learned guests gathered around the host's TV set reluctantly—if not with downright loathing.

After the program, one of the professors said, "Thank you so much, Mr. Brown. You gave me an opportunity to experience something new. I'd never seen a television program before."

"With that point of view on life," said Brown several days later, "what do you teach—and how can you teach?"

Later in the piece, Mr. Mercer cites John's opinion that

TV drama is generally improving. . . . Considering the good things in the medium, he asked, why do some so-called intellectuals look down on it—or rather, refuse to look at it at all?

"It's the coterie mind," said Brown. "Look back through history and you'll find there always was a small coterie that objected to every mass medium. Look at the field of literature today. You'll find snob writers who are unable to write for a large audience, and who are deeply unhappy when another writer is successful. That's not only snobbism; it's inverted snobbism." . . .

"One of the first errors of all mass media is to underestimate the intelligence of the people," he said. "It seems to be an instinctive error with some of those who direct a mass medium to think that their own personal intelligence is higher than that of the public."

As an example from his personal experience of high public intelligence he cited the time when he was teaching at St. Olaf's College, in Northfield, Minn., and T. S. Eliot came to read an essay on poetry and criticism.

"A total of 1,500 persons turned out and listened attentively to him," Brown recalled. "I've never forgotten it. I don't think anyone working in any mass medium should forget it."

Also in July 1957 John gave an interview along the same lines to J. P. Shanley of *The New York Times*. Mr. Shanley quoted John as saying:

I feel this—and I feel it passionately. People who deny themselves television deny themselves participation in life today. They are horse-and-buggy; they are atrophied; they are self-exiled from the world. They suffer from the most painful illiteracy, which is that of the literate. . . .

I have a friend who does not have a television set. One night, when he was entertaining at his home, he said proudly that he did not have one. A guest remarked: "You have gotten as far as using your telephone, haven't you?" I thought the comment was quite appropriate.

At the end of the interview Mr. Shanley writes:

Now engaged in writing his eighteenth book . . . Mr. Brown expects to be busy with it for the next two or three years. The book, to be called "The Worlds of Robert Sherwood," and published by Harpers, will be a comprehensive biography of the late playwright.

In his research, which already has involved 30,000 documents, Mr. Brown discovered an article written by Mr. Sherwood for Scribner's Magazine in 1929.

"It was a prophecy about television, and it was amazingly accurate," Mr. Brown said. "He expressed his horror of the commercials that he expected television would have. But he did foresee its virtues, too."

John's activities off the air during the 1950s were varied, not to say miscellaneous. Some of them must be reported for the record, and the only way to give them a semblance of biographical organization is to treat them—as far as possible—chronologically. It has been mentioned that he was elected to the National Institute of Arts and Letters early in 1950. In 1951, by appointment in February, he became Yale's first Embree Memorial lecturer, and gave a series of seven lectures for drama students. The lectureship grant was provided by the Whitney Foundation in memory of Edwin Rogers Embree, Yale '06, who had been on the administrative staff of the university for twenty years. The lectures were given between April 16 and April 30, inclusive, and the subjects were as follows: "Exit the Ivory Tower," "Problems Presented to and by the Critic," "Irreconcilable Approaches: Ibsen's and Chekhov's," "Professional Man of Genius: G.B.S.," "Broadway Practice," "The Tragic Concept—Old and New," and "Poetic Dramatists in an Age of Prose." From what we know of John's essays and books, we can make a good guess at the contents of some of these, especially the fourth and the seventh; it would be interesting to know what he said about Ibsen and Chekhov, who, by comparison with Shaw and O'Neill, seem to have been neglected in his books.

On January 29, 1952, John was master of ceremonies at the annual dinner of the National Book Awards, when the prizes for what the judges considered the best books published during the previous year in several categories were announced. This was the occasion on which the fiction award went to a best-selling first novel by James Jones. Those who were present will surely remember John's back-handed encomium: "In the opinion of the judges—I repeat, in the opinion of the judges—*From Here to Eternity* was the best novel of the year." (The fiction judges that year were Robert Gorham Davis, Brendan Gill, Lloyd Morris, Budd Schulberg, and Jean Stafford.) An award to which no one except competing candidates could conceivably have taken exception was that for nonfiction, given to *The Sea Around Us* by Rachel Carson. In John's papers there is a brief exchange between him and Miss Carson; he sent her a copy of his introductory remarks and the official citation accompanying the award.

Early in the 1950s the editors of *The Ladies' Home Journal* put in motion a project to assemble and publish an anthology of the best material from the complete files of the magazine, from its inception in December 1883 to the publication of *The Ladies' Home Journal Treasury* in 1956. They called upon John to edit the book, paying him a flat fee of $10,000 but no share in the royalties from sales of the *Treasury*. John was chosen because of his reputation in what by now were several fields; also because he was, as demonstrated by his remarks on television, a man of literary discernment without intellectual snobbery or prejudice against what was popular. He was given a free hand editorially, with of course many suggestions from the editors, Bruce and Beatrice Gould, and the associate editor, Hugh MacNair Kahler. John demonstrated his independence by omitting one piece which the *Journal* editors were particularly anxious to have included: indeed it was a piece written by one of the editors of the *Journal*.

The book is substantial indeed, running over six hundred pages, and is illustrated with characteristic covers and advertisements, many in color, from various eras of the magazine. The authors range from Mrs. Henry Ward Beecher and President Benjamin Harrison, through Kipling and Stockton, to W. H. Auden, Rebecca West, and Isak Dinesen. John began his introduction with this sentence: "To say that I have been a regular reader of the *Ladies' Home Journal* would be as much a lie as to pretend that each night, while waiting for sleep, I reach for Kafka, Kierkegaard, or Sartre." And a bit later:

Mine had been the male error (shared by a surprising number of females) of assuming that there is something embarrassing about being caught alive with a woman's magazine—just because it is a woman's magazine. Each issue of the *Journal* that I bought, as blushingly as a bishop would buy *The Racing Form*, persuaded me I was wrong. In each I always found other things which interested me in their own right and had nothing to do with *la différence* between the sexes so rightly cherished in France and everywhere else.

This was a dozen or more years before Women's Lib. In any event, John went on to give a brief history of the magazine under its succession of editors, mentioning many well-known contributors.

In connection with so-called women's magazines, we may mention John's article "What Makes a Woman Memorable," published in *Vogue* November 15, 1956, and picked up later by *The Reader's Digest*. To a reader today it seems to have been written off the top of his head; it speaks well of Helen of Troy, it quotes Barrie's well-known definition of charm; it does indeed mention George Sand and George Eliot, and the "inability of the French soldiers in *Saint Joan* to express the impact on them of the girl from Domrémy." It does not mention two of the most memorable women John ever knew: Edith Hamilton and Amy Loveman.

From 1951 to 1956, almost coincidentally with his term as Harvard Overseer, John was a member of the Board of Trustees of the Metropolitan Museum of Art. No doubt this appointment came about as a result of his friendship with Francis Henry Taylor, director of the museum. The board is self-perpetuating, with a maximum membership of thirty-five, drawn from various professions and other callings. It has the power of the purse—to raise and disburse funds. It also has the power to elect the director and other officers, including the president, three vice-presidents, the treasurer (who also serves as assistant director); also the power to appoint the chief curator and the departmental curators.

As a member of the board, John was asked to pass on the literary quality of the museum's publications—except the *Bulletins* —but not on the quality of art criticism expressed in them. For the Metropolitan's *Bulletin* of May 1954, he wrote an article about the Grace Rainey Rogers Auditorium, which had recently opened; it is a gracefully written piece of less than a thousand words. It discusses the advantages of the new auditorium over the old lecture hall which it replaced, and proceeds to describe it.

The virtues of the Rogers Auditorium are inescapable and many. Its intimacy is warming (it accommodates seven hundred on the main floor and balcony). Its seats are built on the wise assumption that nature has not done the upholsterer's work for him. Its sight lines are perfect and its acoustics so good that no amplifiers are needed, and a person talking in conversational tones on the stage can be heard with ease in the balcony. . . .

The new Auditorium's function is to supply quarters where music, the spoken word, and the visual arts can live together in a blameless, though creative, *ménage à trois*. . . .

The stage can accommodate a full symphony orchestra of one hundred and sixty instruments plus a chorus. Due to the size of the hall, however, smaller chamber orchestras or choral groups will probably be heard more often. . . . In addition to the facilities for slides and a projection booth with apparatus for showing 35mm. and 16mm. films there is a large television studio. It is adjacent to the stage, and in it the Museum will be prepared to originate programs bringing its treasures directly before the cameras. . . .

The actors in the Grace Rainey Rogers Auditorium will be lecturers, instrumentalists, or vocalists. But one thing is certain. They will provide the passion out of their own caring and share it with those who hear them.

In accepting the appointment, John had written that he agreed, "provided you are not confusing me with John Nicholas Brown, as has happened before." Taylor resigned as director in 1955, and John resigned from the board a year later.

From 1951 an important interest of John's was Recording for the Blind, a nonprofit organization depending on voluntary contributions and voluntary readers. (There is also some help from foundations.) The object is not to duplicate the effort of Talking Books for the Blind, rather it is entirely for the assistance of students. Textbooks are recorded at the request of blind students and the recordings are made available free. The headquarters of the organization are in New York, but there are offices in various other cities; Recording for the Blind finds it particularly useful to have offices in college towns like Princeton, New Haven, and

Athens, Georgia, where on the university faculties someone can usually be found capable of reading, for reproduction, anything from atomic physics to Sanskrit. John joined the board of directors, largely at the behest of two of his friends, Mrs. Donald Oenslager and Mrs. Alfred de Liagre, Jr. Also he made recordings and contributions, as well as writing letters of courteous and irresistible solicitation, in what his friend David McCord, who for years did the same for Harvard, calls the "Language of Request."

John was also for some years a member of the Council on Foreign Relations. This organization had been formed in 1921 as a consolidation of two existing committees. Interest had sprung up in the wake of the controversy over the Treaty of Versailles: by this time it was evident that the United States could not avoid having foreign relations. Membership in the Council is by invitation. Its functions include conferences and publications; it publishes the distinguished quarterly magazine *Foreign Affairs* and books of interest in its field. The records—that is to say, John's correspondence files—do not indicate that he was a particularly active member, though he corresponded from time to time with various eminent members of the Council. The field of foreign relations was not really John's field, except in so far as *Through These Men* entered it. If he had lived to complete the Sherwood biography, he would have been up to his eyebrows in foreign relations. Presumably his election to membership, probably influenced by his friendship with Hamilton Fish Armstrong, editor of *Foreign Affairs,* demonstrates the Council's desire to have a broad representation of distinguished men and women, not necessarily those whose primary interest is in foreign affairs.

John was also a member of the National Book Committee from its inception in 1954. It was created by the American Library Association and the American Book Publishers Council. There are 225 elected members altogether, twenty-one of whom serve as the policy-making Executive Committee. The general idea of the National Book Committee is to encourage reading and writing:

in its own words, "to recognize literary excellence, to promote the fuller use and further development of library services, to work for increased literacy and stronger motivation to read, and to help assure convenient and unhindered access to books and other library materials." To explain further the activities of this organization would lead into a bypath as far as John is concerned. Since 1960 the National Book Committee has administered the National Book Awards, which previously—including the year 1952, when John was master of ceremonies—had been sponsored by certain trade associations.

John's great friend Mrs. Isaacs had retired as editor of *Theatre Arts* in 1946. When she died, at the beginning of 1956, the following clause turned up in her will: "I give and bequeath the sum of One Thousand (1,000) Dollars to PRESTON and MEREDITH BROWN, jointly or to their survivor, as a backhanded expression of thanks to their father for keeping a sagging mind refueled."

On January 13, 1956, John wrote to Mrs. Isaacs's son, Lewis M. Isaacs, Jr.: "That we were devastated by your mother's generosity and her lovely phrasing of the bequest goes without saying. With equal inevitability we were touched, and touched profoundly, by your words and the affection, so strongly shared by us, behind them. . . .

"That I loved your mother, that she shaped my life, started my career, and was essential to my daily living all these later years, you all must know full well. I shall have to control my hands each morning, come nine-thirty, when they reach automatically out of need for the telephone. The need will remain, but so will the joy, pride, and comfort that I had in those talks with her which to me were sources of unfailing stimulation.

"Blessedly, her 'backhanded' remembrance of me in terms of Preston and Meredith was typical of her whole imaginative contribution to life."

On January 1, 1956, John became a member of the Round Table Club, a dinner club whose members were among the most distinguished men in America. It was in 1956 that John did a month's resident teaching at St. Olaf's College, previously mentioned. In John's files for 1956 are two letters from William Faulkner, Xeroxed and evidently sent to all members of a committee headed by Harvey Breit, saying that President Eisenhower wanted to get American writers to encourage other citizens to give a true picture of this country to foreigners. It seems to have been difficult to set a date for a committee meeting. One of Faulkner's letters is mildly—very mildly—facetious. From the creator of Popeye and the Snopeses, it might well have been. There are no replies by John in the file. And at the end of the year David McCord wrote to John: "It is your own fearless way of treating honest work as deserving honest consideration that marks you as a man of letters. . . . Why are so many moderns so cowardly about genuine sentiment?" A final fact for the record: John was appointed to the faculty of drama at the Union Theological Seminary for 1957.

Returning to John's broadcasts—we are now back on the air —there are several that might be mentioned, and two that must be. On January 21, 1955, John was a guest of Edward R. Murrow on the CBS program "Person to Person." After a discussion of his lectures and the books he had recently been reading—with the inevitable reference to Shaw—John told the story of his effort to interest Shaw in the proposed celebration of his ninetieth birthday anniversary, and the elderly gentleman's firm if amiable rebuff—Murrow asked John about his service in the war, and John told of the assignment Admiral Kirk had given him: "It was Admiral Kirk's excellent, I think superb, conviction that this was a democratic war and, therefore, the men that were fighting in it had the right to know why they were fighting and what was taking place about them at the moment of action."

Murrow asked, "John, do you think this theory has some peacetime, even cold war, application?"

John's reply was characteristic of the author of *Through These Men*. The interview took place only a month after McCarthy's censure by the Senate, and when he was rapidly beginning to lose his poisonous influence. It is as pertinent now as it was twenty years ago. This is what John said:

"Never more so than now, never more so than when information is kept hidden, never more so than when people are victims of fear. At the present moment I should believe as a mere citizen and a reporter that the real way for us to win this cold war would not be to take on the manners of our enemies or the people whose system we despise but to be as unlike them in our method as possible, to let the mind range free, because that is the test and persuasion of freedom."

The other important broadcast was an interview conducted by James McAndrew on "Camera 3," also CBS, on December 5, 1965. He spoke of the biography he wrote of Daniel Boone (1952); in 1956 John was to commit himself to the Sherwood project. John told the interviewer that after *Daniel Boone*, which had been more trouble than he had anticipated owing to Boone's longevity (he lived to be over eighty), he had determined never to write another biography "unless it was of a blue baby." Then he walked straight into Sherwood. He was "trapped by the Sherwood papers," fascinated by the multiplicity of Sherwood's careers. "Sherwood," said John, "grew more than any other man of his time."

## Chapter Fifteen

# The Sixties

By now—1960—John was as totally immersed in the Sherwood biography as a Georgia Baptist in the Ogeechee River. He had been working on it much longer than he had anticipated at the outset. It has been recorded that the Sherwood files contained some 30,000 documents,* including letters to and from Sherwood, and there were many other sources of information, mentioned in the author's foreword, which he called "By Way of Introduction." The process of mastering these documents and other sources provides a theme which runs through John's correspondence for a decade. Moreover, there were inevitable interruptions: for instance the bout of pleurisy and pneumonia at the end of 1958. His convalescence was assisted by a cruise to Nassau with Cassie early in January 1959; but after his return, he was obliged to turn down a chance to see a production at Yale because he had not fully recovered.

John's sixties were the decade's sixties. In addition to his profound absorption in Sherwood, he had become a member of the editorial board—the judges—of the Book-of-the-Month Club in 1956. This was a well-paid job, and by no means a sinecure. He was still traveling; early in 1960 he wrote the Griswolds in New Haven a bread-and-butter letter for a Sunday lunch; the letter was written from Louisville.

---

* In one of the Serrell Hillman interviews, John raised the figure to 45,000.

In February 1961, following the sale of *The Saturday Review* to the McCall Corporation, which in turn was owned by Norton Simon, Inc., with the stipulation that Norman Cousins was to continue as editor, John wrote the following reply to an offer Cousins made him, the nature of which can be inferred from John's letter.

"Dear Norman,

"I think you have improved upon Genesis in that enchanting and tempting letter you begat. Don't think that I am not touched, flattered, and honored, or that I haven't been tempted and thought long and hard from every point of view about your offer; an offer, by the way, which I take as just one more proof of your wonderful friendship.

"In your excellent editorial, 'Diary of a Change,' you describe your last three days before the actual signing of the contract with McCall as 'the toughest of my life.' The days since we lunched and your letter came have been among the toughest of mine.

"After searching my soul, conscience, and calendar, I have painfully reached the decision that I cannot, and should not, accept your fabulously generous offer. Let me explain why briefly, though I could do so at chapter length.

"1.   I think I am too old to undertake a weekly page, having, as Hamlet would say, neither the will, the means, nor the strength to do so.

"2.   Remember that I did a monthly column for four years for *Theatre Arts,* a daily column for fifteen years for the *Post* and then the *World-Telegram,* and for ten years, the happiest years, 'Seeing Things' for the SR. I think when it comes to regular column-writing I have had it.

"3.   Then, as to the nature of the column, which we have not discussed. If I touched on a play, I would be inviting Henry's * proper objections—or, indeed, if I wandered into any other departmental field.

---

* Henry Hewes, who by that time had succeeded John as drama critic of *The Saturday Review.*

"4. To do justice to a column, and hence to you and the SR, would mean giving it full and intense attention. Too many columns that I read in newspapers, unless written by specialists about their own subjects, seem to me futile word-wasters in order to be space-fillers.

"5. Mine is already a crowded and committed schedule. The Sherwood book is my passionate absorption. It comes slowly, but its completion in a form as good as I can make it is what I care most about professionally.

"6. I read about twelve books a month for the BOMC. You might say I could write from or about these. The trouble is that I read them usually six months in advance of publication, and by the time they appear I have forgotten them entirely—that is, except for the very, very good ones.

"7. I like lecturing, as you do. I like people, and getting away from New York, and the stimulation that colleges particularly give me, and having the chance, in the quiet of hotel rooms, to catch up on my BOMC reading.

"8. One of the troubles with writing for you the piece you so kindly asked me to do about the probable effect of the new Administration on the literature of the next decade is that the points I would make in that piece are points that I am going to make in my lecture. In other words, people who paid to hear me would, and could, rightly condemn me for repeating myself.

"9. You write not only well but with admirable fluency. Writing is for me the pleasant agony I once described it in the SR as being. As I get older, I am not so certain about there being anything 'pleasant' in it!

"10. Once, years and years ago, I confessed to you that I did not really like writing journalism and that, even when writing it, I was always thinking in terms of a book-to-be rather than the weekly needs of a newsworthy column.

"I guess these explain, and not too briefly, the considerations which have been agitating me these past days and have led me to my decision. Maybe an occasional piece, yes. Let's talk about that sometime when I begin to see real daylight in the Sherwood. I am now just about half through.

"I will never forget your offer and can't say often enough how proud I am of you and what you have done, and how pleased I am that the McCall arrangement, which comes as another proof of your success, has been made to your satisfaction. Don't forget I was devoted to you before you became a millionaire and I have never minded money."

In 1963 Brooks Atkinson, who had retired as drama critic of *The New York Times* and was now writing a column for that paper called "Critic at Large," devoted his space to an imaginary interview with John. This was published in the *Times* of June 25. *Dramatis Personae* had recently been published; so had a book called *Writers at Work,* which was the second collection of interviews from *The Paris Review* published under this title. The Atkinson interview follows.

INTERVIEWER—John Mason Brown, if I may call you that. Your omnibus book "Dramatis Personae" was published simultaneously with "Writers at Work," which consists of illuminating interviews with 14 authors. Since this newspaper is dedicated to all kinds of basic information, including the psyches of authors, I should like to apply to you the techniques of "Writers at Work."

JOHN MASON BROWN—Why, certainly. Since we are old friends, it ought to be fun.

Q. Mr. Brown, why did you retire from newspaper criticism?

A. Why did you?

Q. Answering one question with another is an old Yankee trick. It does not become a cultivated gentleman from Louisville, Ky.

A. Let me point out in a gentlemanly fashion that your question is fully answered in my book.

Q. You mean where you say on page 456: "There was a time when the theater as theater seemed to me all-absorbing. That, however, was before the war"? And on page 455: "Poverty might but horses could not drag me back into daily reviewing and newspaper work"?

A. Certainly. Do I detect in your questioning the petulance peculiar to conversation within the New York Drama Critics Circle?

Q. As the only man ever drafted to serve four terms as president of the Critics Circle, you are entitled to make that remark. Now on page 457 you say you are convinced that "the most challenging function of criticism is rising to appreciation rather than excelling at denunciation." But on page 239 you dismiss Katharine Hepburn's long-legged Rosalind in "As You Like It" with this flip remark: "I cannot help feeling that she mistakes the Forest of Arden for the Bryn Mawr campus." How do you reconcile these two statements?

A. Look, why don't we have lunch some day?

Q. On page 424 you say that a drama critic is like a signpost that points the way but never goes there.

A. Kindly note that I credit Charles Dickens with that statement.

Q. Quite so. But I believe you went where the sign pointed. I have a collection of miracle plays that you edited when you were still an undergraduate at Harvard—very well edited, in fact. In your book you record your fruitful association with G. P. Baker in the study of drama. If I am not mistaken, you acted in plays put on by the Harvard Dramatic Club.

A. The Century would be a convenient place to lunch. It induces good taste in everyone who goes there.

Q. When you acted in a Harvard Dramatic Club play, didn't an apprentice critic for The Boston Evening Transcript say you had "sputtered and spurted"?

A. Aren't you ashamed of yourself now?

Q. In "Writers at Work" it appears that T. S. Eliot and S. J. Perelman, both poets of considerable stature, compose directly on the typewriter. On page 452 you say that you write by snaking across the floor on your stomach: "My desk, a migratory one, is a small piece of beaverboard I push before me." Why did you adopt that water-buffalo method?

A. It's the best way I know to confound bores.

Q. Mr. Brown, I notice in your epilogue that you describe Edward Albee, a practitioner of the theater of the absurd, as "the most gifted of the younger, emerging Americans." But you write eloquently of Jean Anouilh's "Becket," Archie MacLeish's "J.B.," and Robert Bolt's "A Man for All Seasons," which are anything but absurd. Aren't the two statements inconsistent?

A. Consistency is the hobgoblin of small minds, as every New Englander should know. But if I am allowed to look at my own book, you will find on page 541 that I define comparative values by saying that MacLeish, Bolt and Anouilh have made the theater "the dwelling place of wonder" and "this is what the theater has always been at its best."

Q. Criticism at its finest. Now, one final question. You are justly renowned as one of the judges of the Book-of-the-Month Club. How does it happen that your finest book is not a Book-of-the-Month Club selection?

A. Now, really: that's hitting below the Mason Brown line.

Editor's Note—Mr. Brown informs us that he was not present at the above interview.

John wrote to Atkinson on July 1:

"INTERVIEWEE (better known as The Little Man Who Wasn't There): I read a fine piece by some one who was present in a publication which wasn't *Writers at Work*.

"INTERVIEWER: What did you think of it?

"INTERVIEWEE: I have always liked Atkinson better than Brown, and I still do.

"INTERVIEWER: That's just the kind of answer I would expect from a Southerner.

"INTERVIEWEE: It was most ingenious of you to make an absent person talk, and Yankee kind of you to make him talk *in absentia* better than when present. I have long wished you had done my writing for me. From now on I am going to wish that you had done my talking.

"INTERVIEWER: There you go, dripping molasses again. Don't you have any Yankee standards?

"INTERVIEWEE: On page 83 of an excellent book called *Tuesdays & Fridays* [a book by Atkinson: Random House, 1963] I find this line, 'Knowledge is courage.' You have always shown both. I say this in Harvard terms and with a New York accent.

"INTERVIEWER: Shall we go out for lunch?

"INTERVIEWEE: It can't be soon enough to please me. I will stop sputtering and spurting now. But I will start again when I try to thank you for what you did about that absentee landlord in Critic at Large.

"Have a fine summer."

The reception of *Dramatis Personae* was by no means as cozy universally as the exchange between Brooks Atkinson and John. For example, Gordon Rogoff in the *Village Voice* of July 4, 1963, stated:

He [Brown] is less a critic than a genial appreciator, a friendly audience, marked off from the crowd by virtue of that kindly sense of detachment that finally cuts him off from the most terrifying reaches of art. O'Neill is great to Brown because of the largeness of his concerns; and while Brown is never blind to those defects in his heroes that can be indulged with equal pleasantry, he is always blind to the defect of seeing largeness simply as a matter of size.

And here is John Simon in *The New York Times Book Review* of July 14, 1963:

Mr. Brown's equipment includes chatty urbanity, well-informed enthusiasm, a craving for the best and a touching love for the theater that knows no alteration. These are solid qualities, but they are those of the theater buff, the conscientious journalist, the above-average high-school dramatics teacher [actually John taught at Harvard and Yale], the enlightened vulgarizer. . . .

What is most lacking is discrimination. Brando's performance in "Streetcar" was rather less praised, though it was something startlingly new and style-setting, than Cornell's Cleopatra, the remote and asexual tailpiece of an exhausted tradition. Shakespeare is poetry, but so, too, are Arthur Miller's sweaty grapplings with the Poetical. Gielgud's ability "to bring out the song in a poetic speech" comes in for no more praise than "the beauty of [Maurice] Evans' voice," and so on. . . .

Mr. Simon admits that "in other pieces of this book Mr. Brown proves himself a decent cultural reporter and theatrical journalist and publicist"; and in the first paragraph of his review, after quoting Hazlitt's definition of a "commonplace critic as one who 'tells you either what is not true, or what you knew before, or what is not worth knowing,' " he continues: "Mr. Brown—who tells us many things worth knowing, quite a few of which are true, including some that we did not know before—is definitely not commonplace. Neither is he a critic."

Both Mr. Rogoff and Mr. Simon have more to say of a critical nature—no one can doubt that *they* are critics—but enough has been quoted to set forth the case against Brown. John's writings are their own best answer to his critics. No one would maintain that daily—or rather nightly—newspaper reviewing produces much criticism. One may, however, ask if *Letters from Greenroom Ghosts* is not a work of criticism. Also, a considerable number of the pieces John wrote at leisure for *The Saturday Review,* for instance those on T. S. Eliot's plays. Whether or not John was a critic is a matter of opinion; also a matter of definition.

No doubt the publication of *Dramatis Personae* did provide an opportunity for an over-all discussion of John's career. By this time, however, most of the men who might have done a more sympathetic appraisal than those just quoted were John's friends; perhaps they did not feel their position to be sufficiently independent. This is of course conjectural. The nearest thing to such an appraisal that can be found in the files is John Gassner's review in the *Educational Theatre Journal* for December 1963. Mr. Gassner speaks of John's "recovery" of Shaw, Baker, Wolfe, and Robert Edmond Jones, of the enduring value of *The Modern Theatre in Revolt,* and writes: "Mr. Brown could be a lucid scholar when he considered it important to abate his passion for the living moment in order to attend to the living past."

*Dramatis Personae* [Mr. Gassner continues] is the work of a man who prefers appreciation to depreciation and would rather make an art out of the former than self-publicity with the latter. Mr. Brown is a gentleman, as some fresh-as-paint new-generation critics apparently are not. (One of these recently declared in a British publication that he felt like "kicking O'Neill's teeth in" for some infraction of dramaturgy in a late play written while the playwright was suffering from a severe illness.) For Mr. Brown, writing is a civilized activity and not a gutter brawl. . . . Mr. Brown does not dissect plays and performances, he *responds* to them. He is also so painlessly informative, blending information with his afflatus, that he may seem uninformative (except in *The Modern Theatre in Revolt*) to those who have become accustomed to being told that they are being instructed.*

Groucho Marx wrote to John on June 25, 1963:

I'm half-way through your book and it's unquestionably the best thing I've read this year. And that goes for last year, too.

* John himself, in one of the Hillman interviews, said that the word "critic" implies attack or denunciation, which is easier than rising to appreciation.

I think you made a mistake with the title, however. I mean commercially. The average book buyer, as you know, is not a student of Latin, and the ones who can pronounce Dramatis Personae (or even Corpus Delicti) are few, indeed. Therefore, when he goes into a bookstore, fearful of mispronouncing the title, he usually abandons the whole project and winds up with a copy of Hedda Hopper's best-seller. . . .

It would be a genuine literary loss if this book doesn't find the wide audience it deserves.

John replied on July 1:

"Dear Groucho,

"I can't say 'Mister.' Everybody in this country knows you too well for that kind of formality. Now Karl is a different matter, but I have never been on speaking terms with him.

"My sixty-third birthday is coming up this week, and even without your permission I am going to claim your letter as my most treasured present. It is a damned friendly, sensible, and helpful letter, one of the best epistles since St. Paul's, and with him I did not correspond.

"Naturally what you say about the book sets me up no end, and the Viking Press too. Marshall Best there and I did have several talks about the difficulty of *Dramatis Personae* as a title. But we thought, perhaps too optimistically, that, since every high-school student has had to read *Julius Caesar* and has encountered those words above the cast of characters, it ought to be fairly clear. I knew we had been wrong when, a few days after the book came out, I went into a local bookshop and the nice man who runs the place asked me what it meant. I explained to him and even got down Shakespeare to show him. 'Oh, I get the idea,' he said brightly. 'It means the personnel in the drama.' The title I first suggested was one we obviously couldn't use, i.e., *The Portable John*, and no doubt just as well. So here we are, stuck with *DP*, whereas *Corpus Delicti* would have been a better title, and *Flagrante Delicto* better still. Even so, the book for that kind of book is really doing very well. It will never compete with Hedda Hopper and never be a best-seller. But Viking is pleased because there is some life in it, and I am pleased too."

John's London publisher, Hamish Hamilton, who issued almost all of John's books in British editions,* wrote him early in 1963 a long, very newsy letter, inviting Cassie and John to come for a visit, and telling of all the recent activities of the Hamilton family. He began with a sentence that deserves quoting and remembering: "We were never more than intermittent correspondents,† perhaps both feeling that a friendship such as ours can weather long silences and that we can continue our conversation two years latter in the middle of a sentence." John replied with an account of his own doings:

"You are dears to offer us sanctuary in your charming house. If only, if only we could accept! But the schedule remains as insistent as ever—the lecturing, the Sherwooding, the BOMC-ing, and the gerontophixing.

"We did have a lovely break recently, going down to Hobe Sound, Florida, for a week as the guests of the William Burdens. I had two lectures in the neighborhood—one at Palm Beach and one at Miami—so resting, swimming, and working all fitted nicely together. The work was preparation for a telephonic BOMC meeting and reading the galleys of an interim book of mine [*Dramatis Personae*].

"Last night we went to Madeline Sherwood's for dinner with the Lunts, the Don Klopfers, the Jerome Weidmans, and (later) the Dick Rodgerses. . . . It was a charming party, and the Lunts, whom we have seen twice, were in great form. They lunched here a week ago, and Lynnie in the day's full light was miraculous in her beauty. . . . Alfred, though now snow-white-haired and a little plumper, was as always in great form, hospitable to every interest. Lynnie, as usual, was living in that Green Room which is her world and asked Jerome Weidman, 'What do you do?' Exactly as, in our house, she once asked me, pointing to the man

---

* It must be said that John himself crossed the Atlantic more successfully than his books did.
† In subsequent years the Hamilton-Brown correspondence picked up in volume and momentum.

in the corner, 'But who is Archibald MacLeish?' However, they are grand people and I wish they were young again. (I wish the same about myself.) It is as a young, triumphant, swirling couple that I shall always remember them."

A year later (March 5, 1964) John wrote again to Hamish Hamilton, beginning by expressing gratitude for a long letter that had broken a long silence. "I had begun to feel that in some unintentional way I had offended you. Ours is that strange twin relationship of author to friend and publisher which, if the books involved are such dodoes as mine, can cause trouble. I began to sweat it out, feeling that, because of your ardent loyalty, you had taken *Dramatis Personae*. My attendant sense of guilt was heavy. I know how obligated I am to you for your kindnesses in years past and hated to incur any other unpaid debts of friendship. But all this you have never once mentioned to me personally or in print. This caused me alarm, not because I wanted the last book mentioned, but because I didn't want any burr to get in the way of our old friendship. I only hoped to God the damned thing sold enough of the thousand copies you imported to pay back your investment and justify your proven friendship. It does seem to me that we have skirmished ridiculously and evasively as two fact-facing adults in full agreement on every social comment and yet avoiding the affairs which, after all, happen to be the business of each of us. . . .

"To hell with all that, and now to more cheering matters. . . .

"I have been lecturing, West Coast, East Coast, wherever Rand-McNally is, plus a fee. I have had a fine time, especially in universities and colleges. Meanwhile the book [the Sherwood biography] moves. Perhaps you have heard from Cass [Cass Canfield, of Harpers] that it will now be done in two volumes. I don't want to produce one of those hernia-making Schorer-Gelb volumes,* commendable as they are. I am giving up all lecturing next fall

---

* Schorer presumably refers to Mark Schorer's massive biography of Sinclair Lewis, Gelb to Arthur and Barbara Gelb's book on O'Neill—nearly 1000 pages.

until January. Meanwhile we will go to Stonington and dig in here [there?] to meet that most blessed of all writing challenges, a deadline.

"Preston and Meredith are fine. Preston is happily involved in Davis-Polk [New York law firm where he was then employed]; Meredith in his second year at the Law School. Cassie is in the best of health. We both wish that the two of you would come in for an evening with the two of us, with the candles lighted and a fire burning. The fire is always burning here for you and you always light the candles."

Meanwhile, late in 1963, Admiral Kirk had died. John wrote to Mrs. Kirk on November 11:

"Dearest Lydia,

"I haven't written, I couldn't write. I have been trying to do in my minor way what you have succeeded in doing in your giant way—that is, living in a world without Alan. That's a silly phrase. The world for me will always be the world he added to and continues to add to in my own world. I find myself trapped in a growing vacuum. I want to call him. I want him to call me. I want to hear the sound of that resonant voice, to be warmed by his alert interest, and challenged by the darting questions which he asked with those blue eyes sparkling.

"I am only one of the many whose lives he changed. In the books I tried to say what he directed, stood for, and was in public. Private is different. Loneliness is what old people feel more and more when they can't telephone or be telephoned to by a friend, or meet with them for a night off from life which is a reminder of living. I have been engulfed by an emptiness which I can't describe. That emptiness was his fullness, and yours. The two of you came to Cassie and me out of the disciplines of war. Yet he and you, an Admiral and his Lady, survived the war to become our treasured friends. Our lives were charged and enlarged by the way in which you both touched them.

"I have a thousand memories of Alan in action. Alan yodeling at me imperiously when I first reported for duty in London. Alan summoning me to his cabin and confiding in me, with tears in his eyes, that he was to head one of the task forces in Sicily. Alan in the bombings when he stayed at the Connaught. Alan triumphant on the *Augusta,* heading for Normandy and behaving superbly there. Alan fighting a hard battle against the Admirals who fought him. Alan on one foggy night after another riding up and down the curving lanes of England, risking his life because of Austin's reckless driving and his own impatience. Alan with Mac as an inspired junior. Alan grim and determined, his chin squared, as in the unforgettable photograph, facing Omaha Beach. Alan and General Bradley taking a PT-boat between Omaha and Utah again and again.

"Then Alan in glittering whites at City Hall with Eisenhower after V-E Day. Alan at the D-Day anniversaries embodying in one person the courage, the excitements, and the triumph of a great event. Alan at the Embassy in Belgium speaking mesmerizing French to his delighted guests. Alan lunching at the Century with Don and me and Preston and Meredith, young men with whom he was a contemporary and who loved him as Cassie and I did. Alan the force of a country who was the life of a party. Alan national and Alan personal. Alan imperious, demanding, kind, melting.

"The peace continued under his leadership. He went from Embassy to Embassy, from Brussels to Moscow to Formosa. He proceeded as a radiant example of what a knowing America should and could be in action.

"He had a genius for shaping lives. I know he altered mine. No one I have ever known intimately has been to the extent that he was a rudder shifting the course of my own thinking and being. His gruffness could be a growl as commanding as an eagle's cries, his personal kindnesses unfailing. He had the rare gift of being able to plan big things and yet remember little ones.

"I am trying to learn to live in a world without him but of which every day he is a part—living, laughing, considerate, and hotly engaged. The services at the church in Washington and at

Arlington were proper salutes, really ecstatic hymns, to a career of fearless and selfless patriotic service. No Taps can be played on the need for such men.

"Cassie and I both know what you have added to our lives by adding to his. We count ourselves overprivileged to have known you both."

As we have seen, John had become a member of the editorial board of the Book-of-the-Month Club in 1956. Another native of Louisville, Basil Davenport, joined the board at the same time. Davenport had been on the staff of the Book-of-the-Month Club for years, as a preliminary reader—one of those whose opinions determine whether a given book is to be read by the judges or not. (The judges themselves, or any one of them, can decide for themselves in any particular case whether a book is to be considered as a possible Book-of-the-Month Club selection, regardless of the opinions of the preliminary readers.) The other members of the board were Gilbert Highet, Clifton Fadiman, and John P. Marquand. As we have seen, Marquand died in 1960; Davenport died in 1966.

Presumably John's earnings as a judge, well over $20,000 a year, gave him a basis of financial security, a nucleus to which his other earnings could be added. No doubt this was what enabled him to decline the *Saturday Review* offer, when he wrote as he did to Norman Cousins in 1961. He had already written seventeen books, but the income from royalties of a writer of books—with few exceptions, and John was not among them—is precarious.*
By now he had sent *Through These Men* to his publisher, and was absorbed in his work on the biography of Sherwood. Since this—the first volume—was not to appear until 1965, it is evident that the Book-of-the-Month Club appointment came as a godsend.

---

* John's obituary in *The New York Times,* published immediately after his death in March 1969, said that his estate amounted to $750,000. By the time of his death he had received bequests from his Aunt Mary Waite, who died in 1963, and from his mother, who died the following year.

The Club publishes a monthly bulletin for its members, *Book-of-the-Month Club News,* to announce the forthcoming selection and certain other books, called Alternates, which the member may order instead. It also includes a number of short reviews of current books presumed to be of interest to the members but not offered to them on the favorable terms that apply to Selections and Alternates. The descriptions of the Selections and Alternates are written by the judges, who may also write some of the shorter reviews; they are paid extra for what they write for the *News.*

It is interesting to look back over some of John's reviews of books published while he was seated on the judicial bench: books remembered and books forgotten. It should go without saying that these reports are not intended as criticism; they are meant to be recommendations. Marquand, not John, wrote the report on *This Hallowed Ground* by Bruce Catton, selected by the Club soon after John joined the board. In the *News* for May 1957 John reported on *The Turn of the Tide* by Arthur Bryant, a book based on the war diaries of Field Marshal Lord Alanbrooke: "No other book to have come out of [World War II] surpasses it in fascination or historical importance." In the issue for April 1958 he had the happy assignment of the final volume of Sir Winston Churchill's *History of the English-Speaking Peoples:* "Sir Winston has, of course, his own way of writing history no less than of making it."

Two months later he had a less memorable book to deal with, *Seidman and Son* by Elick Moll: "Clarence Day out of Potash and Perlmutter." A very congenial assignment in 1959 was Admiral Samuel Eliot Morison's life of John Paul Jones. Among his praises he inserted the following: "[Admiral Morison] buries once and for all, and with zestfully unblushing detail, the myth that John Paul Jones was ever Catherine the Great's lover. Both of them were otherwise occupied." Two months later he wrote of his friend Margaret Leech's book *In the Days of McKinley:* "Miss Leech has raided what has been widely accepted as a Madame Tussaud interval in our history. She has come out of the waxworks not with dummies but with a host of living, breathing . . . men and women. . . . She is neither a debunker nor an incense-burner."

John could be as passionately against a book as he could be in favor of one, but he gave vent to his opinions on these occasions orally and in private. For instance, when the judges, Brown dissenting, selected a book by James Michener—was it *Hawaii?*— John expressed his opinion to at least one friend in unmistakable terms. A few of his obiter dicta at the judges' meetings have been preserved. Of an unpleasantly realistic novel: "Not an outhouse in the country big enough for it." Of another book: "I read this with morbid interest because I think it is one of the worst books ever to come my way. Give me *The Five Little Peppers* any day." And once he was heard to explode to Basil Davenport: "I wouldn't have expected even you to be so stupid." No one who knew Davenport would have considered him stupid, including John when he kept his temper; on the contrary, he was brilliant. But he was quite as opinionated as John, and one who knew them both can easily conceive that they got on each other's nerves. Both were members of the species *Homo sapiens,* but their utterly different personalities suggest that there may be at least two subspecies.

Apropos of the meetings, a friend once asked John why—since Dorothy Canfield Fisher had been one of the original judges, and after many years on the job had been succeeeded by Amy Loveman—there was no woman on the present board. John replied that the presence of a woman at the monthly meetings would dampen the conversation.

Writing of the Midsummer Selection for 1960 (the Book-of-the-Month Club believes in the thirteen-month calendar), Elizabeth Nowell's biography of Thomas Wolfe, he expressed a universally held opinion: "Wolfe had more genius than he could control." The following year found him writing of books by two distinguished authors, Alan Moorehead and Rumer Godden; later in the year of *Kidnap: The Story of the Lindbergh Case* by George Walker: "A brilliant and absorbing re-creation."

It should be noted that in 1962 John reviewed for the *Book-of-the-Month Club News* Richard M. Nixon's *Six Crises*. That was the year when Nixon lost the election for Governor of California, and told the press, "You won't have Dick Nixon to kick around any more." John's review ignored what his friend Mary Bingham had written of *Through These Men,* quoted earlier. He stated: "[Nixon] comes through its pages as a man of quick intelligence, unflagging persistence and tremendous guts. . . . In spite of what must have been disturbing inner qualms, he faced the country in the 'Checkers' speech."

In the same year John reviewed Steinbeck's *Travels with Charley, The Blue Nile* by Alan Moorehead (he had previously reported on Moorehead's earlier book, *The White Nile*), and a two-volume biography of John Adams. He called *The First Day of Friday* by Honor Tracy "a pot of shamrock that has firecrackers exploding in it." That was in 1963.

In 1964 (incidentally, John did not by any means contribute to every issue of the *News*) the books on which he reported included *The Rector of Justin* by Louis Auchincloss (appropriately, John having sent two sons to Groton); *Corridors of Power* by C. P. Snow; and *My Autobiography* by Charles Chaplin. In 1965, *Max* by Lord David Cecil, and Sorensen's *Kennedy*.

Of all John's reports, the most controversial was that on *Papa Hemingway* by A. E. Hotchner. This appeared in the *Book-of-the-Month Club News* for April 1966, and the issue was accompanied by a notice that delivery of the book to members might be slightly delayed because its manufacture had been held up by a lawsuit. Mrs. Hemingway had attacked the book as both inaccurate and an invasion of privacy. The New York State Supreme Court rejected the application to enjoin publication of the book. This did not assure it a universally favorable reception. John's report, which took Hotchner's book at face value, may be considered, in the light of the criticism *Papa Hemingway* was to receive, perhaps less sophisticated than it might have been; his praise was fulsome and unmitigated. Mr. Hotchner's book, wrote John,

is impeded by no reticence. It shocks, entertains, and it also explains, shuttling from the trivial to the important and the private to the public. This is its point, its value, its fascination, and my belief is that Papa himself, crusty, tender, shockproof, belligerent and sensitive as he was, would have approved of it. . . .

If you mix Boswell and Eckermann with Leonard Lyons and Sheila Graham, and add a pocket tape recorder to bulwark a phenomenal memory, you may have a hint of Mr. Hotchner's manner of dealing with his materials. But you have no suggestion of his writing skill, which, though influenced by Hemingway, is real and very much his own.

And so on.* It makes one wonder why John did not ask for a specialist's judgment before committing himself; he had done so on a previous occasion, received an unfavorable opinion, and the book in question, though it was to become a best-seller, was not selected by the Club.

Of course the *Book-of-the-Month Club News* is not supposed to be an organ of critical opinion, and presumably the other judges, or a majority of them, concurred with John. One recalls the occasion (before John's time) when the Club selected a novel called *Something of Value* by Robert Ruark, which so offended one of the judges—Amy Loveman—that she wrote as cogent a dissent as anything ever turned out by Holmes or Brandeis; and the Club printed it.

But if John did not distinguish himself in his review of the Hotchner book, he had distinguished himself resoundingly on

* Of all the unfavorable reviews of the Hotchner book, perhaps the most devastating, and convincing, is the long piece—almost 5000 words—by Philip Young, published in *The Atlantic Monthly* for August 1966. Mr. Young is Research Professor of English at Penn State and author of a book on Hemingway, published in 1953, translated into several foreign languages, and reissued in a revised edition in 1965.

another occasion—not connected with the Book-of-the-Month Club. For several years he was a member of the advisory board for the Pulitzer Prizes in drama. In 1963 he and his colleague John Gassner of the Drama Department at Yale recommended that the Drama Prize be awarded to Edward Albee's play *Who's Afraid of Virginia Woolf?* They were overruled by the trustees of Columbia University, who make the final decisions, and both promptly resigned in consequence. This was not the first time the trustees had overruled a recommendation of an advisory board. In 1941, at the personal instigation of Nicholas Murray Butler, they refused to give the fiction prize to Ernest Hemingway for his novel of the Spanish Civil War, *For Whom the Bell Tolls,* which contains a scene—and this may have been what offended Butler—in which two of the characters make love in a sleeping bag. As recently as 1962 the trustees had refused to give the biography prize to *Citizen Hearst* by W. A. Swanberg. Parenthetically, Albee was to receive the Pulitzer Prize in 1967 for his play *A Delicate Balance,* and Swanberg the biography prize in 1973 for his life of Henry R. Luce. And Hemingway had won the fiction prize in 1953 for *The Old Man and the Sea.*

# Chapter Sixteen

# If It Be Now . . .

In 1956 John had signed a contract to edit, with commentary, the voluminous letters and papers of Robert E. Sherwood. After he had spent some months looking through the material—somewhere he says that it took him a year and a half, and it might well have taken longer—it became obvious that the book was to be a full-length biography, not merely an edition of letters, however thoroughly edited, however discursively commented upon. But it was not until June 6, 1961, that John wrote to Cass Canfield at Harpers proposing that the change of plan be officially recognized. He pointed out that the idea of the book had changed; the plan for an edition of letters had been "long since" abandoned. Here he speaks of the year and a half of research on the original papers, then the arrival of family papers and letters made available by Sherwood's sister and brother, plus letters of Sherwood's to friends, who had kept them and now offered to lend them to John. Meanwhile John had interviewed friends and acquaintances of Sherwood's in Washington, Boston, London, New York, and other places. He and Cassie had taken a two-month trip to Europe in the summer of 1956, visiting England, Scotland, Belgium, and France. Undoubtedly he found Sherwood material in London.

John thought the contract should be redrawn. He pointed out that he had a living to make. However, he did *not* mention that no advance against royalties had been paid for the Sherwood book. His financial relations with Harpers were unusual, in this and other respects. The first contract he signed with that firm called for an advance against royalties of $10,000, to be applied against *Through These Men* and any other books the author was to write for the publisher. At the time of *Through These Men,* or not long afterwards, Harpers had apparently been expecting John to write his memoirs; on September 29, 1955, Cass Canfield wrote Hamish Hamilton, John's London publisher, that John expected to complete his memoirs in two and a half years. John never wrote his memoirs; nor did he take up another idea of Canfield's, for a book on public speaking, a serious and expanded version of *Accustomed As I Am*—perhaps what is called in the trade a "how-to" book. *Through These Men* earned a little over half the $10,000 that had been advanced. Harpers did not apply the balance to the Sherwood project; evidently the reason was a previous and larger obligation. In a complicated arrangement involving Harpers and the Hearst enterprises, John had signed up, again for an advance of $10,000, to edit a collection of children's books—called at one point in the correspondence "classics of the future," which would have placed John in the dual role of editor and prophet. The idea lost its appeal for him, leaving him indebted for the $10,000. The sum was finally recovered from the royalties on *The Worlds of Robert E. Sherwood.**

To return to John's letter of June 1961. He wrote that he was devoting one week a month to reading for the Book-of-the-Month Club, one week to lecturing, and the rest of the time to Sherwood. He had turned down offers from magazines (not all, however; he had written the piece for *Vogue* on "What Makes a Woman Memorable"). The most important offer he had declined was the one from Norman Cousins; his letter to Cousins has given us

---

* John felt that the portions of his advances unearned by sales were an obligation for him to fulfill—a feeling not universal among authors. His debit balance to Harpers remaining after his death was settled between Cassie and Cass Canfield with generosity on both sides.

in detail the reasons for his decision. John's letter to Canfield says that Cousins would have paid him whatever he received from lecturing for the year. Allowing for the deductions he made for expenses, John estimated that his decision had cost him $22,000.

Meanwhile he had written optimistic letters about the prospects for delivery of the Sherwood manuscript. According to his original contract, his manuscript was due in mid-1958. In April 1958 he thought he would have it done in eighteen months; later he predicted delivery for spring 1961. The publishers received the final chapter in April 1965.

This final chapter was the final chapter of what turned out to be the first of two projected volumes; somewhere along the line it had become obvious that the material was too copious and too interesting to be reduced to a single volume. The subject was uniquely congenial to John. Sherwood had devoted himself to playwriting until World War II; indeed his play *There Shall Be No Night* (produced in March 1940 on the road, before its New York opening; Alfred Lunt and Lynn Fontanne headed the cast) has to do with Russia's attack on Finland in 1939. Soon Sherwood was to enter public service and to become head of the Overseas Branch of the Office of War Information. John's interests were to become broader than they had been when limited by the horizons of the theatre; *Through These Men* represented his breakthrough. Norman Cousins, in his introduction to *The Ordeal of a Playwright* (John's unfinished, posthumously published second volume), was to trace the parallels between the careers of Sherwood and Brown. In private Cousins has said that John's life of Sherwood was his own autobiography.

In February 1957 he wrote to a friend, James Thrall Soby, head of the Fine Arts Department of *The Saturday Review:* * "I am up beyond what remains of the part in my hair, working on a full-scale book to be called *The Worlds of Robert Sherwood.* It requires enormous research and the mastering of some 30,000

* John had introduced Soby to Cousins. Soby retired in 1959.

letters from Churchill, F.D.R., the Lunts, etc., in his personal files." How John could have digested 30,000 (or 45,000) letters in a year and a half is a mystery; his statement must be another reflection of the optimistic attitude he had taken, and continued to take, throughout the assignment. The truth is that John had bitten off more than anyone could possibly chew.

It could have been done given more time; it could have been done given a more ruthlessly selective attitude to the material. Most of the 30,000 letters and other papers John had referred to were from the period of the war and subsequent years; little of John's research on these papers was to see daylight. Of course when he set out he had no way of knowing that time was going to overtake him; by the time he turned in the last chapter of the first volume he had begun to have serious problems of health. By then the form of the biography was fixed, and there was no going back. A more selective view of the material, a more—much more—condensed presentation would have to have been decided upon at the outset. It could not be a retroactive decision.

In any event, John was interested in—fascinated by—everything about his subject. He had reviewed all of Sherwood's plays; he was bound to discuss them again in the biography. Yet a reader who after several years retains the impression that *The Worlds of Robert E. Sherwood* is largely devoted to Sherwood's career as a dramatist is surprised to find, on rereading, that in a book of some four hundred pages it is not until after page 200 that we come to Sherwood's first play, *The Road to Rome*. Up to that point we have his boyhood and education, his service in the Canadian Black Watch during World War I, his early years as a free-lance writer in New York, his friendships with the wits of the Algonquin Round Table, his work on *Vanity Fair* under Frank Crowninshield a few years before John's approach to Crowninshield in the summer of 1923. A drama critic himself, John was especially interested in Sherwood's pioneering work as film critic for the old *Life* magazine; his weekly department began early in 1921. Above all, the book is a personal biography; relationships with family and friends, money matters, two marriages. And the personality of Sherwood is alive on every page. (Incidentally, in a letter to his publishers when the book was on press, John objected to a phrase in the proposed jacket blurb, where Sherwood was called a great dramatist. Major, said John, but not great.)

It seems useless to give a digest of the reviews of *The Worlds of Robert E. Sherwood;* most of them were products of casual journalism. What difference does it make now that the book was praised in Dallas and San Francisco, criticized in Houston and Baltimore? Oscar Handlin of Harvard gave it discriminating and favorable attention in *The Atlantic Monthly.* And Ralph G. Allen, of the University of Pittsburgh, in a favorable review summed it up thus: "It might be argued that no other public entertainer more accurately reflects in his own life the enthusiasms, intellectual and moral, serious and frivolous, that marked American popular thought during the period that began with the Kaiser's War and ended with Hitler's."

Did John work himself to death? He was not a relaxed man. He did customarily take a nap after lunch—a habit that had been necessary in his newspaper years, when he was up well beyond midnight writing his reviews, and that endured thereafter. But awake he was invariably alert, to say the least, usually effervescent. The letter to Cass Canfield of June 6, 1961, gives an idea of John's activity—a life strenuous enough to have drawn commendation from Theodore Roosevelt. A few months after his Sherwood volume was published, he wrote to Hamish Hamilton (November 24, 1965) that he had been hospitalized a *second* time for severe nosebleed. The correspondence files reveal no mention of the previous occasion. The following year he had a prostate operation.

On June 9, 1967, he wrote to Hamish Hamilton: "I seem to have a talent for foolish health problems. During the winter I slipped and hurt my coccyx, which was no fun. That required the support of a cane. Then suddenly a slight occlusion occurred in the vision of the left side of my left eye, which has made me hold the more firmly to the cane (Judge Hand's,* believe it or not, and you can imagine how proudly carried). My eye doctor tells me that within a few weeks I may, or should, regain that side vision. Meanwhile, no pain, only slight alarm, and some curtailment of my newspaper reading.

"But enough of my pygmy woes. The world's in all this Vietnam and Middle East business are all that really matter. . . ." (The sentence is quoted verbatim, and the ellipsis points here are John's own.) The same letter mentions plans for a trip to Holland and London in August, both ways by the Holland-American Line. This trip did not materialize.

Most devastating of all was the gradual onset of Parkinsonism. Although apparently signs of it had been observed in 1966, John did not receive the diagnosis until 1967. During that year John and Cassie visited the MacLeishes at Antigua, where the MacLeishes had a house. During that visit MacLeish noticed John shuffling instead of walking normally; knowing John, he took it for a sort of pleasantry, only to discover that John could not help it. Back in New York, John and Cassie went out for an evening; on returning to their apartment, John fell in the hallway. He attributed the fall to what he had been drinking, but if John ever drank too much (except in Paris in 1922) such occasions were rare indeed. Was the fall that hurt his coccyx related to his Parkinsonism? However that may be, he wrote to Mary Miller and her husband on December 29, 1967: "Let me report on my Parkinson's disease. It's a great comfort to know what has been troubling me. Fortunately, the doctor tells me that he got to my case at an early, and hence propitious, stage. I have not got the shakes and the doctors think I will not. So do I. In other words, everything seems under control and that is good." In April 1968 he wrote to a friend mentioning his operation (presumably the prostate operation of 1966) and proceeded

* Given to John by Mrs. Norris Darrell.

to say: "I have recently been told that I have a mild case of Parkinsonism which they hope to get under control." And the following month (May 27) he wrote to Serrell Hillman: "Since I last wrote you I have had two falls. In one I broke my left wrist, and in the other I cracked a rib.* At the moment I do not have a cast but still carry a cane. I feel much better and will soon be able to get back to Vol. 2 of the Sherwood. God knows when it will be published. I always say 'posthumously,' though I don't really mean it."

Well, it was published posthumously, what John had written of it: five chapters, amounting to about a hundred printed pages. The material was put in shape for publication by John's old friend and long-time editor Norman Cousins, who also wrote a long and informative introduction. Of the five chapters, the first three are largely devoted to an account of the events and the feelings that led Sherwood to write *There Shall Be No Night,* with a discussion of the writing and rewriting of the play. (The full text of the play is reproduced in the second half of the book.) *There Shall Be No Night* had meant a great deal to John when it was produced in London, with the Lunts, during the early months of 1944, while he was there, waiting for D-Day. There is no telling what John would have done with these chapters if he had lived to complete and revise the book; one doubts if he would have cut them.

Chapters four and five introduce Sherwood to Washington; tell of his work for the Committee to Defend America by Aiding the Allies; give an excellent account of his first meetings with Harry Hopkins and President Roosevelt. Hopkins took Sherwood in by pretending to be an isolationist, in order to make Sherwood justify his own interventionist stand. The last completed chapter is largely devoted to Sherwood's relations with FDR, particularly his work as a presidential speech-writer.

So John's biography of Sherwood must remain his Unfinished

---

* On June 2 Brooks Atkinson wrote John: "I'm happy to hear you are movable again."

Symphony, or his Nike of Samothrace—for victory it was, to have done so much against such severe handicaps. When the finished book was delivered to Cassie in 1970, she wrote Cass Canfield: "I think John's writing has strength though he had none left." And Brooks Atkinson wrote: "Since *The Ordeal of a Playwright* is concerned with the responsibility of the individual for the integrity of the state, it represents John Mason Brown, the biographer, and Robert E. Sherwood, the biographee, at their best. Both were citizens of towering character and also of great intelligence and humor. This second volume of Mr. Brown's uncompleted biography of Mr. Sherwood is a poignant reminder that we have lost two vigorous, enlightened men." *

During the years devoted to Sherwood, John found himself increasingly in a mood of reminiscence, as a few of his letters from this period will show. In November 1963 he wrote to his old friend Laurence Stallings (who had given John advice in 1923, on the eve of his *Wanderjahr,* and who was now in California):

"I have had high good fun being with you a lot lately. How? By having been working like a trapped coal miner on a life of Bob Sherwood. Naturally you are part of it, as you are part of mine and part of the lives of hundreds of thousands of book readers, playgoers, and movie fans. I wonder if you realize what you meant both as a friend and as an example to Bob? Imagine my pleasure when, some time back, I came across an entry in his diary for 1936 about the triumphant opening of *Idiot's Delight.* At the curtain's fall, he wrote he 'rushed backstage and thrilled to

---

* At the suggestion of David McCord, we quote a sentence from *The Ordeal of a Playwright*—a comment apropos of the feeling of reassurance Sherwood felt during the opening performance in New York of *There Shall Be No Night:* "Success is electricity, flowing from the stage to auditorium and back again, supercharging the air; failure a tired wind heavy with death." John quotes from a number of the reviews, and says of his own: "I, then on the *Post,* was also enthusiastic, warmly so, although I made some carping distinctions between the eternal and the topical in the drama, which irritated Sherwood. Later in an interview he dismissed these as 'academic twaddle.' He had moved beyond such aesthetic niceties and knew the world had, too. The events of the next two months [late spring 1940] made me see his point."

the sounds of the greatest demonstration any play of mine has ever received. Nineteen curtain calls, vociferous cheers—what I have been hoping for ever since I saw *What Price Glory?* twelve years ago, and decided it would be wonderful to be a playwright.'

"I was there at that opening of *What Price Glory?* and never will forget the excitement of that September night. Nor will I ever forget the glorious privilege of having been with you at Gladys and Bill Ziegler's house over the weekend before. Everybody else had gone off most fashionably for polo on Saturday afternoon. You and I stayed home, by God, and sat it out on a rock near the Sound. I can still see your face as you said, 'I have quite a week next week. On Thursday night a play of mine, *What Price Glory?,* will open at the Plymouth.' By the next Saturday night you were world famous. . . .

"In 1925, when Bob was the movie critic of *Life,* the first serious movie critic in America you remember, he reviewed *The Big Parade* ecstatically. He loved it. As I say in the book, Bob wrote about the film hot from his own recollections as a combatant who had to do some killing himself. The war scenes, he said, actually resemble war. When Vidor [King Vidor, director of *The Big Parade*] (with a bow to you) advances a raw company of infantry through a forest which is raked by machine-gun fire, he makes his soldiers look scared, sick at their stomachs, with no heart for the ghastly business that is ahead. What is infinitely more important, he causes the sleek civilian in the audience to wonder, 'Why, in God's name, did they have to do that?' He has shown an American soldier, suddenly wild with the desire to kill, trying to jab his bayonet into the neck of a German sniper. He has shown the look on the sniper's face and the horrible revulsion that overcomes the American boy. I doubt that there is a single irregular soldier, volunteer or conscript, who did not experience that same awful feeling during his career in France—who did not recognize the impulse to withdraw the bayonet and offer the dying boy a cigarette.

"That long-ago war, which insists upon being present in the memories of all of us who are older, I relived yesterday when in a local bookshop I was hanging with absorption on every page of *The First World War* [a large pictorial history, published some years before the Second World War, with commentary by Stallings]. No book ever had a more ironical title that proved more prophetic. Then, of course, I have been luxuriating in *The Doughboys* [a comprehensive history of the American Expeditionary Force, 1917–18]. What a wonderful job you did, lusty, vital, spilling! Thank you for what you said of Uncle Preston, for the re-creation of the whole war, and your monument to those magnificent young men. And thank you for making a point which I had never seen before: that Wilson, when he went as the Savior of peace to Europe, never went to a battlefield or came closer to combat than a guard of honor. . . ."

On June 8, 1965, he wrote to Brooks Atkinson on the occasion of Atkinson's dropping his column, "Critic at Large," and retiring completely. "The world, God knows, has been bulging with bad news these many months. None of it had for me more poignant personal meaning than the note which followed your 'Critic at Large' on April 30, saying, 'This is Mr. Atkinson's final column.' I won't like the idea of reading an Atkinsonless *Times* any more than I have liked, these past few years, living a personally almost Atkinsonless life.

"Since those distant days at Harvard, you have been very much present in my thoughts and affection. No one in our time has performed for the theatre a critical service equal to yours. No one has had a wider or more deserved influence. And no one has won such merited recognition. What has made your writing stand out is not only its felicity, depth, wit, and warmth. It is all your exceptional qualities as a man who, by virtue of his character, has been a civilizing force in a largely uncivilized world. . . ."

And in September 1966, when Arthur Krock retired, John addressed him as "Dear First Boss":

"Unless my aging memory fails me, it was fifty years ago this summer when, as a red-haired, utterly green kid, I stepped into your office at the *Courier-Journal.* My hope was to become a cub reporter. You asked me, 'Can you type?' When I said, 'No,' your reply was, 'Go in the City Room and learn how.' For a week I tapped out rewrites from the [Louisville] *Times* for the *Courier* or vice versa. That was my beginning for which you have no other choice than to bear full responsibility. I have stood in your debt ever since.

"I liked your turning your back on Browning this morning and preferring instead to depart with the words of the character in the TV thriller, 'All right, officer, I'll go quietly.' However, I am glad the [New York] *Times* ignored your wishes and gave you editorially and in that fine, full news story the tribute you so richly deserve.

"There is so much to remember. The old *World* when, as a college man, I went down to see you and Swope and Laurence Stallings. The parties at Gladys Ziegler's. The dinner party in Washington at Florence Wigglesworth's at which you read a very funny poem to me. . . . The dinner at your house with you and Martha when you exposed my plentiful ignorance in the course of some guessing game, historical or geographical, I've forgotten which. And the sight of you in Chicago's heat in 1952 when, cigar in mouth and your fingers running like Paderewski's over your keyboard, you were typing out a beautifully informed dispatch. . . . I can't pretend to have agreed with you always, but I have always respected your vast knowledge, your incredible industry, and your formidable mastery of your profession. . . ."

On November 12, 1967, the Players Club in New York gave a party in John's honor, called, in the tradition of the Club, a "Pipe Night." (It was indeed a venerable tradition. Originally the members of the club smoked clay pipes on the occasion—hence the name.) In May of the same year a Pipe Night had been given in honor of Alfred Lunt, which John, although not a member of the club, attended as a guest of Richard Aldrich. The day after the party he wrote an account of it to Lynn Fontanne: "I wanted to be among the many who were paying their proper tribute to Alfred.

"Believe me, there were many. Three roomsful, with a healthy supply of standees in the third of these. It was a memorable affair; warm with affection; gay in its spirit; wide in its range. I was overjoyed to have Robeson there. He made it magnificently American. And Bobby Clark, one of the funniest of men! He saved it from being Drama League, and made the tribute come from the whole of show biz. John Gielgud, in a most felicitous speech, linked the two of you with England and your own far-flung dominions. Walter Hampden, very dignified, full of spiritual grace, was an admirable representative of the apostolic succession from Booth. Nor did the fortunate symbolism elude me of having John Mulholland there as a magician to unroll the red carpet for another master of magic.

"Alfred was in great form. I trust he was as touched as I was by the last line of Howard Lindsay's introduction. I mean the line saluting Alfred as 'America's most distinguished actor.' It warmed my heart to see the whole room rise to that and stand in tribute to Alfred both before and after his speech. . . ."

This account conveys the spirit of the occasion six months later, when John was honored. The Pipemaster was Brooks Atkinson, who was introduced by Dennis King, after Mr. King had read a number of telegrams from absentees, including particularly a delightful extravaganza from Katharine Cornell. Atkinson recalled a number of the events which have already been accounted for in this narrative: his own review of the Harvard Dramatic Club production in which John "sputtered and spurted," the early nativity play, John's unique position as the only man who had prepared himself to become a drama critic; he made the point that John's critical career covered "the richest period of the theatre we've ever had." "None of his enemies dislike him," observed Atkinson, and cited John's four-year service as president of the New York Drama Critics Circle. Finally he quoted two remarks of John's on drama critics. First, his comparison of the critic to Mr. Pecksniff; second, John's remark (repeated in the introduction to *Dramatis Personae*) that dramatic criticism was like an attempt to tattoo soap bubbles.

Barry Bingham told stories of John as a boy in Louisville—the gift of books to his sister's friend; the letter to Colonel Watterson; and an occasion when he built a fort in his back yard, hoisted a Confederate flag, and prepared to defend his position, but suffered the ignominy of being called by his grandmother to come in and take a bath. "This," said John, "ended my career as a military strategist."

Marc Connelly told of Professor Baker's suggestion after reading a play of John's; he admired John's writing but not his dramaturgy. "John," Connelly quoted Baker as saying, "did you ever think of writing criticism?" Alfred de Liagre, Jr., described a Town Hall lecture in which he proposed a toast to John as "old Kentucky mushmouth," and spoke of the southern custom of drinking bourbon and Dr. Pepper. De Liagre had questioned John as to his qualifications as a trustee of the Metropolitan Museum at the time of his appointment, and quoted John as replying, "They wanted me for my money." De Liagre concluded by saying of John that there was "no one whose conversation is more entertaining, more amusing, more obscene." Norris Houghton called John "the Judy Garland of the lecture circuit. . . . His performance is as scintillating in private as in public, and never ceases except during afternoon naps." Walter Lord recalled John's rowing him on a pond in the Bois de Boulogne in 1928, when Lord was ten—John must have been on his way to or from Russia.

Marya Mannes read a poem which she called a valentine. Donald Oenslager recalled that John's 47 Workshop one-act play, *The First Day*, had embarrassed John's family; spoke of their European travels, throughout which John carried all the bags because of Don's recent appendectomy; mentioned that during a lecture once John had fallen off the stage, remarked as

he got up, "I shall pick up the subject where I left it."
George Oppenheimer told the anecdote of Thomas Wolfe's play
*The Mountains,* quoted earlier—"God damn yuh, Baldpate, yuh
hemmin' me in." And he added an account of John's performance
in the Workshop production of Philip Barry's *O, Promise Me.* "I
wish I could adequately describe to you John's stage appearance
—impeccably dressed in an ill-fitting tweed, twinkling eyes that
blazed in appreciation whenever he spoke a line, rosy and downy
unshaven cheeks, a military stance as he slouched across the
stage—this was John. He spoke in a low voice so as not to dis-
tract his fellow actors who, in turn, were forced to get their cues
by the touch system. He dominated the stage especially when he
was alone on it."

Richard Watts, Jr., gave his reminiscences of John as a critic
and as a war reporter. Alfred Lunt recalled that John had
visited him in the hospital and contributed to his recovery by
telling "some of the filthiest stories I ever heard." Lynn Fontanne spoke rather casually, and undoubtedly delighted the audience by referring to a review in a publication which she called
*Women's Underwear.*

John's speech of acknowledgment brought the Pipe Night to
a close. He spoke of his experience with the 47 Workshop as
making him see the possibilities in criticism. He recalled that
"the *Post* pinched pennies till they could be heard in Philadelphia." As the *Post* drama critic he had been called upon to write
articles as well as reviews; sometimes he fudged by writing letters
to himself, mostly abusive, from fictitious readers. He expressed
disappointment in the theatre now, that is to say, the theatre
of 1967—he missed the feeling of scale, reach, dimension; he
wanted "anguish that is real; trouble and sweat; and a little
vocabulary once in a while." And he spoke of Shaw at one of his
last meetings as being "hard of hearing—harder of listening."

The apotheosis of the Pipe Night came at the right time,
while John could still enjoy it. His voice, as it comes through on
the tape preserved by the Players Club, is as effervescent as

ever; but for years his friends had been struck by his appearance; he was no longer what he had been—the only word is youthful —through his fifties. Even in the early sixties, when Norman Cousins met him at lunch, "My heart sank," writes Cousins; "for the first time I no longer saw him as eternally young, sparkling, buoyant, but as some one suddenly plunged into old age. He immediately read my thoughts and made some characteristically flip remarks about his age. He said, 'Norman, for heaven's sake take my advice: never grow old, it's a terrible nuisance.' " To growing old there is only one alternative.

After Pipe Night a year stretched ahead, and with it the interminable Sherwood project. John did what he could—the unfinished manuscript of *The Ordeal of a Playwright*—but his strength was giving out. The Parkinsonism became worse, slowly but progressively, and contributed to his declining stamina. Some of his letters concerning his health were quoted earlier in this chapter. A year after Pipe Night he was in the New York Hospital for observation and treatment. Cassie recalls that he went in early in November 1968 and was released for Thanksgiving. He was in Roosevelt Hospital, terminally, early in December, with Asian flu, which developed into pneumonia. After treatment it recurred. There were successive bouts of pneumonia. "He would recover from one episode," writes his physician, Dr. Kenneth T. Donaldson, "only to develop another because of weakness and declining strength." Cassie wrote to Brooks Atkinson, briefly and in distress, that John's mind, that brilliant, coruscating, versatile, spontaneous mind, was affected.

Only a few days before John's death, Cassie went to see him in the hospital, provided with a new joke that Archibald MacLeish had told her, for—they hoped—John's benefit. The joke consisted of a brief dialogue between two octogenarians. First O.: "Are you still chasing girls?" Second O.: "Yes, but I can't remember what for." John responded to this with a smile; he had enjoyed it. But the light did not stay lit. He died in Roosevelt

Hospital in New York on March 16, 1969, in his sixty-ninth year. The final cause of death was pneumonia.

Hamish Hamilton wrote to the present biographer that he still carries with him the tribute to John which Alistair Cooke wrote for *The Guardian*. The last paragraph follows:

It is always a fretful thing to watch a good man of any vitality decline into a small shell of his own self. It was, for too many years, a continual sadness to think of the slow decay of the blithe and irrepressible gentleman from Kentucky, who managed for so many years, and by some subtle chemistry of character, to applaud the brave, to slap down fools without malice, to combine gaiety with goodness, to blast pretension, and leave no enemies.

The services at St. James's Episcopal Church on Madison Avenue made manifest the number and the devotion of John's friends. (Friends were requested in lieu of flowers to send contributions to Recording for the Blind.) The Reverend Dr. Arthur Lee Kinsolving was the officiating minister. As was his custom, he walked from the rear of the church down the center aisle, toward the altar, intoning that most magnificent sentence in the language: "I am the resurrection and the life." After the conclusion of the Order for the Burial of the Dead, Dr. Kinsolving read verses 14 through 40 of the eleventh chapter of St. John. He paused midway to remark that this was the first time he had ever been requested to read this particular passage at a funeral, but John Mason Brown—who had chosen the passage—was an unusual man. Tactfully Dr. Kinsolving omitted the second sentence of the 39th verse. If anybody who ever lived would have enjoyed this elision, it was that same John Mason Brown.

Perhaps he did.

# Books by John Mason Brown

*The Modern Theatre in Revolt.* New York: Norton, 1929.

*Upstage: The American Theatre in Performance.* New York: Norton, 1930; Port Washington, N.Y.: Kennikat, 1969.

*Letters from Greenroom Ghosts.* New York, Viking, 1934.

(Editor, with Montrose Jonas Moses.) *The American Theatre As Seen by Its Critics, 1752–1934.* New York: Norton, 1934; New York: Cooper Square, 1967.

*The Art of Playgoing.* New York: Norton, 1936.

*Two on the Aisle: Ten Years of the American Theatre in Performance.* New York: Norton, 1938; Port Washington, N.Y.: Kennikat, 1969.

(With others.) *George Pierce Baker: A Memorial.* New York: Dramatists Play Service, 1939.

*Broadway in Review.* New York: Norton, 1940; Freeport, N.Y.: Books for Libraries, 1969.

*Accustomed As I Am.* New York: Norton, 1942.

*Insides Out: Being the Saga of a Drama Critic Who Attended His Own Opening.* New York: Dodd, Mead, 1942; New York: McGraw-Hill, 1947; London: Herbert Jenkins, 1947.

*To All Hands: An Amphibious Adventure.* New York: McGraw-Hill, 1943.

*Many a Watchful Night.* New York: McGraw-Hill, 1944; London: Hamish Hamilton, 1944.

*Seeing Things.* New York: McGraw-Hill, 1946; London: Hamish Hamilton, 1946.

*Seeing More Things.* New York: McGraw-Hill, 1948; London: Hamish Hamilton, 1949.

*Beyond the Present.* St. Paul, Minn.: Ampersand Club, 1948.

*Morning Faces: A Book of Children and Parents.* New York: McGraw-Hill, 1949; London: Hamish Hamilton, 1950.

(Editor.) *The Portable Charles Lamb.* New York: Viking, 1949.

*Still Seeing Things.* New York: McGraw-Hill, 1950; London: Hamish Hamilton, 1951.

*Daniel Boone: The Opening of the Wilderness.* New York: Random House, 1952.

*As They Appear.* New York: McGraw-Hill, 1952; London: Hamish Hamilton, 1953.

*Through These Men: Some Aspects of Our Passing History.* New York: Harper, 1956; London: Hamish Hamilton, 1956.

(Editor.) *The Ladies' Home Journal Treasury.* New York: Simon and Schuster, 1956.

(Contributor.) *The Theatre of Robert Edmond Jones,* ed. Ralph Pendleton. Middletown, Conn.: Wesleyan University Press, 1958.

*Dramatis Personae: A Retrospective Show.* New York: Viking, 1963; London: Hamish Hamilton, 1963.

*The Worlds of Robert E. Sherwood: Mirror to His Times, 1896–1939.* New York: Harper & Row, 1965; London: Hamish Hamilton, 1965.

*The Ordeal of a Playwright: Robert E. Sherwood and the Challenge of War.* New York: Harper & Row, 1970.

# Index